Andragogy in Action

Applying Modern Principles of Adult Learning

Malcolm S. Knowles
and Associates

Andragogy
in Action

Jossey-Bass Publishers

San Francisco • Washington • London • 1985

ANDRAGOGY IN ACTION
Applying Modern Principles of Adult Learning
by Malcolm S. Knowles and Associates

Copyright © 1984 by: Jossey-Bass Inc., Publishers
433 California Street
San Francisco, California 94104
&
Jossey-Bass Limited
28 Banner Street
London EC1Y 8QE

Library of Congress Cataloging in Publication Data
Main entry under title:

Andragogy in action.

(The Jossey-Bass management series) (The Jossey-Bass
higher education series)
Bibliography: p. 423
Includes index.
1. Adult education—Philosophy—Addresses, essays,
lectures. 2. Continuing education—Addresses, essays,
lectures. 3. Professional education—Addresses, essays,
lectures. 4. Management—Study and teaching (Higher)—
Addresses, essays, lectures. I. Knowles, Malcolm
Shepherd (date). II. Series. III. Series:
Jossey-Bass higher education series.
LC5215.A53   1984   374   84-47989
ISBN 0-87589-621-9

Manufactured in the United States of America

The paper in this book meets the guidelines for
permanence and durability of the Committee on
Production Guidelines for Book Longevity of the
Council on Library Resources.

JACKET DESIGN BY WILLI BAUM

FIRST EDITION
First printing: October 1984
Second printing: January 1985

Code 8427

A joint publication in

The Jossey-Bass Management Series

and

The Jossey-Bass Higher Education Series

Consulting Editors
Human Resources

Leonard Nadler
Zeace Nadler
College Park, Maryland

Foreword

When Malcolm Knowles asked me to tell how this book came to be, I recalled an evening in New York a few years ago. Several people attending the TRAINING conference had formed a group and gone to a restaurant for dinner. In the course of the evening's conversation, someone inquired if Malcolm—everyone calls him by his first name—was going to be at the conference. After comments about his busier-than-ever work schedule, the discussion turned to Malcolm's impact on adult learning. His classic books, distinguished consulting practice, and warm personal manner were pieces of the conversation, but the highlight was his graduate programs and the students they had produced. Over the years his students have taken his model of adult learning and put it to work in all kinds of organizations, both in the United States and abroad. Working from the inside in a number of human development roles and from the outside as consultants, they have had a significant effect on organizations and the professions of human resource development and adult education. At one point during the evening, I suggested to the others that Malcolm should draw together in a book the experiences of his students as they have applied andragogy. The immediate, unqualified response was that it would be a welcome addition to the professional literature and that it should be done.

The idea for the book remained with me, and I later called Malcolm and outlined the idea—a book of andragogy applications, drawn from his network of students and colleagues, with introduction and commentary from him . . . a book that would build on the foundation he had established in *The Modern Practice of Adult Education* and *The Adult Learner: A Neglected Species* . . . a book that would go beyond principles and models to offer organizational experiences of andragogy in practice, andragogy on the firing line. After I finished, Malcolm expressed his enthusiasm for the idea and immediately gave it the title *Andragogy in Action*. He went on to talk about recent material he had received that could go in the book and began to visualize the structure. After our telephone conversation, he continued to develop the book outline, chose a publisher, and put together all the pieces with his introduction and commentary. The book you have before you is the result of that process.

So, that is the story of how the book came to be—at least the surface story. The other story, and the far more important one, is that through the years Malcolm Knowles has been a seminal figure in shaping our ideas, guiding us to new concepts, advising us on strategies, sharing open dialogues of experience, and always being a learner himself. He has been, in fact, the personification of andragogy. He has initiated, sponsored, and disseminated many of the ideas that we now take for granted. Malcolm introduced and promulgated the concept of andragogy, which probably more than any other force has changed the role of the learner in adult education and human resource development programs. Andragogy values the learner's life experiences and need to be self-directed, draws the learner into a commitment to learn by responding to the learner's needs, and involves the learner in directing the content and process. These concepts have validity now, but when they were introduced they were the cutting edge. Lifelong learning, competency-based learning, self-directed learning, and contract learning are other ideas associated with andragogy that Malcolm has brought to life and elucidated for us. These ideas and their applications are what make this book important. It powerfully illustrates how andragogy can increase individual and organizational effectiveness. Learners in an andragogical program become more competent and confident. The nature of the learning design promotes the efficient use of individual and organizational resources. Andragogy promotes an organizational climate of openness, collaboration, inquiry, creativity, competence, and ultimately success.

Some of us are stone throwers, those who toss ideas into the pool of human knowledge. Some throw stones that land at the edge, making only a few faint ripples. Only a few throw large stones into the middle of the pool, causing potent everwidening circles that touch and affect many. For the last thirty years Malcolm Knowles has been throwing hefty stones. Several of his books are considered classics, remaining in print year after year to influence students and practitioners alike. His graduate programs at Boston University and North Carolina State University have produced many competent students who carry on his tradition of concern for the individual and learning. His ongoing national and international consulting practice has spread the word of andragogy and made organizations more human and effective.

So, the real story of this book is that Malcolm Knowles now offers us an opportunity to learn from the work of his students and colleagues. The persons he has inspired, encouraged, nurtured, challenged, and supported share their experiences as a practical source for us to use as we apply the principles of andragogy. Thank you, Malcolm, for your contribution. You are an Olympian stone thrower. Your thoughts and work will be sending ripples across the profession and beyond for many years to come. You have made us all better learners and facilitators of learning.

Austin, Texas   Ray Bard
August 1984   *President, Bard Productions*

Preface

Word has been spreading in recent years that there is a better way to help adults learn than traditional pedagogy. I have seen a growing hunger on the part of teachers, trainers, and administrators in business and industry, government agencies, colleges and universities, professional associations, religious organizations, voluntary organizations, and even elementary and secondary schools to find out what that better way is. The title of this book is the beginning of the answer—*Andragogy in Action.*

One consequence of this hunger is that I have been spending more and more of my time traveling around the country (and other parts of the world) putting on workshops and speaking at conferences on modern concepts of adults learning—on the andragogical model. One of the most frequent questions people ask in these sessions is, "Who has been applying the andragogical model in institutions and types of programs like mine?" When pressed to explain why they want to know, they give two reasons: (1) they feel more secure about trying out new things if they know others have tried them and found them workable, and (2) they want ammunition to use in persuading their bosses to go along with the idea.

Usually I have been able to give these people the names and addresses of other users of andragogy, but there has been nothing in print to refer them to. Then, in the discussion that

Ray Bard mentions in his foreword, it dawned on me that for almost fifteen years people have been sending me descriptions of programs of all sorts that are based on the andragogical model and that I had an obligation to make them available.

In the course of reviewing over one hundred cases (of which thirty-six have been selected for this book), I have been impressed on several scores. Probably my strongest impression is how ready educators around the world and in every conceivable type of institution have been for a model that would give them a rationale for doing what instinctively they have sensed they would like to do. I have met few teachers or trainers who have felt happy about doing only didactic teaching. Only such a state of readiness would explain the number of people who have been able to apply (or adapt) the andragogical model just from reading about it. I have also been impressed by the number of people who were able to apply the model successfully by virtue of being exposed to it in a one- or two-day workshop. For a long time I had worried about how much good I was doing by putting on short workshops. No longer. Smart people can pick up a new idea even with brief exposure and run with it. Finally, I have been impressed with how imaginatively people have been using the model; I have learned much that has improved my practice from the creative designs and techniques these innovative practitioners have invented.

Several options for grouping the case descriptions were available to me. One was organizing them according to type of activity—courses, workshops, staff development programs, and the like. The problem with that system was that some cases contain several types of activity. Instead, I chose to group them according to institutional settings, since people are most interested in applications of the model in settings similar to their own. But let me warn readers about looking at cases from one type of institution only: settings that are different may yield as many, if not more, applicable ideas. For example, the approach to climate setting in an oral communication course in a community college may give you fresh ideas about climate setting in a management development workshop or a hospital in-service education program. How learners are oriented to self-directed learning in a school of social work may suggest techniques that are applicable to orientation programs in other professional schools and even religious education programs. My introductions to the selections, which are typeset in a sans serif face to distinguish them from the text itself, highlight the special features of each case description. The index will also aid you in locating the wide range of applications of a given type of activity in various institutions.

The book opens with an account of my personal odyssey through the world of andragogy in search of a mastery of "The Art and Science of Helping Adults Learn" in Chapter One. Chapter Two presents applications in business, industry, and government, ranging from teaching technical skills through managerial skills development and using line managers as facilitators of learning to a masters of management degree program. Chapter Three presents applications in colleges and universities, including undergraduate and graduate programs, faculty development programs, courses in science education and public speaking, and a distance education program. Chapter Four presents applications in professional education, including medicine, law, nursing, social work, and school administration. Chapter Five presents applications in continuing education for the health professions, specifically physicians and nurses. Chapter Six contains two cases of application in religious education. Chapter Seven presents three innovative applications in elementary and secondary schools. Chapter Eight is concerned with applications in remedial education—a general educational development (GED) program and a program for teaching English as a second language. Chapter Nine draws conclusions regarding the effectiveness of andragogy in various settings, what we have learned from experience and research about the andragogical model, and what the future may hold.

My associates in this project are the authors of the thirty-six selections, whose titles and affiliations are given in the introductions to the pieces. Many of their contributions were previously published in a variety of journals, newsletters, house publications, and other sources; gracious permission has been given for them to be edited and adapted as part of this integrated volume. Credit lines on the selections identify these sources. Where no credit lines appear, authors wrote their selections expressly for this book, to help show the range of applications for the andragogy model. My heartfelt appreciation to them all.

I close this preface with a clear disclaimer of personal ownership of the andragogical model. I was the first to use the term in the adult educational literature in the United States, but I did not coin it; I stole it from the Europeans. And many other researchers, theoreticians, and practitioners have contributed to it.

Probably the most important contribution this book makes is to demonstrate the power of the notion that people learn best when treated as human beings and that the ultimate purpose of all of education is to empower individuals through a process of lifelong learning. Cumulatively, these selections make a powerful statement.

Raleigh, North Carolina   Malcolm S. Knowles
August 1984

Contents

◆◆◆◆◆◆◆◆◆◆◆◆◆◆◆◆◆◆◆◆◆◆◆◆◆◆◆◆◆◆◆◆◆◆◆

    for Adult Students   273
    *Deborah Arms, Bonnie Chenevey, Carol
    Karrer, Carol Hawthorne Rumpler*

6. Teaching School Administration at
    Cleveland State University   285
    Ernest M. Schuttenberg

Five **Applications in Continuing Education for the
      Health Professions**   297

    1. Self-Directed Learning for Physicians
        at the University of Southern California   299
        University of Southern California

    2. American Nurses' Association's Guide for
        Self-Directed Continuing Education   311
        American Nurses' Association

    3. Teaching Nurses Technical Skills
        at a Metropolitan Hospital   323
        Carol B. Dare

    4. In-Service Nursing Education Through
        Clinical Units   335
        Jessie Albanetti, Donna Carroll

Six   **Applications in Religious Education**   341

    1. The Biblical Andragogy Clinic   343
        Eugene Trester

    2. Adult Education in the Archdiocese
        of Detroit   351
        Jane Wolford Hughes

Seven **Applications in Elementary and Secondary
       Education**   363

    1. Challenging Students to Excel   365
        Maurice Gibbons, Gary Phillips

The Author

Malcolm S. Knowles is professor emeritus of adult and community college education at North Carolina State University and previously was professor of education at Boston University, executive director of the Adult Education Association of the U.S.A., and director of adult education at the YMCAs in Boston, Detroit, and Chicago. He received his B.A. degree (1934) from Harvard College and his M.A. degree (1949) and his Ph.D. degree (1960) from the University of Chicago—all in education. He has honorary degrees from Lowell Technical Institute and the National College of Education.

Knowles's main academic and professional interests have been in the theory and practice of adult education. In addition to administering adult education programs and teaching in graduate schools, he has done consulting and conducted workshops for a wide variety of organizations and corporations in North America, Europe, South America, and Australia. His books include *Informal Adult Education* (1950), *Teaching Adults in Informal Courses* (1954), *How to Develop Better Leaders* (with Hulda Knowles, 1955), *Introduction to Group Dynamics* (with Hulda Knowles, 1959; rev. ed., 1972), *Handbook of Adult Education in the U.S.* (editor, 1962), *The Adult Education Movement in the U.S.* (1962; rev. ed., 1977), *Higher Adult Education in the U.S.* (1969), *The Modern Practice of Adult Education*

(1970; rev. ed., 1980), *The Adult Learner: A Neglected Species*
(1973; rev. ed., 1978), and *Self-Directed Learning: A Guide for
Learners and Teachers* (1975).

During his retirement, Knowles is serving as a mentor for
the Fielding Institute's external degree program in human and
organization development, as national lecturer for the Nova
University Center for Higher Education, as adjunct professor of
the Union Graduate School, and as a member of the Task Force
on Lifelong Education of the UNESCO Institute for Education,
for which he has written a chapter on "Creating Lifelong Learning Communities" for its forthcoming book on lifelong education.

The contributing authors are identified in the introductions to the various selections.

Andragogy
in Action

Applying
Modern Principles
of Adult Learning

ONE

Introduction:
The Art and Science
of Helping Adults Learn

This is a very personal book—a collection of descriptions by people who have personally applied the andragogical model. It seems fitting, therefore, that I present my current thinking about adult learning as a personal account of my wanderings through the morass of learning theory; for, like the wanderings of Odysseus, mine were circuitous, not a direct flight. I see this chapter as a way of introducing newcomers to the world of andragogy with a route map, but those who are already familiar with this world may want to scan the chapter to note certain changes in my current views of adult education.

My First Experiences with Adult Learners

My experience with adult education began in 1935. I had prepared in college for a career in the U.S. Foreign Service, but when I graduated I was informed by the State Department that only the most urgent vacancies were being filled and that only those who had passed their exams in 1932 were being considered. So I had to get a "holding" job for at least three years to support a new wife and hoped-for family. The job I got was as director of related training for the National Youth Administration (NYA) in Massachusetts. The NYA was a work-study program for unemployed youth between the ages of eighteen and twenty-five, with the mission of increasing their employability; I was put in charge of the study half of the program.

I had no formal qualifications for this job outside of leading some boys' clubs in a settlement house. Nonetheless, I sensed that a vocational training program for unemployed youth would have to be different from the prescriptive academic courses that I had taken, although I didn't know in what ways. I tried to find a book that would tell me how to conduct a program of this sort, and I couldn't find one. So I sought out people who were directing adult education programs—including the director of the Boston Institute for Adult Education, a director of adult education in a public school, and a couple of deans of evening colleges—and formed an advisory council to give me guidance. At their suggestion I made an informal survey of a sample of employers to find out what jobs were open and what skills they required. Then I organized courses to provide these skills, employed instructors, found locations for the courses to meet, and published a descriptive brochure. The response to the program was enthusiastic, and many of the youths (especially those between twenty-one and twenty-five years of age) began getting jobs. I loved what I was doing, but I didn't know that it had a name. Then, around 1937, someone asked me what I did. When I told him, he said, "Oh, you are an adult educator." So now I had an identity. He also told me that there was a national organization, the American Association for Adult Education, that was holding its annual conference in New York in several weeks. I attended the conference and was impressed with the people I met there and with their ideas about the differences between adult learners and school children. At that point I joined the association and notified the State Department that I had changed my career goals to adult education and was no longer available for the Foreign Service.

During my five years with the NYA, I observed that some teachers were more effective than others in working with young adults; and I began developing some generalizations—for instance, that the more effective teachers were more interested in their students as persons, were more informal in their manner, involved students more in participatory activities, and gave them more helpful support. But my understanding of the emerging theory of adult education came from two individuals and their books. The single most influential person in guiding my thinking was Eduard C. Lindeman, whose book *The Meaning of Adult Education* (1926) enlightened me about the unique characteristics of adults as learners and the need for methods and techniques for helping them learn. Lindeman was at that time director of educational projects for the Works Projects Administration and thus was in a sense my supervisor. We spent many hours together, discussing what adult education was all about, and I regarded him as my mentor. Dorothy Hewitt, director of the Boston Center for Adult Education, which provided informal courses to the citizens of Boston, was a member of my advisory council and showed me step by step how she planned and managed her program. The book she coauthored with Kirtley Mather, *Adult Education: A Dynamic for Democracy* (1937), served as my how-to-do-it manual. I still reread these two books periodically for inspiration and reinforcement. I marvel that these two early pioneers—especially Lindeman— had insights about adult learning that only recently have been verified by research.

In 1940 I was invited to become director of adult education at the Huntington Avenue YMCA in Boston, and I found myself in possession of a built-in laboratory for applying ideas I was picking up from people and publications and for experimenting with new ideas. The *Journal of Adult Education,* published by the American Association for Adult Education, and the *Adult Education Bulletin,* published by the Department of Adult Education of the National Education Association, were rich sources of information. Both of them frequently ran articles by "successful" teachers of adults ("successful" being defined as the ability to attract and retain students) describing how differently they treated adults from the way children and youth are traditionally treated in school and college. It is interesting to me now, in retrospect, that although there was general agreement among adult educators that adults are different from youth as learners, there was no comprehensive theory about these differences. The literature was largely philosophical and anecdotal and at most provided miscellaneous principles or guidelines.

Getting an Academic Foundation

In 1944 I enlisted in the U.S. Navy and during the next two years had more time to read and think than I had ever had before in my life. I devoured all the books in print about adult education and started trying to work out a comprehensive theory about it. In 1946 I became director of adult education at the Central YMCA in Chicago and enrolled in the graduate program in adult education at the University of Chicago for my master's and doctor's degrees. I was greatly influenced by the intellectual rigor and teaching style of my major professor, Cyril O. Houle. He related to his students as colleagues and demonstrated that principles of adult education could be applied even in a traditional university. At this time also, I experienced the challenge of being a truly self-directed learner in a seminar with Arthur Shedlin, an associate of Carl Rogers.

For my master's thesis, I decided that I would attempt to bring together all the insights, principles, and practices regarding the education of adults that I had garnered from the literature, from other adult educators, and from my own experience, as at least a first step in constructing a comprehensive theory of adult education. When I was about half way through it, Cyril Houle informed me that he had been talking with the editor of Association Press about projects his students were working on and that the editor had expressed an interest in seeing the outline and first couple of chapters of my thesis. As a result, my first book was published in 1950 under the title *Informal Adult Education*. I had been trying to identify the essence of adult education, the thing that made it different from traditional education; and the best I could come up with was "informal." I still had not developed a comprehensive, coherent, integrated theory. But it was a step in that direction.

Into the Larger World of Adult Education

In 1951 I became executive director of the newly formed Adult Education Association of the U.S.A., and my line of vision shifted from individual learners in particular programs to the broad scope of the adult education movement. But three forces kept me thinking about the adult learner. One was my doctoral studies at the University of Chicago, through which I became familiar with the formal theories of learning. My strongest impression was that these theories had all been based on research on animals (mostly rodents, at that) and children, and I had trouble seeing their relevance to what I had observed about learning by adults. In fact, it dawned on me that the educational psychologists had not been studying learning at all, but reactions to teaching. The second force was the research that Cyril Houle was engaged in at the time regarding how "continuing learners"—people who have engaged in systematic learning on their own—go about learning. The results of his study were published in a monograph under the title *The Inquiring Mind* in 1961, and had the effect of redirecting subsequent research by adult education researchers, especially Allen Tough, to focus on the internal dynamics of learning in adults. The third force was my participation in the human relations laboratories of the National Training Laboratories (NTL) Institute of Behavioral Sciences in Bethel, Maine. From this experience I derived a deep understanding and appreciation of the forces affecting learning that are at work in groups and in larger social systems.

In 1960 I was invited to Boston University to start a new graduate program in adult education. During the next fourteen years, I had a laboratory where I could apply principles of adult learning in a university setting; I had time and motivation for doing research; and I had doctoral students to extend and deepen the research. During this period a theoretical framework regarding adult learning evolved. But I didn't have a label for it that would enable me to talk about it in parallel to the traditional pedagogical model. (Incidentally, "pedagogy" is derived from the Greek words *paid*, meaning "child," and *agogos*, meaning "leader of." So pedagogy literally means "the art and science of teaching children.)

I found the solution in the summer of 1967, when a Yugoslavian adult educator, Dusan Savicevic, attended my summer session course on adult learning and at the end of it exclaimed, "Malcolm, you are preaching and practicing andragogy." I responded, "Whatagogy?" because I had never heard the term before. He explained that European adult educators had coined the term as a parallel to pedagogy, to provide a label for the growing body of knowledge and technology in regard to adult learning, and that it was being defined as "the art and science of helping adults learn." It made sense to me to have a differentiating label, and I started using the term in 1968, in articles describing my theoretical framework for thinking about adult learning.

In 1970 I put it all together in a book, *The Modern Practice of Adult Education: Andragogy Versus Pedagogy*. The "versus" was in the title because at that point I saw the two models, pedagogy and andragogy, as dichotomous—one for children, the other for adults. During the next ten years, however, a number of teachers in elementary, secondary, and higher education who had somehow been exposed to the andragogical model told me that they had experimented with applying (or adapting) the model in their practice and had found that young people learned better, too, when the andragogical model was applied. On the other hand, many teachers and trainers working with adults cited circumstances—especially in basic skills training— where the pedagogical model seemed to be required. So the revised edition of the book, published in 1980, had the subtitle *From Pedagogy to Andragogy*.

Toward a Theory of Adult Learning

During the two decades between 1960 and 1980, we gained more knowledge about the unique characteristics of adults as learners and their learning processes than had been accumulated in all previous history. Houle's seminal study in 1961 had stimulated a rash of research by adult educators (Boud,

1981; Boyd, Apps, and Associates, 1980; Cross, 1981; Houle, 1980; Howe, 1977; Knox, 1977; Long, Hiemstra, and Associates, 1980; Smith, 1982; Tough, 1967, 1979, 1982). But knowledge was flowing from other social science disciplines as well. Clinical psychologists and psychiatrists were learning about how to help people change their behavior (Bandura, 1969; Maslow, 1962, 1970, 1971; Rogers, 1951, 1961, 1969, 1980); and, since education also is concerned with behavioral change, their findings were relevant to adult learning. Developmental psychologists were discovering that there are predictable developmental stages during the adult years as well as through adolescence and that the transitions from one stage to another are one of the chief triggers of readiness to learn (Baltes, 1978; Erikson, 1959; Goulet and Baltes, 1970; Havighurst, 1970; Knox, 1977; Levinson, 1978; Lidz, 1968; Neugarten, 1964, 1968; Pressey and Kuhlen, 1957; Sheehy, 1974; Stevens-Long, 1979). Social psychologists were discovering how the conditions of our environment—such as color, population density, stress, social norms, social class, race, and group processes—affect learning (Barker, 1978; Birren, 1969; Bronfenbrenner, 1979; David and Wright, 1975; Deutsch and others, 1968, Lewin, 1951; Moos, 1976, 1979; Moos and Insel, 1974) and how change can be brought about in environments (Arends and Arends, 1977; Bennis, Benne, and Chin, 1968; Eiben and Milleren, 1976; Greiner, 1971; Hornstein and others, 1971; Lippitt, 1969, 1973; Martorana and Kuhns, 1975; Zurcher, 1977). Sociologists were adding to our knowledge about how institutional policies and procedures (concerning, for instance, admissions, registration, financial matters, and reward systems) affect learning (Barrett, 1970; Boocock, 1972; Corwin, 1974; Etzioni, 1961, 1969).

Clearly, by 1970—and certainly by 1980—there was a substantial enough body of knowledge about adult learners and their learning to warrant attempts to organize it into a systematic framework of assumptions, principles, and strategies. This is what andragogy sets out to do. I don't know whether it is a theory; this is a controversial issue, which Cross (1981, pp. 220-228) discusses lucidly and objectively. I feel more comfortable thinking of it as a system of concepts that, in fact, incorporates pedagogy rather than opposing it—a notion that I will develop more fully later. First, I must clarify my current thinking about the pedagogical and andragogical models.

Traditional Learning—The Pedagogical Model

The pedagogical model is the one we have all had the most experience with. In fact, it is the only way of thinking about education that most of us know, for it has dominated all of education—even adult education until recently—since schools started being organized in the seventh century. Stated in their purest and most extreme form, these are the assumptions about learners inherent in the pedagogical model:

1. *Regarding the concept of the learner (and therefore, through conditioning in prior school experience, the learner's self-concept):* The learner is, by definition, a dependent personality, for the pedagogical model assigns to the teacher full responsibility for making all the decisions about what should be learned, how and when it should be learned, and whether it has been learned. The only role for the learner, therefore, is that of submissively carrying out the teacher's directions.

2. *Regarding the role of the learner's experience:* Learners enter into an educational activity with little experience that is of much value as a resource for learning. It is the experience of the teacher, the textbook writer, and the audiovisual aids producer that counts. Accordingly, the backbone of pedagogical methodology is transmission techniques—lectures, assigned readings, and audiovisual presentations.

3. *Regarding readiness to learn:* Students become ready to learn what they are told that they have to learn in order to advance to the next grade level; readiness is largely a function of age.

4. *Regarding orientation to learning:* Students enter into an educational activity with a subject-centered orientation to learning; they see learning as a process of acquiring prescribed subject matter content. Consequently, the curriculum is organized according to content units and is sequenced according to the logic of the subject matter.

5. *Regarding motivation to learn:* Students are motivated primarily by external pressures from parents and teachers, competition for grades, the consequences of failure, and the like.

This may sound like a caricature, but think back to all the teachers you have had. Didn't most of them operate on the basis of these assumptions? Of course, there have always been great teachers who experimented with other assumptions, but in my experience they were few and far between. In fact, teachers have been under pressure from their systems to be loyal to these assumptions, often in the name of "academic standards."

A New Approach to Learning—The Andragogical Model

In contrast—and in equally pure and extreme form—the assumptions inherent in the andragogical model are these:

1. *Regarding the concept of the learner:* The learner is self-directing. In fact, the psychological definition of adult is "One who has arrived at a self-concept of being responsible for one's own life, of being self-directing." When we have arrived at that point, we develop a deep psychological need to be perceived by others, and treated by others, as capable of taking responsibility for ourselves. And when we find ourselves in situations where we feel that others are imposing their wills on us without our participating in making decisions affecting us, we experience a feeling, often subconsciously, of resentment and resistance.

This fact about adult learners presents adult educators with a special problem. For even though adults may be totally self-directing in every other aspect of their lives—as workers, spouses, parents, citizens, leisure-time users—the minute they walk into a situation labeled "education," "training," or any of their synonyms, they hark back to their conditioning in school, assume a role of dependency, and demand to be taught. However, if they really are treated like children, this conditioned expectation conflicts with their much deeper psychological need to be self-directing, and their energy is diverted away from learning to dealing with this internal conflict. As they have become aware of this problem, adult educators have been devising strategies for helping adults make the transition from being dependent learners to being self-directed learners. It has become increasingly widespread practice to include an orientation to self-directed learning at the beginning of an educational activity or program (see Knowles, 1975; and selections 6 and 8 in Chapter Two; selections 1, 2, 3, and 8 in Chapter Three; selections 1 and 3 in Chapter Four).

    2. *Regarding the role of the learner's experience:* The andragogical model assumes that adults enter into an educational activity with both a greater volume and a different quality of experience from youth. The greater volume is self-evident; the longer we live, the more experience we accumulate, at least in normal lives. The difference in quality of experience occurs because adults perform different roles from young people, such as the roles of full-time worker, spouse, parent, and voting citizen.

    This difference in experience has several consequences for education. First of all, it means that, for many kinds of learning, adults are themselves the richest resources for one another; hence the greater emphasis in adult education on such techniques—group discussion, simulation exercises, laboratory experiences, field experiences, problem-solving projects, and the like—that make use of the experiences of the learners. In addition, the differences in experience assure greater heterogeneity in groups of adults. The range of experience among a group of adults of various ages will be vastly greater than among a group of twelve-year-olds. Consequently, in adult education greater emphasis is placed on individualized learning plans, such as learning contracts (Knowles, 1975, 1980; see also Chapter Two, selections 1, 6, and 8; Chapter Three, selections 1 and 5; Chapter Four, selection 3; Chapter Five, selections 1 and 3). But there is a possible negative consequence as well. Because of their experience, adults often have developed habitual ways of thinking and acting, preconceptions about reality, prejudices, and defensiveness about their past ways of thinking and doing. To overcome this problem, adult educators are devising strategies for helping people become more open-minded (Benne, Bradford, and Lippitt, 1975; Davis and Scott, 1971; Ray, 1973).

    There is a more subtle and perhaps even more potent consequence of adults' greater experience: it becomes increasingly the source of an adult's self-identity. Let me illustrate this point. If I had been asked when I was ten years old "Who are you?" I would have explained: "My name is Malcolm Knowles, the son of Dr. A. D. Knowles, a veterinarian; I belong to the Presbyterian Sunday School; I live at 415 Fourth Street, Missoula, Montana; and I attend school at the Roosevelt Grammar School on Sixth Street." My self-identity would be derived almost exclusively from external sources—the name I was given by my parents, my father's vocation, my religious affiliation, my residence, and my school. If I had been asked the same question at age forty, I would have given my name and then recounted the positions I had held with the NYA, the YMCA, the AEA, and so on. Like other adults, I would derive my self-identity from my experience. So if in an educational situation an adult's experience is ignored, not valued, not made use of, it is not just the experience that is being rejected; it is the person. Hence the great importance of using the experience of adult learners as a rich resource for learning. This principle is especially important in working with undereducated adults, who, after all, have little to sustain their dignity other than their experience.

3. *Regarding readiness to learn:* The andragogical model assumes that adults become ready to learn when they experience a need to know or do something in order to perform more effectively in some aspect of their lives. Chief sources of readiness are the developmental tasks associated with moving from one stage of development to another; but any change—birth of children, loss of job, divorce, death of a friend or relative, change of residence—is likely to trigger a readiness to learn. But we don't need to wait for readiness to develop naturally; there are things we can do to induce it, such as exposing learners to more effective role models, engaging them in career planning, and providing them with diagnostic experiences in which they can assess the gaps between where they are now and where they want and need to be (Knowles, 1980).

4. *Regarding orientation to learning:* Because adults are motivated to learn after they experience a need in their life situation, they enter an educational activity with a life-centered,

task-centered, or problem-centered orientation to learning. For the most part, adults do not learn for the sake of learning; they learn in order to be able to perform a task, solve a problem, or live in a more satisfying way. The chief implication of this assumption is the importance of organizing learning experiences (the curriculum) around life situations rather than according to subject matter units. For example, courses that might be titled "Composition I," "Composition II," and "Composition III" in a high school might better be titled "Writing Better Business Letters," "Writing for Pleasure and Profit," and "Improving Your Professional Communications" in an adult education program. I had a terrible time learning to use the computer on which I am writing this chapter because the instructional manual set out to teach me about computers rather than teaching me how to use the computer to compose a chapter.

Another implication is the importance of making clear at the outset of a learning experience what its relevance is to the learner's life tasks or problems. We have a dictum in adult education that one of the first tasks of a facilitator of learning is to develop "the need to know" what will be learned (see Freire, 1970; Knowles, 1980).

5. *Regarding motivation to learn:* Although it acknowledges that adults will respond to some external motivators—a better job, a salary increase, and the like—the andragogical model predicates that the more potent motivators are internal—self-esteem, recognition, better quality of life, greater self-confidence, self-actualization, and the like (Herzberg, 1966; Maslow, 1970). Program announcements are accordingly placing increasing emphasis on these kinds of outcomes.

Choosing Which Model to Use

As I have said, I now regard the pedagogical and andragogical models as parallel, not antithetical. For centuries educators had only one model, the pedagogical model, to go on. Now we have two sets of assumptions about learners. In some situations, such as when learners of whatever age are entering a totally strange territory of content or are confronting a machine they have never seen before, they may be truly dependent on didactic instruction before they can take much initiative in their own learning; in such situations the pedagogical assumption of dependency is realistic, and pedagogical strategies would be appropriate. In many more instances, however, especially with adult learners, the andragogical assumptions would be realistic—particularly if the learners have had some orientation to self-directed learning—and andragogical strategies would be appropriate. There is growing evidence (see Chapter Seven, selections 1, 2, and 3) that the andragogical assumptions are realistic in many more situations than traditional schooling has recognized. For example, children are very self-directing in their learning *outside of school* and could also be more self-directed in school. Children and youth bring *some* experience with them into an educational activity, and this experience could be used as a resource for some kinds of learning. Children and youth also are more ready to learn when they experience a "need to know" than when they are told they have to learn, and we can expose them to life situations through which they will become aware of what they need to know. Finally, children and youth are naturally more motivated by intrinsic rewards than by external pressures; it is schools that have conditioned them to be otherwise (see Chapter Seven, selection 1).

Implications for Program Design

The pedagogical and andragogical models result in two very different approaches to the design and operation of educational programs. The basic format of the pedagogical model is a *content plan,* which requires the teacher to answer only four questions:

1. What content needs to be covered? The implication is that it is the teacher's responsibility to cover—in the classroom or through assigned reading—all the content that students need to learn. So the pedagogue constructs a long list of content items to be covered. (This requirement seems to me to place an unfair burden on the teacher to master all

the content and to doom the students to be limited to the teacher's resources.)

2. How can this content be organized into manageable units, such as fifty-minute, three-hour, or one-week units? So the pedagogue clusters the content items into manageable units.
3. What would be the most logical sequence in which to present these units? It is the logic of the subject matter that determines the sequence, not the readiness of the learners or other psychological factors. So, in mathematical or scientific content programs, the sequence is typically from simple to complex; in history it is chronological.
4. What would be the most efficient means of transmitting this content? With highly informational content, the preferred means would probably be lecture or audiovisual presentations and assigned reading; if the content involves skill performance, it would probably be demonstration by the teacher and drill by the students.

In contrast, the basic format of the andragogical model is a *process design.* The andragogical model assigns a dual role to the facilitator of learning (a title preferred over "teacher"): first and primarily, the role of designer and manager of processes or procedures that will facilitate the acquisition of content by the learners; and only secondarily, the role of content resource. The andragogical model assumes that there are many resources other than the teacher, including peers, individuals with specialized knowledge and skill in the community, a wide variety of material and media resources, and field experiences. One of the principal responsibilities of the andragogue is to know about all these resources and to link learners with them.

An andragogical process design consists of seven elements:

1. *Climate setting.* What procedures would be most likely to produce a climate that is conducive to learning? In my estimation, a climate that is conducive to learning is a prerequisite to effective learning; and it seems tragic to me that so little attention is paid to climate in traditional education. I attach so much importance to climate setting that I devote about 10 per-

cent of the time available in an educational activity to this element, and most of the case descriptions in this book do, too. In planning procedures for climate setting, I give attention to two aspects of climate: physical environment and psychological atmosphere.

In regard to *physical environment,* the typical classroom setup, with chairs in rows and a lectern in front, is probably the least conducive to learning that the fertile human brain could invent. It announces to anyone entering the room that the name of the game here is one-way transmission, that the proper role of the student is to sit and listen to transmissions from the lectern. I make a point of getting to a meeting room before the participants arrive, and if it is set up like a classroom I move the lectern to a corner and put the chairs in one large circle or several small circles. My preference is to have the participants sitting around tables, five or six to a table. I also prefer meeting rooms that are bright and cheerful, with colorful decor.

Important as physical climate is, *psychological climate* is even more important. Here are the characteristics of a psychological climate that is conducive to learning as I see it:

• *A climate of mutual respect.* People are more open to learning when they feel respected. If they feel that they are being talked down to, ignored, or regarded as dumb, and that their experience is not valued, their energy is spent dealing with this feeling more than with learning.

• *A climate of collaborativeness.* Because of their conditioning in their earlier school experience, in which competition for grades and teachers' favor was the norm, adults tend to enter into any educational activity with a rivalrous attitude toward fellow participants. Since, for many kinds of learning in adult education, peers are the richest resources for learning, this competitiveness makes those resources inaccessible. For this reason the climate-setting exercise with which I open all my workshops and courses puts the participants into a sharing relationship from the outset.

• *A climate of mutual trust.* People learn from those they trust more than from those they mistrust. And here we who are put in the position of teacher or trainer of adults are at

a disadvantage, for students in schools learn at an early age that
on the whole teachers are not very trustworthy. For one thing,
they have power over students; they are authorized to give
grades, to determine who passes or fails, and otherwise to hand
out punishments and rewards. For another thing, the institutions in which they work present them in their catalogues and
program announcements as authority figures. And it is built
into the bloodstreams of those who grew up in the Judeo-
Christian democratic tradition that authority figures are to be
mistrusted, at least until they are tested and their degree of
trustworthiness determined. In my workshops I try to convey in
various ways (for instance, by encouraging participants to make
decisions and by lending them my books) that I trust participants and hope thereby to obtain their trust.

   • *A climate of supportiveness.* People learn better when
they feel supported rather than judged or threatened. I convey
my desire to be supportive by accepting learners with an unqualified positive regard, matching any diagnosis of a weakness
with a valuing of a strength, empathizing with their problems or
worries, and defining my role as that of a helper. But I also organize them into peer-support groups and coach them on how
to support one another.

   • *A climate of openness and authenticity.* When people
feel free to be open and natural, to say what they really think
and feel, they are more likely to be willing to examine new
ideas and risk new behaviors than when they feel the need to be
defensive. In school we often have to pretend to know things
that we don't or to think things that we don't or to feel things
that we don't, and this interferes with learning. If the teacher or
trainer demonstrates openness and authenticity in his or her
own behavior, this will be the model that participants will adopt.

   • *A climate of pleasure.* Learning should be one of the
most pleasant and gratifying experiences in life; for, after all, it
is the way people can become what they are capable of being—
achieving their full potential. It should be an adventure, spiced
with the excitement of discovery. It should be fun. I think it is
tragic that so much of our previous educational experience has
been a dull chore.

• *A climate of humanness.* Perhaps what I have been saying about climate can be summed up with the adjective "human." Learning is a very human activity. The more people feel that they are being treated as human beings, the more they are likely to learn. Among other things, this means providing for human comfort—good lighting and ventilation, comfortable chairs, availability of refreshments, designation of nonsmoking areas, frequent breaks, and the like. It also means providing a caring, accepting, respecting, helping social atmosphere.

A climate-setting exercise designed to bring these characteristics into being is described in Chapter Four, selection 6, and other climate-setting strategies are described in Chapter Two, selection 8; Chapter Three, selections 7 and 8; and Chapter Eight, selection 2.

2. *Involving learners in mutual planning.* What procedures can be used to get the participants to share in the planning? I sometimes have subgroups choose a representative to serve on a planning committee to meet with me to discuss where we should go next. Frequently I will present several optional possibilities for activities and ask the groups to discuss them and report their preferences. There is a basic law of human nature at work here: people tend to feel committed to any decision in proportion to the extent to which they have participated in making it; the reverse is even more true—people tend to feel *uncommitted* to any decision to the extent that they feel others are making it for them and imposing it on them.

3. *Involving participants in diagnosing their own needs for learning.* What procedures can be used for helping learners responsibly and realistically identify what they need to learn? One of the pervasive problems in this process is meshing the needs the learners are aware of (felt needs) with the needs their organizations or society has for them (ascribed needs). A variety of strategies are available, ranging from simple interest-finding checklists to elaborate performance assessment systems, with a balance between felt needs and ascribed needs being negotiated between the facilitator and the learners. I frequently use a model of competencies, which reflects both personal and organizational needs, so that the learners can identify the gaps

between where they are now and where the model specifies they need to be (see Knowles, 1980, pp. 229-232, 256-261, 369, 371).

4. *Involving learners in formulating their learning objectives.* What procedures can be used to help learners translate their diagnosed needs into learning objectives? See the following section on learning contracts.

5. *Involving learners in designing learning plans.* What procedures can be used to help the learners identify resources and devise strategies for using these resources to accomplish their objectives? See the following section on learning contracts.

6. *Helping learners carry out their learning plans.* See the following section on learning contracts.

7. *Involving learners in evaluating their learning.* Evaluation of the accomplishment of objectives by individual learners is treated in the following section. But evaluation is also concerned with judging the quality and worth of the total program. Assessing individuals' learning outcomes is a part of this larger evaluation, but more than this is involved in this process. This book is not the place to go into detail about the complex process of program evaluation, but I would be remiss if I neglected to call my readers' attention to the fact that a major turn in our very way of thinking about evaluation has been in progress in the last few years. This turn, away from almost exclusive emphasis on quantitative evaluation toward increasing emphasis on qualitative evaluation, is described in Cronbach and others, 1980; Guba and Lincoln, 1981; Kirkpatrick, 1975; and Patton, 1978, 1980, 1981, 1982.

Using Learning Contracts to Provide Structure

Learning contracts are an effective way to help learners structure their learning. Some people have difficulty with the term "contract" because of its legalistic flavor and substitute "learning plan" or "learning agreement" for it. But "learning contract" is the term most often found in the literature.

The procedure I use in helping learners design and execute learning contracts is as follows: (1) Each learner translates a diagnosed learning need into a learning objective that describes the terminal behavior to be achieved (which is appropriate for most basic skills learning) or the direction of improvement in ability (which is appropriate for more complex learnings). (2) The learner next identifies, with the facilitator's help, the most effective resources and strategies for accomplishing each objective. (3) The learner then specifies what evidence will be collected for indicating the extent to which each objective was accomplished. (4) Finally, the learner specifies how this evidence will be judged or validated. After the learners have completed a first draft of their contracts, they review the drafts with small groups of peers and get their reactions and suggestions. Then I review the contracts to make sure that the required objectives of the program are included, to suggest other resources, and to determine whether I can agree with the learners' proposals for collecting and validating evidence of accomplishment. Once I approve a contract, the learner proceeds to carry it out, with me always available as a consultant and resource. The resources specified in the contracts include group activities; information inputs by me or other specialists, peers, or individuals in the community; and independent study. When the contracts are fulfilled, the learners present me with their "portfolios of evidence," which often include papers, tapes, rating scales by judges or observers, and oral presentations. I indicate whether I accept the portfolio as fulfilling the contract or, if not, what additional evidence is required for my acceptance.

I use learning contracts in almost all of my practice. Students contract with me to meet the requirements of the university courses I teach. (Incidentally, even though there may be a number of unnegotiable requirements, the means by which students accomplish required objectives can be highly individualized.) Students going out on field experiences, such as practicums or internships, contract with me and the field supervisor— a three-way contract. I also use contracts in short-term workshops, but in these the learners leave the workshop with a contract specifying how they are going to continue to learn on their own. Finally, I use learning contracts in the in-service education programs I am involved in; many physicians, nurses, social workers, managers and supervisors, and educators are using learning contracts for their continuing personal and professional development.

More detailed descriptions of contract learning can be found in Knowles, 1975, pp. 25-28; 1978, pp. 127-128, 198-203; 1980, pp. 243-244, 381-389; and in Chapter Two, selections 1, 6, and 8; Chapter Three, selections 1 and 5; and Chapter Five, selections 1 and 3, in this book.

Ways of Using Andragogy for Education and Training

The andragogical model has been widely adopted or adapted in a variety of programs—from individual courses at every level of education to total programs of in-service education, undergraduate education, graduate education, continuing education, human resources development, continuing professional education, technical training, remedial education, and religious education. It appears in almost every kind of institution, including elementary and secondary schools, community colleges, colleges and universities, business and industry, government agencies, health agencies, professional societies, churches, and voluntary organizations—in North America and around the world. "Andragogy" was so recently introduced into our literature (a decade and a half ago), though, that it does not yet appear in a dictionary. But it will before long.

As Cross (1981, pp. 227-228) states, "Whether andragogy can serve as the foundation for a unifying theory of adult education remains to be seen. At the very least, it identifies some characteristics of adult learners that deserve attention. It has been far more successful than most theory in getting the attention of practitioners, and it has been moderately successful in sparking debate; it has not been especially successful, however, in stimulating research to test the assumptions. Most important, perhaps, the visibility of andragogy has heightened awareness of the need for answers to three major questions: (1) Is it useful to distinguish the learning needs of adults from those of children? If so, are we talking about dichotomous differences or continuous differences? Or both? What are we really seeking:

Theories of learning? Theories of teaching? Both? (3) Do we have, or can we develop, an initial framework on which successive generations of scholars can build? Does andragogy lead to researchable questions that will advance knowledge in adult education?" Actually, a growing amount of research is being done, which I shall summarize in the last chapter. But I agree that andragogy's greatest impact has been in action.

TWO

Applications
in Business, Industry,
and Government

I have often wondered why, among the many kinds of organizations I work with, those that seem most consistently open to new ideas and approaches are business and industry—especially large corporations. My guess is that the answer is competition. In order to be competitive, corporations must keep up with, if not get ahead of, their rivals in the marketplace. And in the case of productivity and sales, the effectiveness of personnel is at least as critical as machinery and advertising. For this reason, corporations have been among the most innovative in applying modern concepts of adult learning in their human resources development programs.

This chapter opens with a description of the American Management Associations' master's degree program in management, which is organized around two of the newest ideas in education—andragogy and competency-based education. Next, it presents the General Electric Company's unique andragogical approach to program design (selection 2). It then investigates the relevance of the andragogical model to highly technical training in one of the country's largest accounting firms (selection 3) and to the training of line supervisors and managers as people developers in a manufacturing company (selection 4).

23

After a brief discussion of self-directed learning in a bank (selection 5), it examines the implementation of the andragogical
model in training for automation in an insurance company (selection 6) and in training customers to operate highly technical
equipment (selection 7).

Turning to government agencies, which have a somewhat
less glowing record of innovation, the concluding selection describes a creative approach to management development from
the Queensland Public Service in Australia.

1

Master of Management Program at the American Management Associations

Tony Daloisio, Marsha Firestone,
Harry F. Evarts

This is a case description of a master's degree program in management that was consciously based on the andragogical model. The program officially opened with its first regular class on January 26, 1981, after a six-year developmental period that included an extensive research study into the competencies possessed by managers who were outstanding performers.

Tony Daloisio and Marsha Firestone were members of the faculty of the Institute for Management Competency of the American Management Associations in New York City at the time their article was written. Harry F. Evarts is group vice president, research and development, of the AMA.

Special features:

- Competency-based education
- Performance assessment both for admission and graduation

Adapted from an article by Tony Daloisio and Marsha Firestone, "A Case Study in Applying Adult Learning Theory in Developing Managers," *Training and Development Journal*, 1983, *37* (2), 73–78; copyright 1983, *Training and Development Journal*, American Society for Training and Development; reprinted with permission, all rights reserved; and from a paper presented by Harry F. Evarts, American Management Associations, to the Academy of Management, August 1982, with permission.

- Recognition of learning through prior experience and training
- Use of individualized learning plans (learning contracts)
- Systematic feedback
- Provision of a variety of learning experiences
- On-the-job application

The Competency Program offered by the American Management Associations (AMA) is a case study of the application of the purposes, processes, and assumptions regarding adult learning developed by Malcolm Knowles. A nontraditional approach to graduate management education, the program is designed to help managers become more effective. As a base, a behavioral research firm (McBer & Company of Boston) identified what makes a manager effective. Its study of over 2,000 managers in a variety of jobs and organizations delineated eighteen generic management competencies. An applicant to the program is assessed through audio- and videotaped operant exercises and special tests. The assessment determines the extent to which the applicant possesses and uses the program's skill and knowledge competencies. Six weeks after the initial assessment, the applicant returns for feedback on the test results. Students learn about the competencies by attending didactics, participating in group discussions, meeting individually with faculty advisers, and sharing examples of the competencies with group members. Based on the understanding of their performance in the assessment process, the students, with the aid of their faculty adviser, design a competency development plan (CDP) or syllabus for an independent course of study. Students then work one-to-one with the guidance of a faculty adviser to carry out their plans on the job.

Model of Competencies

The research into the competencies of high-performing managers identified eighteen generic competencies, which cluster into four groups. These competencies constitute the foundation of the Competency Program (for complete definitions and descriptions, see Boyatzis, 1982):

Goal and Action Management Cluster

Efficiency orientation
Proactivity
Concern with impact
Diagnostic use of concepts

Directing Subordinates Cluster

Use of unilateral power
Developing others
Spontaneity

Human Resource Management Cluster

Use of socialized power
Managing group process
Positive regard
Accurate self-assessment
Self-control
Stamina and adaptability

Leadership Cluster

Self-confidence
Conceptualization
Logical thought
Use of oral presentation

Faculty and Students

Faculty are required to meet specific criteria. All have a doctoral degree. All have been managers during their careers. Each has expertise in a specific relevant field. All have had interactive teaching experience, and each possesses the competencies needed to deliver the program.

Students must have managerial responsibilities in organizations willing to provide both financial support and opportunities to practice competencies on the job. Most of the participants have reached the managerial level by virtue of their technical expertise in their areas of specialization. Many are outstanding sales people, computer technicians, or production specialists. Few have been trained to be managers.

Assessment Process

The first step in the program is to identify the competencies a student has as compared to those contained in the model. Each applicant takes part in several operant exercises, which are video- and audiotaped. During these exercises a number of different opportunities are available for competencies to be demonstrated. In addition to these exercises, students are further assessed through the use of a special battery of tests, by which AMA is able to evaluate their traits, motives, learning styles, cognitive abilities, and interests. Knowledge competencies are tested by both objective and case study exams. The process is extremely thorough, requiring five days, and generates a large amount of information.

Participants work individually to think through priorities for self-development and to establish specific behavioral objectives. They consider short-term job-related needs as well as long-term career objectives. They present these objectives to the faculty adviser during an individual counseling session and then to their study group for reality testing.

Feedback Process

Six weeks after the assessment, students return to receive feedback. The amount of information about each necessitates that one week be devoted to presenting the feedback and integrating the material with the competency model. In addition to reviewing audio- and videotapes as a major aid to learning, students spend significant amounts of time on a one-to-one basis with the faculty.

Competency Acquisition Process

The goal of the program is for students to acquire and use the competencies in the model. AMA incorporates the six stages of adult competency development:

1. Recognition of the competency.
2. Understanding of the competency.

3. Assessment of the competency.
4. Experimentation with demonstrating the competency.
5. Practice using the competency.
6. Application of the competency on the job.

The first three stages begin during Feedback Week. The distinctive aspect of this competency acquisition process is the final three steps. This program guides the individual through all steps in the process in a unique faculty/student relationship. The faculty are available at all times to work with and guide the students on a one-to-one basis.

Learning Plans

The last three steps of the competency acquisition process are continued with the use of individualized learning plans, first drafted during Feedback Week. Students create their own independent course of experimentation and practice in the use of knowledge and skills they have not yet acquired or demonstrated. Although the students design the plans, they do it with professional guidance from the faculty.

The learning plan (or contract; see Knowles, 1975) is composed of several distinct but interrelated parts: the statement of specific learning objectives; a measurable outcome that addresses the question "How do I know that I have accomplished the objectives?"; target dates for completing the various objectives; and means or activities that will be used for accomplishing the objectives.

Once the learning plans are completed and approved, students carry out their own learning process while on their jobs.

Resources

An inventory of all existing relevant learning resources is made available to faculty and students. Students choose their learning experiences from university business courses, AMA seminars, in-house programs at their work site, cassettes, and textbooks. This design is intentionally planned for maximum flexibility in permitting students to choose their own time and place for learning.

AMA offers several skill courses that are not readily available elsewhere. They include such areas as Developing Leadership Competencies; Developing Influence Skills; Maximizing Managerial Objectivity, Influence, and Power; Coaching and Appraisal Skills; Enhancing Executive Presence; Executive Group Dynamics; Goal and Action Management; Directing and Developing Subordinates; Superior Communication; and Developing Managerial Flexibility.

Documentation of Performance

Program completion requires use of competencies on the job. Documentation of performance may be considered analogous to the final exam in a traditional course of study. It is proof that an individual has acquired the ability to use the competencies on the job and is the final step in the competency acquisition process. The Documentation of Performance is submitted in a portfolio which is modeled after the legal process. It requires both physical evidence and relevant and reliable testimonial evidence to be submitted for each competency. The evidence is subsequently evaluated by a faculty panel for acceptance or rejection.

Completion Requirements

In order to complete the program, students are required to demonstrate competencies during assessment as well as to submit documentation that they have used the competencies on the job. The competencies must be demonstrated a minimum of thirty-two times during assessment, and they must be documented a minimum of twenty-two times on the job. In sum, there are fifty-four units of evidence required to earn a Master of Management degree.

Conclusion

Adult education and training have come of age. The interest in adult education has necessitated reviewing the assumptions underlying adult learning, as well as the processes used in helping adults develop. The following comments from the program highlight conclusions about the effectiveness of applied theories of adult learning:

> From the underlying assumptions of the andragogical model, some of the concepts seem to work in the program while others do not. Two problematic areas relate to the self-concept and motivation of the learner. Many participants remain accustomed to externally directed techniques. Motivation is at its highest point at the conclusion of "Feedback Week." Participants leave enthusiastic about the learning process; however, their motivation for involvement decreases with time.
>
> With respect to process elements of the andragogical model, specific areas are problematic. For example, the learning plans are not always carried out in a systematic manner. Time limitations and work activities often take precedence over these learning plans. As the distance from feedback increases, participants become less committed to the process.

Those assumptions and process elements of the andragogical model that work effectively support the continuation of the Competency Program. Program designers are currently rethinking techniques to resolve the problematic areas.

2

Managerial Skills Development
at General Electric

Edward H. Thorne, Jean L. Marshall

Adapting the andragogical model to a manufacturing setting, the General Electric Company in Cincinnati, the authors set out to create an environment in which a program for developing management skills could thrive. They demonstrated particularly the effectiveness of using teams of managers in assessing needs, planning the program, designing and implementing learning modules, and evaluating results as a way to ensure a quality program and management commitment.

Edward Thorne held a variety of managerial jobs in industry, including assignments in manufacturing, engineering, and personnel relations, before joining General Electric Company in Cincinnati as manager of organization and manpower. Jean Marshall worked in General Electric's Aircraft Engine Group (AEG) in employee training and development and later became the ombudsperson for the Evendale plant, responsible for helping resolve problems between the employees and their managers.

Special features:

- A stated program objective and philosophy
- Creating an educative environment
- Getting group commitment
- Achieving group-centered action

Adapted from "Managerial Skills Development: An Experience in Program Design," by Edward H. Thorne and Jean L. Marshall, copyright 1976. Reprinted with the permission of *Personnel Journal*, Costa Mesa, California (January 1976, pp. 15–38); all rights reserved.

- Program evaluation and revision
- Manager/instructor teams
- Professional packaging
- Program design
- Needs assessment
- Learning modules

Exhibit 1 displays an overview of our experience in designing a managerial skills development (MSD) program.

Exhibit 1. Stages in Designing a Managerial Skills Development Program.

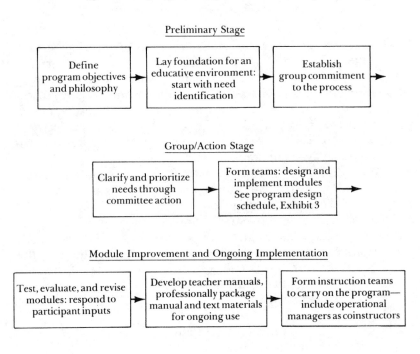

Preliminary Stage

| Define program objectives and philosophy | Lay foundation for an educative environment: start with need identification | Establish group commitment to the process |

Group/Action Stage

| Clarify and prioritize needs through committee action | Form teams: design and implement modules See program design schedule, Exhibit 3 |

Module Improvement and Ongoing Implementation

| Test, evaluate, and revise modules: respond to participant inputs | Develop teacher manuals, professionally package manual and text materials for ongoing use | Form instruction teams to carry on the program— include operational managers as coinstructors |

Program Objective and Philosophy

A democratic philosophy is characterized by a concern for the development of persons, a deep conviction as to the worth of every individual, and

faith that people will make the right decisions for
themselves if given the necessary information and
support [Knowles, 1970, p. 60].

We think that all educational programs must start with a
basic stated objective and philosophy. We had no difficulty in
defining our objective: to provide skills training that would
meet managerial needs. Our philosophy was more difficult to
define: we subscribed to the adult education philosophy. Our
challenge was to adapt the adult education model to the indus-
trial setting.

The andragogical model stresses the importance of building an educative environment in any institution or organization
concerned with helping people learn. Knowles (1970, p. 60)
lists four basic conditions of an educative environment:

• Respect for personality.
• Participation in decision making.
• Freedom of expression and availability of information.
• Mutuality of responsibility in defining goals, planning and
  conducting activities, and evaluating.

Where can an environment such as this be found, especially in industry? Our answer is to build it. Acting on the premise that environment is largely what people make it, we set out
to create an environment in which the MSD program could live
and flourish.

Building an Educative Environment

For if one thing stands out about adult learning, it is that a self-diagnosed need for learning pro-
duces a much greater motivation to learn than an
externally diagnosed need [Knowles, 1970, p.
284].

First, in keeping with Knowles's concept of respect for
personality, we brought together our personnel relations people
to pool perceptions of the middle managers who wanted skill

development training. We concluded that managers are self-directing adults who can best identify their own training needs. We also perceived them to be a resource for designing an adult education program to meet those needs. We recognized that, as participants in an adult education process, managers had to be involved in the development of the program from the very beginning.

Hence, our next step in building the educative environment was to hold a series of informal meetings, limited to less than fifty middle managers per session. All 1,500 of the plant's middle management were invited; approximately one third attended. The objective of the meetings was made clear in advance: to discuss skill development needs, especially those related to personnel practices. Top-level personnel relations managers conducted the meetings and led the discussions. At the end of each meeting, those present were asked to fill out a questionnaire and return it before leaving.

The questionnaire (Exhibit 2) was designed for use as a self-diagnostic tool. It included a checklist of typical development needs to spark the managers' thinking. Space was provided for managers to identify and add more of their own personal needs. Every manager attending the auditorium sessions completed the questionnaire. As a result, we derived a representative indication of the managers' self-perceived needs. In keeping with Knowles's second condition for an educative environment, participative decision making, we also involved a large number of managers in making a decision relative to their most pressing training needs. These preliminary activities laid a firm foundation for building the MSD educative environment.

Group Commitment

The questionnaire served an additional purpose. The final question asked managers to indicate their willingness to participate in further need clarification and in the development of a training program responsive to those needs. Approximately 60 percent of the managers indicated willingness to assist in this process. We later followed up with a representative group of

Exhibit 2. Questionnaire on Development Needs.

Check the items which indicate your needs:

_____ Increased skill in conducting performance appraisals and providing suggestions for your employees' continued growth and development.

_____ More knowledge about exempt compensation practices and procedures.

_____ A better understanding of promotion and placement systems.

_____ Increased ability to assist your employees with determining career paths and with developing action plans for achieving career goals.

_____ Improved decision-making and problem-solving ability.

_____ A better understanding of managerial and leadership styles.

_____ Greater sensitivity to others and more effective interpersonal skills.

_____ More knowledge about techniques for work planning and goal setting.

_____ Increased understanding of team building and motivation techniques.

_____ Improved communication skills, including oral, written, and listening ability.

_____ More information about the financial aspects of management, such as cost savings, manpower planning, and budget reviews.

_____ Increased knowledge of employee benefits.

_____ Improved interviewing, evaluating, and assessment ability.

_____ Better planning and organizational skills.

_____ Greater understanding of AEG and GE from a business and organizational standpoint.

Please indicate other areas of interest and needs—

Would you be willing to work with others to further define managerial skills needs and to help develop a meaningful program which would respond to those needs? (Please check ____ YES ____ NO).

Name _____ Mail Drop _____

---

these willing middle managers to confirm their commitment and involvement.

Throughout this process we were careful to keep upper management informed of what was happening. Program success clearly depended upon their commitment, support, and sense of ownership. There is little doubt in our minds that a successful program must have the backing of the people who make financial decisions as well as commitment from those who will directly benefit from the program.

Group-Centered Action

The group-centered method is one in which the members select the subject for discussion, carry it through, make decisions, develop conclusions, and implement the outcomes [Kemp, 1964, p. 21].

Now, having stated a program philosophy, laid the groundwork for an educative environment, and established group commitment to the process, we moved on to the next step: group action. Initially, four committees were selected, each consisting of fifteen middle managers and three personnel relations representatives. The four committees met separately with the common assigned task to:

Identify the four top-priority skill development needs, using questionnaire results as a guide. The questionnaire provided information on how many people thought that a specific need was important; the committees assessed the importance of each need to the business.

Set four more priorities for later module development.

Select representatives to design the first four top-priority modules.

The next phase of module development involved subcommittee action. Each subcommittee was comprised of three operating and two personnel relations people who represented each fifteen-member committee. Subcommittees met as a total group to review the process to date, further define the top priorities, and regroup into four design teams according to individual interest in top-priority items.

The four top-priority needs were:

Motivation and Communication

Career Development

Work Planning and Performance Appraisals

Compensation

Each design team was charged with the task of designing a "module" that would meet one of those four needs. A module was defined as a learning experience consisting of three sessions or less, not to exceed nine hours. A tight time schedule was established for completion of module design. The schedule was evaluated by each team and modified to enable the teams to achieve the high standards they set for themselves.

Before the four design teams began to work, they were provided with a "gallery walk" to review the readily available resources pertinent to their topic. The term "gallery" refers to a collection of materials on display in a large room. Included were flip chart listings of consultants, programs, and other resources. This gave the teams a starting point and helped fulfill the third condition of Knowles's educative environment: availability of information. Subsequent investigations by team members included field trips, consultation with "experts," a review of additional literature, a look at what other companies were doing, talks with sales representatives of packaged programs, and a study of adult education techniques such as games, videotapes, and role plays.

Following the investigations the teams began a series of meetings to develop and refine assigned modules within the agreed-upon time frame. In the early stages of program development, team members were concerned because they did not perceive themselves as having enough knowledge to design a meaningful learning experience. Some wanted to bring in an "expert" to do the trick for them. However, as involvement increased and program development progressed, more self-confidence and real feelings of accomplishment became apparent.

Program Evaluation and Revision

Andragogical theory prescribes a process of self-evaluation, in which the teachers devote their

energy to helping the adults get evidence for themselves about the progress they are making toward
their educational goals. In this process the strengths
and weaknesses of the educational program itself
must be assessed in terms of how it has facilitated
or inhibited the learning of the students [Knowles,
1970, p. 43].

Once completed to the satisfaction of each team, modules were evaluated and refined twice. Members of the original
fifteen-member committees attended in a participant's role.
Their responsibility was to critique the program through a rediagnosis of learning needs and to recommend program improvement. In cases where original members were not available,
other managers who had previously expressed needs and interest in the process were involved. Once the recommended changes
were incorporated, modules were "complete" and the original
contract with all teams came to an end. Two major problems remained unsolved, however, and the design teams were called
back into action. (1) An ongoing instruction team had to be
established and trained to carry on the program. (2) Program
packaging was needed to give the program an added touch of
professionalism.

Manager/Instructor Teams

We decided through committee action that ongoing MSD
instruction teams would remain in place to ensure proper training of the new teams. Using key managers as instructors was
viewed as having payoff in training the manager to work more
effectively as a team leader, developing group rapport or team
building, providing ongoing reinforcement of course materials,
establishing strong ownership ties, and setting up an "expert" in
each area who could act as a resource for others who might
need help in putting skills development learning to work.

Professional Packaging

Packaging involved renewed team action and overcoming
inertia generated by original contract "completion." Inertia was

overcome, and teams met to develop and provide an abstract of course objectives and content, a teacher's manual to ensure on-going process and materials integrity, and a "text" of reference materials with at least short-range applicability.

With the packaging of the modules, the MSD program design was complete. Based on our adult education philosophy, a supportive educative climate had been established, group commitment to the process was achieved, and "needs" had been mutually identified. Through team action, training modules were developed, assessed, and packaged, and instructor teams were trained (Exhibit 3). The learner was involved throughout the process and, as a result, acquired a considerable amount of expertise while designing a learning tool for use by others.

Our Assessment of the MSD Experience

The positive aspects:

- Our process from beginning to end involved both operational managers and personnel relations people. The pooled experience, knowledge, and resources of these two groups resulted in an enriched end product.
- Ownership never became an issue. The usual suspicions of an "ivory tower" production were never generated. From the very beginning, the program belonged to those who requested, designed, and experienced it—the operations managers.
- Our process was adult education oriented all the way.
- Program design of MSD was based upon real and immediate needs. Shop conditions, managerial problems, and business needs were taken into consideration. Hence, the program had applicability and relevance.
- Although the primary emphasis was on experiential learning, the finished product contained substantial content, such as exposure to contemporary theories of the behavioral scientists; a broader knowledge of our compensation system; and increased understanding of effective approaches to performance appraisals, career discussion, and communication.

Exhibit 3. The Initial MSD Program Schedule.

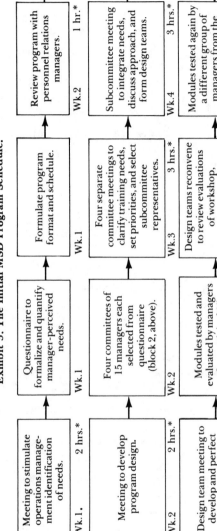
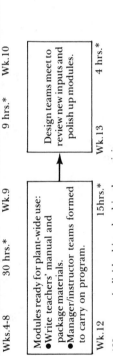

Meeting to stimulate operations management identification of needs.	Questionnaire to formalize and quantify manager-perceived needs.	Formulate program format and schedule.	Review program with personnel relations managers.
Wk.1. 2 hrs.*	Wk.1	Wk.1	Wk.2 1 hr.*

Meeting to develop program design.	Four committees of 15 managers each selected from questionnaire (block 2, above).	Four separate committee meetings to clarify training needs, set priorities, and select subcommittee representatives.	Subcommittee meeting to integrate needs, discuss approach, and form design teams.
Wk.2 2 hrs.*	Wk.2	Wk.3 3 hrs.*	Wk.4 3 hrs.*

Design team meeting to develop and perfect training modules.	Modules tested and evaluated by managers from original 15-member committees.	Design teams reconvene to review evaluations of workshop, recommend redesign, prepare to test second trial run.	Modules tested again by a different group of managers from the original 15-member committee.
Wks.4-8 30 hrs.*	Wk.9 9 hrs.*	Wk.10 6 hrs.*	Wk.11 9 hrs.*

Modules ready for plant-wide use: •Write teachers' manual and package materials. •Manager/instructor teams formed to carry on program.	Design teams meet to review new inputs and polish up modules.
Wk.12 15hrs.*	Wk.13 4 hrs.*

*Hours per individual involved in the activity.

Drawbacks in the program:

- Our timing left something to be desired. Program design took place during the summer vacation period, with resultant problems in getting teams and study groups together. Lots of substitutions were necessary, interest fell off, and patience wore thin. Also, due to a reshaping of the plant work force, managerial attention was split between commitment to the MSD program and to primary job problems. Naturally, job pressures were continual problems in our program development efforts.
- Once the "contract" agreements with the team members were met, everyone breathed a great sigh of relief and relaxed. We then tried to introduce new tasks and found that the letdown and inertia resulting from job completion were almost too great to overcome. It's easier to negotiate a "complete" contract at the onset than to start the momentum rolling again once it has stopped.
- All of the original fifteen manager-members of our teams were not kept up to date on what their representative subcommittees were doing; hence, they got lost in the shuffle and lost interest. The learning: Total, not partial, team involvement is crucial.

In summary, we believe that principles underlying the development of MSD are basic to any adult training. The success of such a program depends upon a democratic and supportive climate. The effectiveness of an adult education process varies to the extent that the educative environment has been developed. As previously stated, however, an environment is largely what you make it, and using the adult education approach to design a managerial skills development program may be a first step in creating a climate in which it can flourish.

3

Teaching Technical Skills
in a National Accounting Firm

Fredric H. Margolis

One of the frequent comments I hear in my workshops is "I can see how the andragogical model would work in 'soft' content areas like management development, but would it work with 'hard' content, like technical skills?" In this selection the author describes what he has learned in applying the model to training programs for technical personnel in one of the large national accounting firms. He emphasizes the necessity of teamwork between an adult education consultant and a technical expert in designing programs. In a personal letter to me at the end, he describes how he has applied this process to other technically oriented firms.

Fredric Margolis is an independent consultant in training design, training delivery, organization development, and conflict resolution based in Washington, D.C. He is a frequent presenter at meetings of the American Society for Training and Development.

Special features:

- Discovery learning
- An andragogical checklist
- Motivation
- Selection of content
- Selection of methods
- Course writer/technical expert teams

Adapted from an article, "Discovery Learning and Technical Material," *Northeast Training News*, November 1981, © 1981 Warren/Weingarten, Inc.; and from a personal letter dated April 15, 1983. By permission.

This article is about a revolution, a revolution that is going on right now. It's similar to the one that started a few years ago when management training curricula switched from an information-based (pedagogical) approach to a "discovery learning" (or andragogical) approach. This time the revolution is taking place in the training programs for people engaged in high technology and professional areas such as computer science, accounting, insurance, real estate, law, and medical science.

Traditionally, the training programs in these areas have focused primarily on a straightforward conveying of information. The approach seemed logical because the people working in high technology and the professions have a very simple need, the need to stay current with their fields. Their abilities depend on their knowledge of their subjects. Accountants cannot issue reports on financial statements unless they know recently issued principles of accounting. Accurate tax services cannot be offered if new tax laws are not understood. Hence, both learners and instructors expect the training to consist of a simple process of acquiring information.

But simply teaching the prescribed knowledge is not sufficient. If you are involved in information-based training programs long enough, you begin to hear revealing comments from managers and participants.

> "These people have learned the principles, but they don't know how to apply them."
> "This training program doesn't reflect the real world."
> "Some of the information was useful, but most of the session was over my head."
> "I knew most of that stuff before I came to the course."
> "Too many lectures and slides. After a while, it all seemed the same."

Many trainers have realized that relying primarily on the process of conveying information is not as effective as they want. Even slides, movies, and occasional discussions are limited in what they can do.

An Andragogical Revolution

The revolution started when some organizations started using job-related "discovery learning" approaches in their training programs. I was asked to be a consultant to such a company, which developed over seventy-five professional and high technology courses. The subsequent six years of helping them develop their courses taught me a lot about the andragogical approach.

The first problem I encountered was explaining the differences between information-based and "discovery learning" approaches. "Discovery learning" is the essence of andragogy. It is not easy to explain all the differences between andragogy and pedagogy, and there is much room for misinterpretation; so my initial job was to develop a checklist for determining the degree to which a program is information based or andragogically based:

1. Are participants given presentations, films, or readings, followed by a series of problems or cases to which they apply that information?
2. Are participants given problems or situations to analyze or solve, followed by the information needed to analyze or solve the problems?
3. Are problems or cases designed primarily to help participants understand the concepts?
4. Are problems or cases designed primarily to help participants do their work more effectively?
5. Is 50 percent or more of the training time used by participants to actively engage in problem solving, analysis, or decision making—usually with the help of other students?
6. Is the primary job of the instructor to present information, discuss questions, or pose reinforcing questions to the class?
7. Is the primary job of the instructor to help, consult, advise, and pose problems to be analyzed (both individual and in small groups) and then manage an interactive discussion?

There could be more questions, but by now you've got the point.

An andragogical approach:

- Emphasizes the skills of analysis and decision making through a series of job-related cases or problems.
- Establishes a learning approach rather than a teaching approach by a series of planned structured activities enabling the learner to acquire the appropriate knowledge.
- Is a practical, job-based approach which keeps the learners constantly aware of the value of the training program to them and their work.

Applying Andragogy

If you want to use the checklist on your own programs, the odd-numbered questions tend to get "yes" answers when the program is information based. The even-numbered questions tend to get "yes" answers when the program is more andragogical.

If your answers are mixed, review the questions again. Perhaps you missed a subtle issue. If your answers are still mixed, then you may have a little of both in your programs. You are on the road to revolution yourself.

Armed with the knowledge of the differences between information-based programs and "discovery learning," the next step is to work with technically knowledgeable people to write the courses. When I first started working with technical people, my responsibility was to help them (1) select the content, (2) sequence the content, (3) select methods which emphasized discovery learning, and (4) write the course so they or others could teach it.

Here are some other issues we confronted:

Motivation. We started with the idea that most professionals are motivated to work and motivated to learn. The motivation to work is stimulated by having interesting work to do, progressing in the profession, receiving financial reward, and getting appreciation and recognition from supervisors and clients.

The motivation to learn is closely tied to the motivation to do better work. Training courses must tap into this aspiration.

Courses that are seen by learners as closely tied to present or future work responsibilities are considered relevant; those that do not appear to be related to work content or processes may be seen by trainees as peripheral or "academic."

Inappropriate, boring, or seemingly peripheral training programs can actually reduce or temporarily extinguish the motivation that participants bring with them to the course. So competently designed training programs build on the existing motivation through careful selection of content and methods.

Selecting the Content. Different methods of carrying out a need diagnosis can be used, depending on the type of course, experience of the learners, and how frequently the course is to be offered.

Regardless of the diagnosis method, however, you must use the technical experts in the process because they are the ones who know what the trainees have to learn. On the other hand, the need diagnosis method should only identify what the learners need to know for their present jobs or work they will be doing in the near future. Anything else is going to undermine motivation.

You will find that most technical people have difficulty in limiting the content of a course. They want to include "everything." The best way to deal with this impulse is to use challenging questions: Why do the trainees have to know that? If they know this, how will it help them on their jobs? If they don't know this, how will it affect their work?

Selecting Methods. The general labels that trainers use for interactive methods don't always work for technical experts. The words "case," "discussion," or "question-and-answer session" do not convey to the technical people any picture of the learning that will take place. The challenge is to create specific activities that will obviously help participants improve the skills of analysis and decision making they need.

I tried to meet the challenge by developing a series of specific activities or tasks for each course, using a standard format:

1. A brief introduction and explanation.
2. Detailed specific instructions for the participants to follow.

3. The participants' active engagement in these activities—
   whether small-group discussion, question-and-answer sessions, or whatever.
4. A sharing or synthesis by the participants.
5. A summary or presentation by the instructor, based not on
   prepared texts but on some of the comments produced in
   the activity. This can also incorporate examples, presentation of principles, or practical experiences.

An activity should be selected according to the extent to
which it achieves the intended learning goals; is job-related; requires investigation, analysis, creativity, or decision making; is
challenging; requires new thought or synthesis and not simple
regurgitation; and is seen by participants as helpful to their
technical and professional development.

Resources Needed

In the process of discovery learning, the central person is
the course *writer*. This person must have competence in the
technical aspects of the course as well as competence in andragogical methodology.

The writer's technical competence is supplemented by a
consultant who is *technically expert* in the content area. The
technical expert assists in deciding on the content and final approval of the technical aspects.

The writer's methodological competence is supplemented
by a consultant who is experienced in *andragogical methodology*. This person helps determine the sequences of methods to
accomplish the learning goals and is responsible for checking the
methodological approach.

Usually, instructors for high-content courses are technically competent people who lack experience in teaching an andragogical course. The course, then, must be written with great
detail and attention given to managing the discovery learning
process as well as outlining the content that has to be learned.
And no matter how explicit the course design is, there must be
an instructor training course emphasizing the skills of presenting

and managing the five-step activity format mentioned above, as well as the skills of facilitating group discussion.

Just because the content of a training program is very technical or dense does not mean you have to rule out the excitement and effectiveness of discovery learning. In our project we developed seventy-five courses, of which a few were:

Computer Modeling

Making Computer Hardware/Software Choice

Advanced Statistical Samplings

Corporate Reorganizations and Business Acquisitions

Auditing Hospitals and Medical Services

The Principles of Escrow

When the training director of this firm was asked why his company switched from an information-based to an andragogical approach, he answered, "It works. Knowledge increases and is better retained when information is applied to job-related situations. We also found that the skills of analysis, problem solving, and decision making were improved when participants actively engaged in job-related problems. Most important, confidence and ability increased when participants successfully demonstrated professional competence in job-related situations in the training course."

After reading this selection, I wrote to Fred Margolis asking if he would write me a letter describing how he was applying the andragogical model to technical and professional training in other contexts. Here is his reply:

In the past three years I have worked with three organizations—Price Waterhouse, Du Pont, and the World Bank—helping them develop technical professional courses. Over 125 courses involving more than 2,200 classroom hours have been designed. The technical content included the more basic subjects—such as the policy and procedures for filling out required Internal Revenue Service reporting forms; determining whether a business should be organized as a corporation, a partnership, or a sole proprietorship; and financial management for nonfinancially trained managers—as well as more complex subjects, such as statistical sampling in the audit process and financial application system effectiveness review.

Each of these organizations has a different mission, structure, and set of educational needs. The courses differ widely in content and focus. Yet there are some similarities of experience. An examination of these common experiences might offer guidance for implementing the andragogical approach elsewhere:

- Each organization has a commitment to providing a superior service or product to customers or clients.
- There is a dedication to developing and keeping competent professional staff.
- The professional staff have a strong commitment to their own continued professional development.
- Each organization was dissatisfied with the result of courses which primarily relied upon lecture presentations.
- The content experts are in-house members of the professional staff and understand the unique ways the content is applied in their organizations.
- The content experts were responsible for producing the courses. The methodological consultant helped apply the andragogical principles.
- The content experts found that between ten and fifteen hours were required to produce each course hour.
- The instructors for these courses are drawn from the professional staff of the organizations and are active practitioners in their technical field.
- All instructors attend an instructor training program. The content includes (1) increasing the instructors' ability to focus on what gets learned rather than what gets taught; (2) making learning-oriented presentations; (3) giving instructions for small-group or individual activities; (4) group dynamics; (5) managing a large group sharing or reporting process; and (6) the interpersonal skills of training including the

do's and don't's of asking questions, the ability to evidence understanding, the process of paraphrasing, summarizing, and extending.

I'm not sure that all of these factors are necessary to ensure success, but they were present in each situation where the andragogical approach was used.

The advantages to the organizations include:

- The courses are seen by participants as directly related to their work, which results in increased motivation and attention to learning.
- The courses focus on increasing participants' ability in improving their professional judgments and decision making, resulting in increased professional ability on the job.
- Having content experts who are active practitioners teach the courses results in a richer, more highly relevant experience for the participants.
- After the content experts have developed a course, they find that less consultant help is needed for developing future courses.
- Though the instructor training course (two to three days in length) is focused on helping instructors teach a specific course, the skills learned are applicable to other courses and other areas.

The major disadvantage is:

- The developing of the course takes the time and active involvement of busy practitioners or managers who often would prefer to assign that task to others.

As each organization or department has experience with this process, it quickly becomes the preferred approach.

4

Line Managers
as Learning Facilitators
at an Equipment Manufacturer

Bernard S. Fabian, Barbara Mink

A major aspect of current thinking about human resources de-velopment is the notion that the most pervasive resource for the development of employees is their daily work experience. The chief responsibility for employee development, according to this line of reasoning, rests with the line supervisors and man-agers. The problem is that supervisors and managers have been trained to supervise work, not to be educators. Accordingly, they often lack the skills required for people development. This selection describes a program instituted by Joy Manufacturing Company to provide its supervisors and managers with these skills.

Bernard S. Fabian is manager of employee relations at Joy Manufacturing Company, Pittsburgh, and Barbara Mink is a consultant with OHRD Associates, Inc., Austin, Texas.

Special features:

- Creative use of a management steering committee
- Development of a competency model
- The role of training in company reorganization
- Matching training to positions
- Training managers as facilitators of learning
- Constructing course modules
- Module outlines and review form

Several years ago the Machinery Division of Joy Manufacturing Company, an international company that manufactures large underground mining equipment, found that a major customer/ sales problem had developed in its three marketing units. Each sales unit had the potential of contacting the same customer: one sales unit selling new mining machines, another sales unit selling complete machine rebuilds and rebuilt parts, and yet another unit selling new parts. Each of these sales units had reporting relationships in different parts of the company and sometimes had goals that conflicted with one another. The company was in competition with itself. As a result, a decision was made to develop a regional structure to consolidate the three marketing functions with the support functions of manufacturing and warehousing into the same business unit.

Step 1: The Management Steering Committee

A Management Reorganization Steering Committee, consisting of five senior executives in the business units involved and an external consultant with a long-term relationship with the company, began to develop the new organizational structure. After meeting for approximately thirty to forty hours over several months, the steering committee developed a reorganized business unit that would eliminate conflict and establish mutual goals. At this time the steering committee expanded to include a human resource development (HRD) professional who would assist in developing the interventions necessary to achieve the goals of the reorganization.

Step 2: Development of Skill Dimensions Matrix

The steering committee determined that it was critical to develop a method and process for identifying the needed skill dimensions for the salaried positions in the new organization. Initially, forty-five skill dimensions for the first-line regional managers were established. The process was reviewed and revised and the skill dimensions reduced to a more manageable number. When the skill-dimensioning process proved workable, it was then used to determine the job skill dimensions for positions on the staff of the regional managers and ultimately for all salaried positions within the reorganized business unit.

The next step of the process required that each skill dimension be defined in terms of degree of importance to a job, skills required within the dimension, and degree of proficiency necessary. The steering committee developed a matrix of skill dimensions, which was integrated with the hiring and promotion practices. As a result of this process, it was recognized that significant training would have to occur within the organization to bring potential internal candidates for specific positions up to the proficiency required by the skill dimensions.

Step 3: Skills Organized into Courses

From the job dimension information, the steering committee developed a list of desired course contents, similar to a college catalogue, which was matched, in matrix form, with internal candidates for various positions. Initially thirty-two courses were identified. Several have subsequently been added as other development areas have been identified.

Step 4: Selection of Delivery Method for Courses

When the course/candidate matrix was completed, the steering committee concerned itself with how the courses would be presented and who would present them. Presenter alternatives that were reviewed were: using company instructors, using outside seminars, hiring educational professionals, or contracting with a local college for the development and presentation of the identified courses.

After review and discussion by the steering committee, it was decided that, as far as practical, the courses would be taught by internal company personnel. Managers working in the areas identified in the course matrix would be selected as instructors. This meant that the managers chosen would be required to delve even more deeply into their area of expertise and become "peer experts." They would also need coaching on

course material development and presentation skills in order to
fulfill the role of instructor. The steering committee selected
twenty-five instructors and decided on a competency-based
model of instruction as the instructional design mode.

Step 5: Training of Managers/Instructors in Adult Learning Principles

Once the instructors and the course development model
were selected, the external consultant and the human resource
development professional developed two workbooks—one on
competency-based instructional design and one on course presentation skills. (Outlines for these workbooks are included in
Appendixes A and B.) At this point the Joy Manufacturing
managers chosen as instructors were themselves the adult learners. The first seminar on the design of competency-based instruction was delivered as a model to the instructors, to exemplify how they should employ adult learning techniques in the
teaching of their courses. The instructors developed preliminary
drafts of their material during the seminar. It was a different
and sometimes difficult process for some of them. The seminar
was very different from those that they had had in their past
formal learning experiences.

During one portion of this seminar, the new instructors
were given a learning-style inventory. (From this point in the
case example, the term "instructor" will refer to the Joy Manufacturing managers who were selected to deliver the courses in
the reorganization process. The term "consultant" refers to the
persons conducting the seminars for the instructors.) Their
scores and learning style were discussed and shared with the rest
of the participants. The diversity of styles in the seminar helped
to make the new instructors aware that they would have an
equally diverse class of learners for their courses and that they
must develop their course materials to include a variety of instructional strategies to accommodate the learning diversity.

Step 6: Courses Prepared and Reviewed

At the completion of this introductory three-day program, the instructors continued developing their individual
courses from the drafts generated at the seminar. During the de-

velopment period (approximately three months), the instructors communicated with the HRD professional and the external
consultant. As various components of the course materials—or
modules as they were called—were developed, they were sent to
the HRD professional and to the external consultant. Each
module was reviewed by several persons utilizing a developed
Module Review Form (see Appendix C). Also during this period,
the Joy Manufacturing personnel who were to be trained by
the new instructors were each given a learning-style inventory.
The scores and learning styles were compiled and sent to the instructors for consideration in revising the modules.

After the modules were revised, they were sent to the
steering committee, who also reviewed them. Acting as mentors
with the new instructors, the steering committee members made
suggestions, offered assistance, and generally gave support.

Step 7: Training Managers/Instructors in
Course Presentation Skills

After the objectives and content were developed for the
modules, the instructors attended a three-day seminar on presentation skills. The seminar was designed to model various
forms of information presentation. The instructors utilized a
variety of resources and methods to develop a short segment of
their course. This course segment was videotaped, played back,
and reviewed by peers and consultants. The presenter then was
given the opportunity to revise the presentation, based on the
peer/consultant feedback. The revised version was videotaped,
played back, and reviewed a second time.

Step 8: Courses Presented and Results Evaluated

A course schedule was developed for the entire range of
courses. All the courses were delivered twice, many three times,
over the next two years. Revision material was collected by the
instructor, and the modules were reworked on the basis of the
feedback.

Each time a course was delivered, the class also included
some of the new instructors as learners. The sense of peer group

learning was extended into every course presented at Joy Manufacturing. The participants in each class have come from all areas of the new business unit and from many different locations throughout the United States.

The success of the project can be attributed to dealing with the new instructors as adult learners and using the andragogical model for them to employ when facilitating their own courses. Each seminar they attended in preparation for instruction was task centered and revolved around a problem-solving format.

The process that has developed from the initial problem within the sales units has brought about a methodology for employee development that has become widely accepted and institutionalized throughout Joy Manufacturing: employee needs can now be easily identified by using the skill-dimensioning process; training for future manufacturing development or promotion can be foreseen and planned for; on-site experts can be developed and utilized for the future; and the senior executives have a process for developing and fine-tuning their own management skills.

The process for employee development is also being used in response to changes in technology, new product design, and new product development, as well as for new people entering the business unit.

Appendix A. Module Outline:
Competency-Based Instructional Design.

Table of Contents

Appendix B. Module Outline: Presentation Skills.

Table of Contents

Appendix C. Module Review Form.

Module: _____   Reviewer(s): _____ ‾‾‾‾‾‾
                                                     Date

Author(s):_____   _____ ‾‾‾‾‾‾
                                                     Date

_____

Review Question	Comments
COVER SHEET	
1. Is the cover page complete (contains module title, program, target group, organization, instructor, working time)?	
PREASSESSMENT	
2. Are the prerequisite skills (if any) necessary for a learner to master the module specified?	
3. Are the pretest items consistent with the stated competencies?	
4. Are the criteria for judging acceptability of learner pretest responses clear?	
INTRODUCTION/RATIONALE	
5. Is the introduction concise, interesting, and clear?	
6. Does the rationale clearly state the importance of the material being dealt with in the module?	

This form or parts of this form are not to be duplicated without written permission of the author, Barbara P. Mink.

(continued on next page)

Appendix C. Module Review Form, Cont'd.

Review Question	Comments
COMPETENCIES	
7. Are the competencies behaviorally stated?	
8. Is there an appropriate mix of competencies (affective, cognitive, psychomotor)?	
9. Is the order in which the competencies are stated appropriate?	
10. Do the competencies consider the on-the-job and/or future professional requirements that will be expected of the learner? Do they consider: knowledge needed? skills needed? attitudes needed?	
11. Is the level of mastery stated in the competencies appropriate?	
LEARNING ACTIVITIES	
12. Is the size of the learning activity steps appropriate?	
13. Do the practice items accurately measure learner mastery of competencies?	

Appendix C. Module Review Form, Cont'd.

Review Question	Comments
LEARNING ACTIVITIES, CONT'D.	
14. Is immediate knowledge of practice exercise results provided for the learner?	
15. Are the types of learning activities appropriate?	
16. Is there a variety of learning activities utilized (discussions, film, role play, visuals, demonstrations, lecture)?	
17. Is the material presented on the page in an interesting and clear manner—liberal use of spacing, diagrams, charts, highlighting methods?	
18. Have copies of transparencies and support handouts been included?	
19. Are the instructions to the learner clear?	
20. Is the content of the module technically accurate?	
21. Is instruction responsive to individual learner needs (personalized)?	

(continued on next page)

Appendix C. Module Review Form, Cont'd.

Review Question	Comments
LEARNING ACTIVITIES, CONT'D.	
22. Can the learner dictate his or her own: learning approach sequence or pace content	
23. Is a glossary included (necessary)?	
24. Are any other supplementary materials appropriate for this unit? If so, list relevant materials.	
POSTASSESSMENT	
25. Do the module posttest items accurately measure learner mastery of the stated competencies?	
26. Are the criteria for judging acceptability of learner posttest responses clear?	
REVISION/GENERAL	
27. To what extent is learner feedback used to review and revise learning activities/materials?	
28. Would you have approached the teaching of this content differently? If so, what changes would you have made?	

Appendix C. Module Review Form, Cont'd.

Review Question	Comments
REVISION/GENERAL, CONT'D.	
29. If material was to be added to this module, what would it be?	
30. If material was to be deleted from this module, what would it be?	
31. What do you consider the especially good aspects of this module to be?	
32. Do you believe that this module would prepare a learner to function effectively on this topic outside a formal learning environment?	

33. Other comments:

5

Self-Directed Learning on the Job
at Lloyds Bank of California

Lloyds Bank of California

A simple little announcement in the "Education Officers' Newsletter" provides a vignette in the life of an employee who engages in a self-directed learning project with his employer.
Special features:

- The self-directed learning approach
- Managers as facilitators of learning
- Contract learning
- Educational brokering
- Goal setting
- Mutual responsibilities of learner, manager, and educational officer

---

Do you realize that half the knowledge a person has acquired at age twenty will be obsolete at age thirty? Do you realize that the 1970s have brought to us more answers than any other era in history? Do you know that, if an individual were to read all the learning material available today, it would take that individual over one hundred years, full time, to read it?

Perhaps when you graduated from your last school you felt you had built a foundation of knowledge that would assure you of a successful and meaningful future. Today change is the only constant in our lives, and we need to take the responsibil-

Reproduced, with permission, from *Action Line*, the Education Officers' Newsletter, Lloyds Bank of California, August-September 1978.

ity for coping with that change. As our lives become more complicated, we cannot always depend on others to tell us what we need to learn and how we should go about learning it. The self-directed learning concept begins with the premise that the individual is aware of the need for learning and is master of his or her own education.

It involves self-assessment: first reviewing present performance, then determining where best to invest energy in improving current performance and meeting future goals. The learner sets measurable objectives and gains agreement from his or her manager on standards which will prove to both that the agreed-upon objectives have been attained. The agreement between employee and manager is known as a "learning contract." A third individual known as a "facilitator," helps to provide avenues for learning. As education officer, you can be an excellent resource in facilitating the self-directed learner.

Let's take an example of the "self-directed learning" approach:

> *Step 1:* Jay Smith is a consumer finance officer in a large branch. When his job performance is reviewed, his manager says that Jay has the potential to be a branch manager. He suggests that Jay would be a better manager if he improved his organization and communication abilities and learned to set objectives with more clarity. Jay agrees.
>
> *Step II:* Jay establishes goals with his manager. He says that in six months he will prove that he is better organized by meeting all deadlines and by accomplishing all the proper "homework." He will prove that he communicates better by testing his listening ability with subordinates and peers. He will also test his ability to get his point of view across by asking his manager to pick groups of people to whom he will make presentations. The manager will then survey the listeners. Jay's manager agrees that, if he can accomplish these goals successfully, Jay will have shown improvement.
>
> *Step III:* Jay goes to his education officer and asks for at least five avenues to help him de-

velop his management skills. The education officer tells him about three classes, four seminars, several books and periodicals, cassette tapes on management, and clubs that specialize in management development. He also suggests that Jay get signed up for the next task force on "organization." Jay picks the avenues that he feels will best teach him.

Step IV: Jay now goes to his manager with the total package, explaining the avenues he wants to use and the measurable objectives that they have already discussed. Thus, Jay and his manager have a learning contract. They will meet periodically to see how Jay is progressing. They may alter the contract from time to time.

A learning contract, the focal point of self-directed learning, is a means of blending job requirements and corporate goals with the individual's personal goals and objectives. It makes visible the mutual responsibilities of the manager, the employee, and the facilitating education officer in meeting the goals. The vital ingredient is the individual's self-direction. Individuals learn because they have had input on how they learn and how they demonstrate that their education has improved performance.

6

Introducing Data Processing
at an Insurance Company

Roger Sullivan

One of the consequences of our moving with increasing speed into the "information society" is that traditional instruction-oriented training cannot keep up with the need for continuous day-in and day-out development of personnel. The knowledge explosion and technological revolution are happening too fast. Workers become obsolete too fast. This selection describes how the data-processing installation of Commercial Union Automation Services, Inc., applied the andragogical model to solve this problem. Specifically, employees are oriented into a process of continuing self-directed learning; a system of varied learning resources is made available; managers are trained to engage with their workers in assessing learning needs and developing plans for meeting these needs; and a learning and resource center markets the concept, nurtures the environment, and provides methodology and resources.

Roger Sullivan was director of the Education and Learning Resource Center of the Commercial Union Automation Services, Inc., Boston, during the initiation of this program.

Special features:

- Orientation of new employees
- Creation of a learning and resource center
- Development of an option-mix approach to training resource use
- Competency-based education
- Assessment of learning needs
- Contract learning (learning plans)

73

- Training managers as facilitators of learning
- Getting support of senior management
- Guidebook for employees

This is a description of a program developed and implemented over a four-year period between 1978 and 1982. Its purpose was to introduce an andragogical learning environment into a 500-person data-processing installation in a large insurance company in the Northeast. The result satisfied management, drew favorable comments from employees, and was rated as very effective by outside observers.

One of the current advantages of implementing adult training in the workplace is that a large number of workers are becoming interested in careers and growth rather than just jobs. When organizations and training managers recognize this fact, they are in a position to take advantage of it in designing training programs. Their objectives then become:

- To identify organizational competency needs.
- To create a learning environment in which these competencies can be attained.
- To provide employees with an understanding of why it is to their benefit to take advantage of all resources offered to attain the competency levels required.

The following elements were addressed by Commercial Union Automation Services in order to attain these objectives:

- Creation of a learning and resource center (Education Center).
- Development of an option-mix approach to training resource use.
- Implementation of a job analysis and individual needs assessment system.
- Development of programs and materials for the attitudinal and skill training to prepare managers to use the process.
- Preparation of a guide for employees to aid them in understanding the self-learner role and the resources available for learning.

Orientation of New Employees

What we told employees when they visited the Education Center on their first day of employment was "You are entering an adult learning environment. This is a very participative process. We realize that you are interested in a career rather than just a job. We will help you become aware of the skills and knowledge you will need on your growth path with us. We will expect you to participate in certain training at each step. We will recommend other training and will support you with both direct resources and recommendations for additional resources. We will not test you in your classes. Rather, we will expect you to use your training as an opportunity and gain from it the information you need for your own competence and future career growth. Your test will be on the job. If you are able to carry out your functions competently as a result of the training, then your manager will recognize this and consider it in growth appraisals. If you fail to take advantage of the resources offered, then you will not become competent, not progress, and probably not be with us in the future."

The Learning and Resource Center

We chose to create what we termed a learning and resource center (within our Education Center) as opposed to a training center. The learning and resource center does contain two well-equipped meeting rooms, but it also contains a room with eight video-viewing units for self-learning multimedia activity, a large library of audio cassette packages, and a library with books and programmed instruction courses. In addition, there is a current periodical library and a technical manual reference library. The audio cassette, programmed instruction, and book libraries are designed for take-out use as well as internal use, and materials and cassette players can be signed out by employees for outside use. The multimedia area contains about 200 modules, most of which are on a rental-contract basis. Over 5,000 modules can be procured as requests are made from catalogues available.

The subject matter of this resource center encompasses

both the technical and nontechnical (from interpersonal to management subjects) training needs of the staff.

Lists of all materials are available to all personnel; and monthly notices posted on department bulletin boards and sent to all managers list new acquisitions or focus on particular aspects of the collection.

The center is open from 7 A.M. to 5 P.M. and, with prior arrangement, later. Personnel can use the center before or after work or at lunchtime. They can also come in without prior arrangement and use the libraries or the two video displays which are set aside for reference and update scanning any time they wish to. These services are in addition to the scheduled use of the video facilities and meeting rooms for planned training.

If personnel become aware of video courses (from the catalogues) that are of value or of books that should be in the library, they can recommend these and we provide them.

An Option-Mix Approach

We recognize that there is no one way that is the most effective method of learning. Different people learn best in different ways, and some subject matter lends itself to certain formats. Our objective is to provide people, whenever possible, with the most effective learning format for them. We are providing learning experiences for over 350 different job functions, and there is no way in which an on-premises instructor staff could provide that range of learning cost-effectively.

We provide learning experiences of the following types:

Self-study programmed instruction courses and books.

Audio cassette self-study packages.

Multimedia modules for individual or group study.

Internally developed courses.

Courses taught on premises by outside vendors.

Participation in consortium training with other companies.

Participation in outside courses, workshops, and degree programs with tuition reimbursement.

Job Analysis and Individual Needs Assessment

On the assumption that employees—if they are to become self-learners—must be aware of the prospective growth paths open to them and the competency needs related to each path, we analyzed all the major jobs in the data-processing environment. We determined the general accountabilities of each job and defined the actual functions to be performed to attain each accountability. Finally, we defined the competencies associated with each function. We then created a master matrix for each prospective growth path, from entry level to management. We listed all the functions in that entire growth path, in categories such as basic technical, communication, supervisory, and various technical specialty areas. We use this matrix in the following ways:

- When new employees visit the Education Center as a part of their orientation, we provide them with a profile form that lists all these functions. We ask them to rate each one that they have had any prior experience with on a four-level scale: (1) Conceptual understanding and awareness only, (2) Able to use under supervision, (3) Able to use without supervision, (4) Able to coach or instruct others in. We also ask them to list their major or most current learning experience in each area. This form provides the new employee with an idea of the types of knowledge and skills needed for future growth in comparison with present knowledge and skill; it also provides the employee's supervisor a basis for developing a training plan with the employee.
- We provide the managers with a list of all functions, their associated competency needs, and a cross-index of the files showing recommended skill level required.
- We keep a copy of this matrix in the Education Center as a basis for maintaining an individual educational record system.

The manager meets with the employee and reviews the profile and, if need be, further discusses the employee's previous experience in light of the needs of the unit. If, as a result of this review, any changes are made to the profile information, the manager forwards this information to the Education Center. The manager and employee then discuss training needs and set up a personal learning plan for the period until the next semiannual needs assessment. The manager notifies us at the Education Center of the training needed, and we work with him or her to identify resources and construct a schedule.

Twice a year each area carries out an individualized needs assessment of all staff members, with managers at each level assessing the persons who report directly to them. Managers are provided with a kit containing an updated training status for each employee reporting to them, procedures for carrying out the assessment, and a personal planning form for each employee. The manager revises the employee's training status in light of three kinds of projected training needs: (1) needs to perform presently assigned functions competently, (2) needs for potential growth/promotion planned in the period, (3) known unit needs for new projects during this period.

A meeting is held with the employee, and the projected training is discussed. The employee is able to comment on the plan and share his or her thoughts regarding modifications. Upon agreement, a plan of both formal and on-the-job training for the period is drawn up, using the training plan form. Review dates are set to ensure that training is followed up.

Managers forward a copy of this matrix (a master chart with spaces to "X in" the planned training for each employee) to the Education Center. These are compiled into a master chart showing all training needs, which serves as a foundation for identifying the priorities, number, and types of training needed in the area and the most effective method of delivery. Courses can then be scheduled, or recommendations for the use of self-study aids can be made.

Manager Training and Materials

A critical facet of this process is involving line and staff managers in the plan, so that a self-learning environment can be implemented and maintained. The first stage of this process is a training session for managers, which includes the following elements:

Understanding the concepts of adult learning.

Understanding the personal benefits to the manager of having a competent staff.

Understanding the importance of reinforcing the self-directed learning concept within the unit.

Skill in constructing individualized training plans.

Skill in using the individualized needs assessment materials.

Understanding the roles of the employee, manager, and Education Center in developing competencies.

A *Manager's Education Manual* is distributed, and regularly updated, to reinforce the information included in the sessions. Meetings are held with senior management to discuss policy and to ensure that personnel development is given a major emphasis in appraising managers. Senior management must support this process through understanding the long-term benefits of investing time and resources for training.

Additional materials are provided to aid managers in supplying on-the-job training experiences to complement the formal training. The materials include guidebooks related to coaching and counseling, guidebooks related to developing on-the-job training experiences, and a course on preparing and delivering internal unit classes.

An ongoing program to market the benefits of the education process includes a range of activities from bulletins and guidebooks to talks with individual managers and open-door services for employees.

Guidebook for Employees

It is important that we ensure that the individual employee sees participation in this program as beneficial from a personal standpoint. It is likewise important that the employees see themselves as in control of their overall direction of growth. To further these ends, each employee is given a guidebook, *Employee Personal Development Guide for Self-Learning Planning,* containing the following sections:

The Personal Development Concept

Becoming a Self-Learner
    Defining objectives
    Defining learning needs to fulfill objectives
    Self-evaluation
    How to learn

Available Opportunities for Self-Learning

Recommended Areas of Self-Learning

Conclusion

It is the combination of all these components of the total process that has made this program successful. Top management, managers, and employees all have to provide positive support based on an understanding of the benefits to be obtained by each. The Education Center acts as the catalyst to market the concept, nurture the environment, and provide the methodology and resources required.

7

Product Use Training
for Customers at Du Pont

Glenda M. Green

One of our largest corporations faced a special problem when it
brought to market a complicated new clinical analyzer—a machine used to analyze a variety of body fluids simultaneously.
The problem was how to train customers—mostly medical technicians with a variety of years and kinds of experience—in the
shortest possible time to use the machines. The customer training group was also committed to applying principles of adult
education. This selection describes the andragogical system designed by the training design and customer training group at
Du Pont.

Glenda Green was a training specialist in the Clinical Systems Division of Du Pont Company in Wilmington, Delaware, at
the time this selection was written.

Special features:

- Individualized, self-paced learning
- Orientation of learners to learner-controlled learning
- Modular learning guidebook
- Computer-assisted learning
- Self-check quiz feedback
- Use of videotapes
- Climate setting
- Hands-on laboratory
- Instructors as facilitators of learning
- Adaptation to varied backgrounds

This selection appeared previously, in modified form, in the Du
Pont publication *aca*® *Update.*

In 1981 the Customer Training Center of Du Pont Company's Clinical Systems Division introduced a new approach to training for the aca (registered trademark of Du Pont Company) discrete clinical analyzer. Using the latest advances in training techniques, the program is individualized to allow trainees to work independently at their own pace to acquire the necessary skills and knowledge to operate and maintain the aca analyzer.

In designing this program, the training design staff utilized the basic principles of andragogy. Specifically, trainees are seen as self-directed, problem centered, participating adults who are encouraged to answer some of their own questions from their own experience. Since customers know that they are responsible for operating the aca analyzer on their return, they come to the program motivated to learn.

Prior training programs had followed the more traditional lecture approach and were group paced, instructor dependent, and content centered. Trainees worked two to an instrument and, regardless of their previous experience, were exposed to the same basic information and procedures. Customers rarely used their own experience or participated in the learning process as they now do. Consequently, customer response to the new learner-controlled course has been very positive.

A Variety of Learning Resources

The course begins with an explanation of the learner-controlled concept. The different learning media are reviewed: computer-assisted lessons, videotapes, computer and written exercises, selected text readings, and "hands-on" practice. Customers then tour the training center, participating in demonstrations of the equipment and the aca analyzer. In addition to instrument and chemistry manuals, each customer receives a guidebook, a major tool that directs the learner's progress through the course. Each section or module in the guidebook defines what the learner will do and which resource will be used. The guidebook also contains selected readings highlighting information in the instrument and chemistry manuals. Its many self-check quizzes validate and reinforce the learning process.

Once the tour and orientation are complete, the four-day course begins.

Customers enjoy the PLATO (registered trademark of Control Data Corporation) computer lessons, since information is presented both creatively and interactively. The terminals are located in individual carrels, ensuring privacy. Experienced users can skip over basic sections and take a quiz instead. The procedure demonstrates an important principle of adult learning: the learner is allowed to participate actively in the learning process and in the evaluation of that process, so that the learner's understanding is constantly checked. Corrective feedback is always provided when needed, helping to build confidence or identify areas that need review.

Computer-assisted learning is compatible with adult learning characteristics. Because it is individualized, it can deal more effectively with the considerable differences in experiences and rates of learning in the training population. Rapid learners can now move on to new material while slower learners can review or repeat information and proceed at a pace they can handle.

Videotapes demonstrate both scheduled and unscheduled maintenance. The action and "close-up" photography help the customer identify and find hard-to-reach areas on the instrument. Typically, a procedure is viewed on videotape and immediately practiced on the instrument.

Obviously, the most important resource in this course is the aca analyzer itself. This learner-controlled course has increased the amount of individual "hands-on" time compared with the former course. Most customers like to work alone with the instrument, to gain as much experience as possible, but some prefer to work with a partner. The course is flexible enough to accommodate both preferences.

Training Center Design

Physical comfort and variety are emphasized at the Training Center, which is designed so that customers move from one location to another to use the available media and equipment. Adults enjoy this mobility, and the physical activity stimulates body functions, keeping learning at a high level.

The reading room provides a quiet place for study and review throughout the week. The instruments are located in a large, spacious laboratory where instructors, acting as facilitators, are positioned in a central location. The audiovisual room contains a variety of AV equipment and computer terminals arranged in individual carrels. Finally, there is a comfortable open lounge—perhaps the most important room of all. It is here that customers discuss their progress, share helpful hints, and exchange ideas with each other and the training staff. Refreshments are available at all times. Frequent short breaks are highly recommended by the staff. Customers enjoy having the freedom to determine when they need a break.

Changing Instructor Role

In this type of learning system, instructors become facilitators of the process. Their primary function is to guide the learning process, rather than manage the content of the course. Much interaction occurs between the staff and customers—typically in a one-to-one situation. The instructor acts as a resource person who uses questions to help the learners answer their own questions from personal experience. The learners are responsible for managing their own progress and for achieving their own goals through self-direction and evaluation. The responsibility for the outcome of the training program is shared between the learner and instructor.

Contact with a facilitator always occurs at the end of a module. Customers often clear up minor points or comment on their progress. This contact gives the customer a sense of accomplishment and the staff a way to track learner progress.

A Typical Module

In any given module, the customer may use several media and resource materials to achieve an objective. For example, the Non-Enzyme Calibration Section of the guidebook directs the customer to read about calibration and answer specific questions. A PLATO lesson, simulating the instrument, then presents the mechanics of calibration, reviews its purpose, and questions the learner. Finally, customers perform the calibration procedures on an aca analyzer. This process of reading information in the guidebook or manuals, seeing it on PLATO or a videotape, and practicing it on the aca analyzer reinforces the concepts needed to become a competent operator.

Creative Educational Experience

The Clinical Systems Division's training design and customer training groups designed and developed this highly successful learner-controlled course. The creative use of a variety of resource materials and media captures the interest of the customers as they go about establishing their own pace in a user-oriented course. The division of the course into well-defined modules provides flexibility and a means for dealing with experienced users, who can skip familiar material and spend more time on difficult areas or areas of interest. At the same time, someone with no experience will find all the information and practice necessary to become a competent operator. Whatever the prior level of proficiency in the operation of the aca analyzer, participating in the computer-assisted, learner-controlled training course is a unique and rewarding adult education experience.

8

Management Development at a Public Service Board

Catherine Sinclair, Robert Skerman

Here is an especially comprehensive and innovative application of the andragogical model from "Down Under." The detailed way in which the procedures used in this program are described make this almost a how-to-do-it manual that can be used in designing programs in a variety of settings, public and private. Its central thrust is self-directed learning.

Catherine Sinclair and Robert Skerman are senior consultants with the Queensland Public Service Board in Brisbane, Australia.

Special features:

- Workshop design
- Needs assessment
- Individualized learning
- A case for residential programs
- Climate-setting techniques
- Provision of a variety of resources
- Role of learner in self-directed learning
- Use of peer resources
- Stages in movement from dependency to self-direction
- Staffing an andragogical program
- Program evaluation

Excerpted, with permission, from a report, *An Alternative Design for Management Development in the Queensland Public Service*, published by the Queensland Public Service Board, Brisbane, Australia, October 1981.

The design described in this paper is based on andragogical principles. It was evolved from initial experiences in two separate one-week residential workshops, both utilizing a self-directed approach. The first was in the form of a follow-up program for managers who had experienced a "traditional" management training program. The contract for this follow-up course was to provide a "Management Skills Workshop." The second instance of using the self-directed approach was in the residential phase of a three-stage traditional management program. The design was offered as an alternative to a continuous group approach to interpersonal development.

From these two initial applications, a design for a comprehensive Management Development Program based on self-directed principles evolved.

The goals of the Management Development Workshop were defined as follows:

1. To provide an environment where participants take control of their learning process.
2. To provide a wide range of resources to facilitate the individual learning process.
3. To encourage the development of initiative, autonomy, and risk taking in seeking out learning opportunities.
4. To allow maximum opportunity for participants to achieve individually set goals, relevant to their own learning needs or the needs perceived in the systems they manage.
5. To maximize the use of participants' own internal motivation and felt needs.
6. To provide a design where participants adopt a learning pace and style appropriate to their own background.
7. To provide an environment in which individuals are stimulated to explore new possibilities.

The stages of the workshop are shown in Figure 1.

The Information Session

The objective of this session was to provide information regarding the workshop and its philosophy. Potential participants could then make an informed choice.

Figure 1. Stages of the Workshop.

Information Session	Two-hour meeting of potential participants to provide information on the overall seminar design and the philosophy of self-directed learning.

Decision to participate.

Needs Analysis Day	Participants utilize a process provided by staff to develop specific learning goals.

2 weeks

One-Week Residential Workshop	In the learning environment, participants have access to material resources provided (as well as staff and other participants to achieve their own goals). A climate of trust, mutuality, and sharing is encouraged. Goals are reevaluated and reset during and between stages.

2 weeks

One-Week Residential Workshop

3 weeks

Three-Day Nonresidential Workshop	The final workshop is of a shorter duration and is nonresidential to help participants involve environment in the application of their learnings, or to consult specialist staff with skills not available at the residential workshop.

Information was given on:

Alternative forms of management training available to managers, including the traditional management training design.

Specific information on the self-directed learning design,

with emphasis on the responsibility of the participants regarding their learning.

The staff for the workshop: their interests and backgrounds, including areas of expertise and qualifications.

Small groups were formed to discuss the information given and to share thoughts and feelings. A plenary session integrated this process and brought questions of clarification. Individuals were then given the option of participating.

Needs Analysis Day

This was the first occasion on which the participants for the course met in the context of a learning group. Staff took responsibility for providing a process for the day, to stimulate individual goal formation. The increasing uncertainty for managers of the 1980s was highlighted. In addition, the following elements were included in the Needs Analysis Day:

Time for "getting to know you" activities.

Information on goals and objectives and how to state them. Emphasis was placed on the fact that goals will differ from individual to individual, depending on their degree of specialization.

Presentation of a systems model of an organization (to stimulate awareness of potential areas of need in the manager's total area of responsibility).

Identification of possible career paths for the individual and what new skills may have to be acquired.

Identification of managerial situations where the individual performs well and situations where the individual could improve.

These elements were introduced during the day, with time for individual reflection or discussion in pairs or small groups (at the individuals' discretion).

The final suggestion by staff was for goals to be placed in order of priority, written down, and shared by posting on the wall. This provided information to each individual on other participants who had similar goals. The sharing process was optional. It encouraged the formulation of logical "links" for formation of pairs and small groups in the first workshop, and the publishing of goals served to enhance personal commitment to them.

The Residential Workshops

Learning Environment. The residential phases were designed to create for participants an environment conducive to learning. A diverse range of material and human resources were provided and review sessions were structured to confront the learning process.

Climate. The residential stages in the self-directed design serve primarily to promote the creation of a climate conducive to learning—specifically, a climate that is informal, mutually respectful, consensual, collaborative, and supportive. The development of these characteristics is helped in a live-in setting. Experience in the pilot programs has reinforced the value of the residential phases. Minimum disruptions to the learning process occur, time is available for reflection and integration of learning, and a supportive community spirit is developed.

Physical Layout. The major consideration in the selection of a residential venue is the availability of suitable conference facilities. The design is resource intensive, and space for adequate display of the material resources is required. Space for the following activities is also required, and combinations of these activities need to be able to proceed concurrently: large-group work, small-group work, paired discussion, individual study, film screening, and video role plays.

Material Resources. Resources covering some fifty topic areas were gathered. The inclusion of topics was influenced by the Needs Analysis Day and by the knowledge and experience of training staff. A wider range of topics was presented than indicated by the Needs Analysis Day.

Resources were gathered from a variety of sources, with emphasis placed on obtaining a wide variety of types of resource within a topic heading. Since various learning modes were provided, participants could choose the types of resources best suited to their learning styles.

For each topic area, materials were assembled in a range of the following formats: printed handout materials, reference books, self-scoring instruments, structured experiences, films and filmstrips, audiotapes, and videotapes.

Staff as a Resource. Staff for the workshop identified themselves as resources to be used by participants according to their learning goals. To assist this process, staff listed their areas of expertise and posted them in the room where other resources were displayed.

Staff also declared the times when they were available—namely, from 8:30 A.M. to 9:30 P.M. If the situation and energy warranted, however, they were willing to work beyond 9:30 P.M.

As an extension of staff knowledge of resources and skills, a list of topic areas that could be explored experientially in groups was posted. If a specific topic—such as group dynamics or conflict resolution—was desired, the initiating participant organized a group of interested people.

Participant Role and Responsibility. All decisions are made by the course participants. These decisions include:

1. The initial decision to participate in the course.
2. Determining personal goals for learning.
3. Deciding on content areas covered during the course.
4. Deciding sequence of content.
5. Time utilization during the course. The participant decides on all aspects of time usage except for a daily one-and-a-half-hour process review and mealtimes—usually a function of the venue of the program. This choice includes decisions to use time for work and play.
6. Choice of learning mode. Resources are provided in diverse formats and these can be chosen individually, in pairs, or in groups, all with or without a staff person.

This total control by the client ensures that learning is relevant as determined by the client for his or her own situation. This enhances the practical application of skills learned and maximizes the effect for the participants, since all their time can be used for personal goals. Thus, the participant is moving in a learning environment in response to internal motivation, tailoring a program for personally identified needs, and choosing and using individual strengths as a learner.

The Participant as a Resource. Participants bring a wealth of experience and skill to a workshop. This is recognized in the design. Participants are asked to post their skill and knowledge areas in order to provide a wider range of human resources and to encourage sharing of knowledge. This process in itself is a learning experience for some participants, who may realize for the first time that they have personal skills. Enhancement of self-esteem can result.

Initiating the Residential Workshop. The first residential workshop commenced with a total community where the following aspects were addressed:

Administration details for the venue (mealtimes, house rules, and the like).

A discussion on self-directed learning and its principles.

An explanation of the layout of the resources, the variety of learning modes available, the use of self-scoring instruments, and the use of audiovisual equipment.

Clarification of the staff role as resource persons who will respond to specific requests for information. Staff declared availability times (8:30 A.M.-9:30 P.M.). Staff would not take responsibility for organizing participants' learning but were happy to facilitate according to participants' requests.

A discussion on participant responsibility for use of their time at the workshop.

A statement of one compulsory time period per day (3:30 P.M.-5:00 P.M.) for a learning process review, which all participants were to attend. This meeting provided a time when staff could challenge and confront participants with respect to their learning process, and participants could share their reactions to the workshop.

A discussion on extending available resources through identification of human resources present, and subsequent request for staff and participants to post lists of resource areas.

A request that participants post their goals for the week (identified on the Needs Analysis Day).

Following this initial meeting, participants began seeking out their own needs from the learning environment.

Learning Process Review. This was the only compulsory time of the workshop and was set down for one and a half hours per day. The purpose of the review was to share perceptions regarding what was happening, check progress and problems, and provide a time for staff to fulfill their stated responsibility for facilitating the learning process.

The following questions were posted, to stimulate individual thoughts for sharing:

What didn't I do today that I could have done?

Whom or what did I avoid?

What stopped me?

What "messages" did I get to be motivated to do anything?

How many initiatives did I take toward others?

How much of today did I spend doing what *I* wanted to, not what was expected of me by others (this group, the staff, my organization)?

How do I rate my involvement in the workshop so far?

What is my level of commitment to my goals?

How will I operate differently tomorrow?

How do I feel right now?

These sessions tended to provide participants with a better understanding of personal struggles regarding taking charge of their own learning. A sense of mutuality and increased trust levels also tended to develop.

As these sessions continued during the week, staff provided observations and information on the process of the workshop as it became relevant or apparent.

Characteristic Behaviors During the Workshop. After the initial contract-setting meeting, participants tend to explore the range of resources. Movement is halting and often uncertain. Patterns associated with anxiety relief tend to become apparent. For example, participants struggling with the process tend to join activities initiated by others.

During the early phase of the workshop, participants with a specific "learning block" may recognize the need to work with a staff member to resolve it. A learning block may be either work related or personal and is an issue that, until confronted, will make it difficult for the participant to engage in further learning. This phenomenon is explained to participants in the first process review.

As the week progresses, small groups, large groups, both with and without staff, tend to form with increasing frequency. The length of existence of such groups tends to be for one and a half to two hours, before they disband and new combinations form around new topics.

Individuals begin to notice (or have pointed out by staff) cyclic energy patterns. The tendency is to work up energy to confront some learning, spend one to two hours in a high energy level while actively learning, then enter a recovery period (of about an hour) before further active work can ensue. The recognition of this process can stop individuals from fighting it and can help maximize the use of energy during the workshop.

The student dependency on the teacher that may develop in more traditional programs does not become apparent—probably because the control remains with the individual. However, individuals still cluster into groups with a sense of interdependence.

The second-week residential tends to be a demanding one for staff. Participants have a grasp of how to use the design, trust levels are already established, and groups around learning topics tend to form early in the week. A much higher level of learning takes place, at higher risk levels. The variety of work and the amount of interest and energy exhibited are both exciting and demanding.

The final three days of the design are not residential. Here participants tend to work in a more task-oriented framework, utilizing work environments and people resources relevant to work projects they have undertaken.

Staffing the Workshops. The successful implementation of this design is largely dependent on the appropriateness of the staff.

Staff require a philosophy consistent with the andragogical principles of the design; a comprehensive knowledge of organization development, managerial skills, interpersonal skills, intrapersonal processes, and group dynamics; personal skills of facilitation, counseling, and communication; and the ability to solve problems and to impart this skill by example to participants.

During the workshop, particularly in the initial days of the first residential, there is much pressure on staff to provide the structure and make learning choices for the participant. This severely tests the philosophical stance of the staff person. For the sake of the goal of learning how to learn, staff must remain firmly as facilitators of the learning process, and respond only to participant-initiated requests for content delivery.

The training of staff for successful participation in this design would probably need to focus heavily on examination of personal values relevant to teaching adults.

Evaluation of the Design

Participants were asked to evaluate the usefulness of the design on a range of dimensions:

Impact on managerial effectiveness.

Achievement of goals.

Taking responsibility for one's own learning.

Degree of availability of staff, resources, other participants.

Effective use of time.

Extent of initiative taking.

Extent of opportunity to use preferred learning mode.

Extent of flexibility of program.

Appropriateness of environment.

The overall evaluation by managers was very positive. The highest ratings were given to "impact on managerial effectiveness" and "extent of flexibility." The main comments centered on the cost effectiveness of the program in that time was not wasted on areas already known to participants.

A follow-up evaluation to assess the long-term impact is planned.

THREE

❖◆◆ ❖◆ ❖◆ ❖◆ ❖◆ ❖◆ ❖◆ ❖◆ ❖◆ ❖◆ ❖◆ ❖◆ ❖◆ ❖◆ ❖◆ ❖◆ ❖

Applications
in Colleges
and Universities

Established originally for the exclusive purpose of serving teen-age youth, our institutions of higher education have, within the past decade, become institutions serving predominantly adult learners. As Cross (1981, p. 3) points out, "For most of the years of this century, the United States population has been numerically dominated by young people. With the exception of the World War II years, children under the age of fifteen have always been the largest single group in the nation. . . . In 1980 numerical dominance shifted to those between the ages of fif-teen and twenty-nine. By the year 2000, the largest age group will be thirty- to forty-four-year-olds, with a rising curve for forty-five- to sixty-four-year-olds." We have shifted from a youth-centered to an adult-centered society—with drastic impli-cations for our whole educational enterprise.

As the pool of teenagers has begun to shrink, colleges and universities have aggressively been recruiting adults to maintain tuition income as a matter of economic survival ("The Coming Enrollment Crisis," 1983). And they have found the adult population most responsive, for in a world of accelerating change—especially with the knowledge explosion, the techno-logical revolution, and the entry of women into the work force

in massive numbers—adults have become aware that higher education is a matter of survival for them, too. So college and university campuses have been flooded with a "new clientele"
(Vermilye, 1974)—adult learners.

This chapter presents descriptions of a variety of responses
by institutions of higher education to this new situation. Selection 1 describes the innovative program of undergraduate education at Alverno College, which has the development of lifelong
learners as an explicit objective and which provides a progressive
sequence of learning experiences for transforming dependent
youth learners into self-directing adult learners. An approach to
helping entering students at Mercy College make the transition
to behaving as adult learners—and helping the faculty learn how
to treat them as adult learners—is described in selection 2. An
adaptation of this process to an external degree program is presented in selection 3. The special challenge of preparing traditional faculty members, whose experience has been only with
teaching teenagers, to adapt to the unique characteristics of
adults as learners is explored in selection 4 at the University of
New Hampshire, in selection 5 at Gordon College, in selection 6
in the universities of Brazil, and in selection 7 among college
lecturers in Africa. The focus then shifts to the application of
the andragogical model to particular subject matter courses: a
science course in selection 8, a course in oral communication in
selection 9, and an imaginative application to one of the pressing social issues of our time—environmental protection—in selection 10. The final selection describes how one of the key concepts in adult learning—learner involvement—was applied in
establishing learning groups in distant communities.

It is perhaps a sad commentary that, of all our social institutions, colleges and universities have been among the slowest
to respond to adult learners. But the case descriptions in this
chapter indicate that a movement in that direction has begun;
with models of the sort presented here, the pace may accelerate.

1

Self-Directed
Undergraduate Study

Georgine Loacker, Austin Doherty

Alverno College in Milwaukee has developed an approach to undergraduate education that attempts to reconcile the requirements of academic rigor with an increasing delegation of responsibility to the learner. One of its explicit goals is to produce lifelong learners. The use of three levels of learning contracts provides a vehicle for organizing sequential learning experiences. This selection describes the process through which students earn degrees and follows three students anecdotally through this process—providing one of the clearest descriptions of what happens inside the learners as they learn to be self-directing that I have seen. You will be intrigued by the new meaning it gives to the competencies a liberal education should provide.

Georgine Loacker is professor of English and chairwoman of the Assessment Council, and Austin Doherty is academic dean at Alverno College, Milwaukee.

Special features:

- Three levels of learning contracts
- Sequence of progress toward self-directed learning
- Diversifying learning environments
- Gearing learning to developmental stages
- Assessments as learning experiences
- Dealing with reentry anxiety of older women
- Contract learning
- Transferable learning
- Use of community resources
- Experiential learning

101

At Alverno College we have been working for a decade now to be equally explicit about the goal toward which the learner works—self-directed learning—and about the environment and the services we as educators will provide. We have done this by agreeing on college-wide definitions of the abilities we seek to help the learner develop and by entering into three levels of contract with each learner. At the first level, the "college contract," we specify the college-wide abilities and the various kinds of learning experiences we will "deliver" to help develop them. The learner accepts these goals and our services by enrolling in the college. At the second level, the "program contract," learner and educator work regularly (for instance, each semester) to negotiate her particular program, selecting courses and other learning experiences designed to help her develop the particular abilities relevant to her career goals as well as those required by the college for general education purposes. At the third level, the "course contract," the learner decides which of the abilities offered in a particular course or learning experience she will agree to focus on. At this level as well, each educator specifies the learning opportunities that will be used to help develop an ability as well as the criteria by which its achievement will be judged.

We have also spent the last ten years at Alverno diversifying our learning environments and our learner populations. Besides the familiar model of full-time undergraduate studies, we now offer the whole range from a three-session career counseling relationship (one of several dozen short-term workshops and series in our Telesis Institute) to varied certificate and associate's programs as well as an intensified baccalaureate curriculum in a weekend time frame for working women. Ten years ago we served women almost exclusively in the traditional eighteen to twenty-two age range; today more than 70 percent of our 1,400 degree and certificate students are older than that, and our 2,000 nondegree learners range across the life span.

Amid all this diversity, we have been struck by a consistent sequence in which our diverse learners progress toward self-direction. This seems to occur as the learner encounters three basic issues: (1) that learning is a change in the self; (2) that newly learned (or newly recognized) abilities can be adapted to varying situations, where they have the power to change the environment; and (3) that one can take charge of the learning process, integrating and to some extent directing the changes in one's self and one's world. Stated as propositions, these issues may sound fairly simple. But almost every learner, we have found, undergoes a real struggle in discovering these principles and making them into habitual operating assumptions.

As a framework for reviewing the multilevel contracts we create with each learner, we would like to focus on this developmental pattern. We can most vividly illustrate it by sharing the "case studies" of three diverse learners (names and identifying references have been altered to protect privacy) as they move through these three phases. Alongside the case studies at each phase, we will briefly indicate how our learning designs and contracts meet the learner where she is developmentally and urge her to move forward toward self-direction.

Phase One: Internalizing Learning

In this phase the learner relates learning to herself in two senses. First, she comes to see that the self is the locus of learning and that information or processes "out there" are important in learning only after they are "taken in" and alter the learner's perceptions and abilities. Second, as a result of the first kind of internalizing, she begins to consider learning an important issue and to count it as one of her own major goals. We use a special kind of learning experience, which we call assessment, to encourage both kinds of internalizing.

Before each semester begins, we ask every new degree or certificate student to write a letter to a fictitious national women's magazine editor who is doing a story on "How Women Choose Colleges." Students not only demonstrate their writing skills in these letters; they also reveal much that is helpful about their views of themselves and their learning.

Jean, entering college directly from high school, expresses typical anxiety about making one of her first major life decisions:

Last year I reached that all-important time
in my life when I was to select the college of my

choice. I had always been made aware that I would
need a college education, and was continually reminded of the good grades I was to keep up and
the money I was to save. Now I started searching
for "my" school.

I knew I wanted to live on campus. Things
weren't going all that smoothly for me at home,
and my first concern was to find a college that was
not too terribly far, but far enough so that I could
be on my own. I also wanted a small school where
I could get personal attention, and one with a good
program in my major. These restrictions narrowed
my choice to four schools.

I had also heard good things about Alverno's
program. So I attended the Sleeping Bag Weekend,
and during my two days there I met many other
girls who had come to look the college over. We
were taken on a very informative tour and got to
meet many students and faculty members. I fell in
love with the place. I was making a fast decision,
but I knew it was in fact the right one.

Emily, undertaking a part-time program of day and evening courses, focuses more on her needs and the decision to return to school:

I graduated from high school and married
my high school sweetheart that summer. . . . Two
children and sixteen years later, I found myself
wondering who I was and what I was going to do
with the rest of my life. I felt the need to go out
and make something of myself: to reach out and
touch the lives of others.

I needed to go back to school. For me, that
was the major decision. Choosing Alverno was the
easy part.

For one thing, it would hardly do for me to
pack up and move to another city or state. Also, I
knew I wanted a small, caring atmosphere that had
a feeling for the particular problems of women returning to school. Above all other considerations, I
wanted a college that would be interested in helping me to develop into the best person I could become.

I had heard about Alverno from friends who attended. I liked the fact that so many of the students were women like myself. Then, when I went in for a MAP [career counseling] interview to look at my career choices and plans, my adrenalin really started to flow. I loved every minute of it. I thought, "They are really interested in me as a person."

I look forward to my education at Alverno with a sense of security and eagerness to apply myself.

Pat, enrolling in the intensive Weekend College program (twenty to forty weekends of up to twenty-two class hours each), looks at the careful juggling of constraints required to go back for a degree:

I have been actively involved in the business world for ten years now. I have taken night classes and company seminars, and have moved up through every job to a management position.

I'm now ready for the next step, but it isn't there. I'm at a dead end. It's college time—time to obtain that magic piece of paper employers find so essential.

But I don't want to spend the next ten years in night school studying things I'm not interested in just to get a degree.

Clearly, these three learners come out of different life experiences and reflect very different expectations of college-level education. For all their individual differences, however, they share some important learning needs.

Most critical at this point is the fact that none shows any clear concept of learning or commitment to it—a rather startling fact, given its central role in the college experience. Both Jean and Pat seem to view education almost wholly in externalized, instrumental terms: they expect to move through a "program" of "studying things," after which they will receive a "magic piece of paper" that enables them to pursue their chosen careers. Emily, her attention drawn inward by her shifting life roles, shows some awareness of education's impact on the self; but hers is an unspecified faith that if the process includes personal attention and support, it will somehow help her to become more fulfilled as a person.

The problem these three share is one common to most learners at this point: they do not understand that the learning process will change them or, suspecting that, cannot imagine how that change will take place. Such learners need to experience learning as an active, self-transforming process; and they need tools with which they can understand their experience, perceiving and analyzing the learning process for themselves.

It is not that they have never learned before—but that they have had no way to understand how they were doing it, either at the time or afterward. Their inability to analyze learning experiences seems in fact to be but one particular instance of a more generic problem: an inability to analyze subjective experience. Learners at this point, regardless of age or education, find it difficult to break down an experience (especially a powerfully felt one) into constituent parts, or to sort a subjective response or judgment from its global statement into separate, specific criteria.

Our task as educators, then, is to provide learners at the outset with experiences and tools that will enable them to analyze and understand their learning—and, by extension, their experience in general. The vehicle we use for this at Alverno is what we call assessment. Assessment is not only how we measure successful completion of each part of a learning contract; it is also a key learning experience in itself.

Essentially, in assessment we create small, focused experiences where the student turns her attention toward how she is learning as well as what she is learning. We break down the unmanageably large concept of "learning" by identifying a particular ability that is to be learned in each situation—it might be "observation" in an introductory science lab, or "addressing the audience" in a writing workshop. We then create a number of specific criteria by which to estimate whether that ability is being demonstrated. These might include:

"Observing" in the Lab	*"Addressing the Audience"*
Identifies major visible stages of a chemical reaction.	Identifies audience's knowledge/attitudes in notes or elsewhere.
Notes sounds and odors produced.	Directly addresses audience in text.
Gathers tactile evidence where possible.	Indirectly appeals to audience's knowledge/attitudes in text.
Uses appropriate measuring tools for volume, weight, temperature.	Uses language particular to this audience.

The learner then performs the task in the situation (doing the lab experiment, writing the letter draft). Afterward she applies these criteria to assess how effectively she is using the ability in question and receives careful individual feedback from assessors (usually her instructor, community professionals in her field, and/or her peers) who apply the same criteria.

The criteria do not, of course, represent a complete model of the learning process; nor do they exhaustively define the ability in question. What they do provide is a heuristic; applying even these few criteria to her own performance, the learner is practicing the art of analytically breaking down one of her experiences. Simultaneously, looking reflectively at her performance by means of the criteria enables her to move from her own global sense of "how she did" to specific elements. Using the criteria in successive assessments, she begins to see her own developing ability in specific detail.

The beginning learner's encounter with assessment is always a powerful experience, often an unsettling one. It abruptly shifts her attention from a text or teacher to herself, something she has seldom if ever been asked to do in a formal learning situation. It directs her focus toward an active process rather than a body of data. Yet it also provides her with tools that will enable her to operate effectively in this new context—the criteria themselves, supportive personal feedback, and our careful modeling of the criteria's use as we assess alongside her. Rapidly she begins gaining a sense of how to look at her learning in this new way.

For our degree and certificate students, the first assessment comes in the day-long series of exercises from which we have already quoted Jean's, Emily's, and Pat's letters. We initiated this Entrance Assessment several years ago, partly to acquaint the student with assessment by direct experience (in addition to having it explained in orientation and preentry advising sessions) and partly for diagnostic purposes. Since then this combination of writing a letter, delivering a short videotaped speech, reading and interpreting an academic article, hearing and interpreting an academic lecture, and preparing and reading quantitative graphs—then assessing each of these—has proven an invaluable opportunity for beginning learners to become aware of their own learning.

Jean recalls coming into the Entrance Assessment experience while still in her last term of high school:

> They had a get-together for all incoming freshmen, to orient me and my family to the whole new outlook. They talked about assessments, they talked about criteria and validations. It still left me confused, but it made me start looking. It was just like "I'm stepping into a whole new world."
>
> Then we came in for one day in the spring and were bombarded with sheets and tests and making that speech. That basically scared me. I didn't know if this was what college was going to be like, and I didn't know if I wanted to stick to it.
>
> But then, when I got the feedback on my speech—well, I was in debate for two years in high school, and it really excited me to see that you could break it down into all these parts of a speech. I'd never done that before. I thought they were going to tell me, "Your speech was good" or "Your speech was bad." But they really made some concrete statements about it.

Emily's recollections focus on the anxiety felt by the returning woman who has been away from schooling for many years:

> I never had to make a speech in my life—and we had to give one in front of a video machine! It was the most terrifying experience I had ever had in my whole life.
>
> Then you sit there and watch your speech, and you think, "Oh, my God, I did this and this and this wrong," and you don't concentrate on anything you did well. But they stress that, more than they do your weaknesses. I think that's really important, especially when you're just beginning.

Pat, having been immersed in the world of business, focuses on adapting to a strange environment:

> We sat in the auditorium our first day here. I remember thinking, "What are they talking about?" It was really very threatening and challenging. It was like going into a different culture.
>
> Then we had these assessments—speaking, writing, listening, and so on. I remember the tension of thinking someone would be looking over my shoulder at every word, everything I said or did. But when I sat down with the assessor, she put me at ease right away. She asked if I knew why we were going through this process, and I actually didn't. So she went through it all, point by point. And after we'd gone through the criteria, and looked at my strengths and weaknesses, I did. I felt I'd actually learned something about myself.

Throughout her courses and other work, the learner will encounter assessment again and again. In fact, since it is the major means by which we accredit each learner's progress, as many as a half-dozen assessments for a variety of abilities are offered in every course.

Shortly after this initial assessment experience, therefore, the learner engages in her first contract-writing session. In a consultation with her staff adviser, she designs her program contract for the first semester. They negotiate not only which courses she will take but also—based on the Entrance Assessment diagnostic information—any abilities she will need to give immediate attention to developing through special learning experiences. At the same time, they write her course contracts. From among those abilities and levels the instructor has identified as central to each course, the learner selects which ones she will undertake to develop and demonstrate as the course progresses.

Implicit in the college contract is our responsibility, as educators, for maintaining the "viability" of the abilities we have identified as learning goals within each program. We do this in part by collaborating with hundreds of regional professionals in all fields, as co-assessors of our learners' demonstrations and as mentors for their off-campus internships. Each program and department also relies on the regular review and counsel of an advisory committee, including business and professional people from relevant fields. Most important in this "quality control" area, however, is our major commitment to ongoing program evaluation, embodied in the multidimensional studies of our learners in and after college conducted by our Office of Research and Evaluation (Mentkowski and Doherty, 1982). Within this context of constantly reevaluated abilities, the learner selects when and where in her program she will develop those she needs for general education and for her particular career goals.

The terms of each of the learner's course contracts are actually set forth in two documents. First is the instructor's syllabus, spelling out among the course goals and procedures each ability level offered, the learning experiences that will help the learner develop it, and when and how it will be assessed—including the criteria to be used. To this the learner adds her signed learning contract form, specifying which abilities and levels she will endeavor to develop and demonstrate.

Her official academic record is a computer-generated matrix that lists which courses she has taken or is taking, which ability levels she has successfully demonstrated, and which ones she has currently under contract and where. (Unsuccessful attempts are not officially recorded, though they are used in advising.)

As educators we take much of the initiative in this early phase of the learner's growth toward self-direction. We decide which abilities to offer in each course and learning experience, we create the assessment exercises, and we define the criteria. As she assesses herself, the learner works in something of an apprentice role at first, with our assessment always there alongside hers as a model and a stimulus for dialogue. Even in her contract writing, the learner has a limited range of options from which to choose at the beginning of most programs. Soon after her work is well under way, however, the learner in a certificate or degree program does have the option to renegotiate any of the several course contracts she has made. Within the context of her longer-term commitments, this encourages her to begin taking responsibility for evaluating the pace and direction of her learning and taking a degree of control.

Gradually the learner begins to see her own learning as the unifying theme of her diverse experiences. Jean vividly relates the shift from seeing learning as external to seeing it as internal, and the empowering awareness that she is changing:

> When I came here, I thought everyone had the knowledge, and I had to find the people who had the knowledge in order to get brains, education, talent. As I struggled through this learning process, I realized that the stuff is inside me—and that people can help me bring it out and hone it down so its rough edges are gone, and considerably expand it.
>
> That's what changed about me. It shocked me to find I have a brain. It's the greatest to be able to say, "I can do it," or "I think I can do it," or "If I can't do it I'm going to know why."

Emily reflects a similar sense of elation:

> When I first saw that matrix of competences, I wondered, "How do you ever get these skills?" It's a painful process in the beginning, and I guess I did go through a period of negativism.
>
> But you get this constant practice, and the process is practice. Practicing something, it be-

comes a part of you. And once you get into the
system you realize, "Well, now I can do this and
this and this—and I couldn't when I first came
here."

For Pat, too, tangible evidence of her own learning helps
make sense out of an unfamiliar and challenging environment:

At first I was overwhelmed by this approach
to learning. I thought, "How am I ever going to be
able to understand this? What is it good for?"
A few weeks into the semester, I realized
that I do have skills. But I still didn't know where I
was going. So I sat myself down with all the syllabi
and materials they hand out, and I just read. I read
for a whole day until it started making sense.
Since then, I haven't really had any problems. I know I'm learning. And I'm being taught a
way to learn, not just facts or information.

This ability to see her own learning, and to see it as a process in which she changes, constitutes a major milestone for the
learner. It is a deep shift in her modes of self-perception, and it
has strong impact on her attitudes about learning. She comes to
own learning as an important issue in her life, and to own the
learning she has seen taking place within herself.

Being able to see her learning, however, is not the same as
being ready to take full control of directing it. The learner who
has successfully grappled with this first phase still has some major work to do in order to become an effective self-directing
learner.

Phase Two: Transferring Learning

Discovering that her learning isn't "out there" but that it
occurs within her, as a change in her perception and abilities, is
the most difficult hurdle for the beginning learner. After it,
usually in fairly short order, comes her second major insight:
that her learning is something she can carry with her from situation to situation, adapting it for use in each new setting.

In the first phase, assessment enables each student to discover that learning is personal. In the second phase, her learning contracts enable her to discover that learning is portable.

The learner in a degree certificate program may, for example, have successfully demonstrated the ability to observe in an introductory science lab exercise. That will be duly entered on her matrix. In order to be fully accredited, however, she must also demonstrate her observing skill successfully in at least two other settings. In a music class, that might mean identifying the major segments of a work and learning to note significant shifts in key or mode, in tempo, and in dynamics. In a course in social policy studies, she might be asked to apply a framework that distinguishes "event" from "issue" from "structural problem" when she reads a newsmagazine article.

We have built the college contract into our long-term programs to require this multiple demonstration at almost every level of almost every ability. Our reasons for insisting on this multiplicity are two. First, we want to be sure—and we want the learner to be sure—that she indeed has command of the ability in question. Her demonstrating it in several different settings allows us to infer that her success is not an artifact of the situation, or a lucky imitation, or a misreading by the assessors. Second, we want to be sure that each learner experiences herself using an ability like "observing" within very different analytical systems, looking at quite dissimilar kinds of material in different environments. We want her to see that her ability, once developed, goes with her wherever she goes and can be translated into a wide variety of languages and situations.

This is not quite as easy for the learner as it seems. The languages of the academic disciplines differ considerably, for one thing, and the learner is at first too busy learning these different languages to see their commonalities. This only increases her tendency to recall and describe the things she has done in terms of the settings in which she did them, a human trait familiar to anyone who has interviewed a job applicant or tried to help a returning housewife translate "child rearing and homemaking" into transferable skills.

At first the learner has a similar difficulty in generalizing a newly demonstrated ability from the specific situation in which she herself first became aware of it. Our insistence in the college contract on multiplicity provides her with the experience that will enable her to generalize; our consistent use of a language that transcends our disciplinary dialects—the abilities and subabilities we have identified as educators—provides her with the *tools* she needs.

In the science lab, while she has been consciously learning to describe a chemical reaction and to use certain lab measuring equipment, she has also been aware that she is "observing." And it is "observing," not describing the actions or measuring chemicals, for which she receives her contract credit. Simultaneously, in her music class, she has been consistently reminded that finding the elements of a musical form is an instance of "observing," and in her social policy course she has been learning to use the event/issue/problem framework as an "observing" technique.

Emily, the housewife returning for part-time study, recalls that "It took me that whole first semester to get acclimated to concentrating on my abilities rather than just on content." Early in her second semester, her vision of her "abilities" began to come together: "In my psych class, we were working on how you do an experiment, and I suddenly realized I was doing the same thing again—looking at the pieces, at the behavior, and trying to infer what patterns there were. . . . It was just the same as reading an article, or looking at a painting. They weren't just parts of a category, they were the same thing—and that's why they were all called analysis."

Closely allied to the insight that her learning is transferable is the discovery that it is usable—that the learner can, as an act of conscious intention, adapt an ability she has developed elsewhere and apply it to the present situation in order to influence the outcome. This key step toward informed control of her own learning is illustrated in Jean's recounting of her experience with some of the subabilities we have identified within "effective social interaction":

In the New Student Seminar, we did several group interactions. After the first one or two, I could see I wasn't doing much to lead the group along. So on the next one, I worked at doing that. And I got it pretty well. I was able to keep an eye on our job as well as my own assignment and remind people when we needed to move on ("evaluating"). I even helped out at "closure," getting people to agree on a next meeting.

I felt good about that. And what really made me feel good was in my management class later that semester, when four of us had to give a panel. . . . No one was too eager to be in charge, but I finally said I would do it. . . . And I just used my interaction skills—my "summarizing" and my "evaluating" and so on—and I kept the group moving right along. It worked.

As these examples indicate, we must back up what we require in the contract, not only with a transdisciplinary language but also with specific supports to the learner. Not many learners, even in this second phase, can be counted on to reach Emily's spontaneous insight in the midst of a class exercise. Most learners need the tools tangibly available in the form of "all the syllabi and materials they hand out," as well as in guided experiences like Jean's seminar and simulations that help each learner perceive, understand, and begin to take control of her learning.

Phase Three: Directing Learning

In the first phase, the learner focuses primarily on herself, looking there for the changes that constitute learning. In the second phase, her attention shifts toward the various academic disciplines—the course settings in which she secures her new abilities and across which she learns to transfer and use them. In the third phase, the learner begins to move off campus and focus on nonacademic environments. Taking her abilities into settings that are not designed for her learning, she is challenged to integrate and use her abilities independently and to assume more of the initiative for planning and evaluating her development. She begins to develop the autonomy and flexibility essential to effective self-directed learning.

As in the second phase, we use the requirements of the

college contract to ensure that each learner has the *experiences* that will challenge her to make this last major step toward self-direction. We also try to provide the *tools* and support systems that will enable her to take up that challenge successfully.

For the learner in a weekday degree or certificate program, the first major out-of-class challenge comes as early as her third semester. We have created a required half-day simulation called the Integrated Competence Seminar (ICS), which involves each learner in sustained role taking across a series of individual and group exercises. As she works with her peers to resolve a number of problems on behalf of a fictitious organization, each participant must select, combine, and apply the several abilities she has so far developed.

While this simulation gets careful assessment and feedback, we do not use it as some sort of "summative" accrediting judgment. It exists simply as a catalyst. Nonetheless, Jean's reactions typify the initial resistance the ICS frequently receives:

> I know they probably told us about the ICS back in Freshman Seminar. But when we actually came to it, I was furious. Here it was almost the end of the semester, and suddenly we're going to have to take this huge assessment on all our abilities at once.
>
> "What are they trying to do?" I said. "I've been assessed for these things already! Are they going to take them away?"

Actually, we find this kind of resistance encouraging, since it dramatically expresses the learner's growing sense of investment in her learning. And the resistance quickly dissipates as she gains a new awareness of herself operating more independently. "I had to set my priorities right away," Emily recalls, "because I had this stack of things on my table. And I thought, 'Wow! I want to be a professional woman, and look at all the things I'm going to have to do!' Then I started to pull together all the qualities I needed." For Pat feedback afterward brought the picture into focus: "The integrated assessment was tough, but I felt pretty good about what I'd done. When we went over it, my assessor was a woman who works at the phone company. She kept relating the things I'd done to situations she was familiar with in her work, and it made me realize, 'This is it. This is the kind of thing I want to be doing in my work. I want to take charge of a problem and use the abilities I know I have, and have the company recognize it.' "

This catalytic experience prepares the learner for her primary encounter with learning in nonacademic environments: her OCEL (Off-Campus Experiential Learning) field internships. In the OCEL program, learners in every major select and negotiate for placements relevant to their career goals in local corporations and hospitals, agencies and clinics, civic and commercial and professional organizations. Each OCEL intern works part time for a semester or more under real time constraints, with the organization's ability to meet certain of its goals depending on her performance. She has the supervision of an "on-site mentor" trained by our faculty and participates weekly in the OCEL seminar, which provides three important learning supports: (1) The faculty introduce a series of conceptual and practical tools, and exercises in using them, to help her handle the often overwhelming experience of her field setting. (2) The learner is required each week to log key on-site experiences according to a guided format that directs her in analyzing her environment and her performance and impact in it. (3) Her peers provide a secure setting in which she can introduce insights, questions, and conflicts and expect to receive sympathetic but seriously analytical assistance. The seminar thus involves each learner in repeated cycles of experiential learning, from active on-site engagement to reflective analysis and critiquing and then back again.

By feeding her learning—both practical and theoretical—back into her performance week after week, the learner frequently makes dramatic gains in her ability to contribute effectively at the work site. Equally important, and more enduring, are the gains she makes in being able to direct her own learning.

The learner's ability to perceive and assess patterns in her learning, as well as in her actual work performance, is a key development in this third phase.

We still provide the framework, of course. We require
OCEL as part of the college contract, design the seminar support system into the program, screen possible sites, and train
on-site mentors. We provide regular input of new tools for learning, from techniques for "reading" institutional environments
to role-playing important encounters, and we still guide the
learner's reflective analysis via the log format. But she has now
reached the point where she defines virtually as many of the
learning contract's terms as we do. At every stage it is the learner who exerts the critical initiative, from negotiating for her
internship to defining its learning goals and measures, from
evaluating both her performance *and* her learning to setting new
directions for both.

Conclusion

The learner who has worked her way successfully through
the challenges involved in each of these three phases is ready for
self-direction. In fact, she is already operating as a self-directing
learner in extended "real-life" professional situations as well as
on campus—while her educators, in both settings, function more
and more as mentor-colleagues and less and less as directive
guides.

When the learner reaches this point, the essence of our
multilevel learning contract with her has been fulfilled. She has
effectively acquired and demonstrated the ability to direct
learning—to construct learning experiences (even in nonacademic environments), to define learning goals and measures, to
observe learning and assess its growth and direction, and to interpret future learning needs and options.

Ironically, it is at this point that the learner is for the first
time really ready to enter into a learning contract as a fully cog-
nizant and competent equal party. Until now, she has been
entering into learning contracts with the "informed consent" of
the layperson. But she now has a practiced understanding of her
own learning and a demonstrated ability to guide it that is in
kind if not yet in degree, equal to that of her educators. She is
now a junior peer in a sense, and her own educator.

It is gratifying to see learners of all ages and backgrounds reach this point, in their infinitely individual ways. But it is also sobering to realize that, at this point or very soon after, they leave us. We can take comfort that our learners emerge far better equipped than if we had ignored the issue of self-direction and left them to deal with it all after graduation, or if we had simply thrown them from the outset into a "trial by immersion" without supports or guidance and without recognizing the developmental process necessary to achieve self-direction.

We hope that what we have learned about learners' development toward self-direction will be of value to our colleagues in adult education. And we warmly welcome the collaboration of colleagues in medium- and short-term programs who are addressing the developmental needs of the learner with self-direction as their goal. That would add greatly to what we, as educators, can bring to our learners when we sit down with them to create a design for their learning and to what our learners, through the working out of that design, take into their lives.

2

Helping Adults
Reenter College

Margaret Coe, Ann Rubenzahl,
Vicki Slater

Adults who have been away from academia for some time frequently experience high anxiety on reentering the hallowed halls. They worry about being embarrassed by asking dumb questions or giving dumb answers; they wonder whether they can learn as well or as fast as the younger students; they fear that they might fail or get low grades. And many faculty members are uneasy with the increasing number of "oldsters" in their twenties, thirties, forties, and older, appearing in their classrooms. Most colleges that are catering to adult students in response to the dwindling pool of teenagers are experimenting with ways to smooth the reentry process for returning adults.

One of the best-planned programs of this sort that I have encountered is described in this selection. It outlines the Adult Entry Program that was launched for the students and a series of workshops to prepare the faculty for its "new clientele."

The authors are members of the staff of the Center for Lifelong Learning, Mercy College, Dobbs Ferry, New York.

Special features:

- Parallel scheduling
- Eight-week terms
- Extension centers
- Redesigned courses
- Faculty development workshops
- Self-directed learning
- Evaluation
- Profiles of reentry students
- Attrition and retention

121

Mercy College is an independent, coeducational, nonsectarian commuter college with its main campus located in Dobbs Ferry, a suburban community north of New York City. In the years since 1972, the college has grown from 1,500 to more than 9,500 students. It offers associate, baccalaureate, and graduate degree programs as well as noncredit courses and programs.

Much of Mercy College's growth is attributable to the implementation of three delivery approaches in the 1970s that made it accessible to the adult student: parallel scheduling, eight-week terms, and the opening of extension centers. Parallel scheduling was designed to accommodate students such as policemen or nurses, who work rotating shifts and need flexible hours. Parallel classes are taught in both day and evening sessions by the same instructor, and students may attend class in either session. Eight-week terms were introduced (to supplement the more traditional sixteen-week semester) to permit students to carry a full load of course credits for the semester while enrolling in only two courses per eight-week term and attending only two evenings per week. Five extension centers (one now a branch campus) were opened to make a college education more convenient and accessible, especially for adults. These innovations led to the Academy for Educational Development's 1979 award to Mercy College for innovative solutions to critical problems in higher education.

In 1980, the year the college created an Office of Continuing Education, the only needs that remained were redesigned courses and special counseling support to help the new, anxious adult student through the first semester. Thus, an Adult Entry Program was created by the Office of Continuing Education, and a Title III grant proposal was written in an effort to get seed money for a program "designed to assist the adult who is returning to education in overcoming the barriers . . . which exist by providing counselors and a special sequence of courses taught by faculty who have been specially trained in adult learning theory and techniques." Monies were granted by Title III to fund the first year's expenses for these services. Monies were also granted for additional support services, such as special help for the learning-disabled adult, tutoring, and a homework hot line. Another goal was to study the specific causes of adult attrition and make recommendations for reducing this attrition.

Ten Adult Entry Program courses were planned: one, an orientation course, to be created; the other nine, existing college courses to be modified by application of techniques that facilitate adult learning. The newly created course, "Career and Life Planning: College Orientation for Adults," had as its objectives:

1. To become comfortable and involved in the course and with each other
2. To understand the ongoing process of career choice
3. To set career and educational goals, and to make career and educational plans to meet those goals
4. To learn how to be a self-directed learner
5. To learn other college survival skills (such as study skills, time management, reading, and note taking)
6. To become acquainted with Mercy College's services, procedures, personnel
7. To understand the process of self-growth and development
8. To meet an individual, significant learning objective

The other nine courses that were planned for inclusion in this program were introductory courses in English, psychology, speech, math, philosophy, and education (reading improvement).

Faculty Workshops

To meet the proposal's objective of creating a learning environment that reflects the learning needs of adult students, a faculty training program was developed to provide faculty with knowledge of current adult learning theory and methods of facilitating adult learning and persistence. The tangible results of the faculty training program were to be (1) redesigned course outlines for the ten courses in the program, and (2) publication of these outlines in a faculty handbook.

Under the direction of the Office of Continuing Education, the faculty training program took the form of a series of workshops, to be attended by faculty and interested staff of Mercy College. The core of participants were those faculty members selected by their chairpersons to take responsibility for redesigning the relevant Adult Entry Program courses. In three cases the chairpersons themselves made this commitment. Malcolm Knowles was selected as the facilitator of these workshops and consultant in planning course outlines. Other faculty and staff members who had a special interest in the needs of the adult learner were invited to attend. These participants included the Title III grant coordinator, the director of libraries, the assistant dean for academic advising, the assistant dean for college opportunity programs, the assistant dean for academic affairs, and the coordinator of College Skills Programs (placement testing and remedial services).

In consultation with Knowles, it was decided to hold five workshops, a month apart, starting in November 1981 and completing in March 1982. The first workshop would be on a Saturday, to allow meeting for a full day. The other four would be on Friday afternoons, when most faculty members would not be teaching.

At the first workshop, Knowles put into practice the principles of andragogy and self-directed learning. The participants were divided into small groups at tables forming a horseshoe. Knowles requested that each person share his or her learning needs with the small group and that each group should choose a spokesperson to report these questions or goals to Knowles and the large group.

In his role of facilitator, Knowles set the climate by modeling andragogical techniques, encouraged group interaction by not presenting himself as the only expert to answer questions, and offered himself as a resource by providing information and suggesting readings. The small-group evaluations of this workshop indicated that some participants were experiencing tension and resistance to the process. Requests were made for more "nuts and bolts" and information from Knowles that was specific to the needs of Mercy College's adult students. A possible explanation is that a few faculty members were interpreting the very existence of these workshops as a negation of their many years of successfully and sensitively teaching adult students. Rather than being perceived as an opportunity for further learning and honing of skills, the workshops were producing anxiety and criticism.

To deal with these issues and to foster the involvement of participants in the planning of each forthcoming workshop, a task force was formed of several volunteers from the participants of the first workshop. At the first task force meeting, an outline of Knowles's suggested plan for the December workshop was presented for the task force's approval or amendments. Also on the agenda was provision for discussing the reactions to the previous workshop and planning how to meet the communicated and perceived needs. This agenda was typical of the ones for future task force meetings—evaluating the previous workshop and planning the upcoming one.

Beginning with the second workshop, focus was put on sharing progress in developing the new course ("Career and Life Planning: College Orientation for Adults") or the redesigned course outlines for the other nine courses. Knowles was available as a consultant, to explain techniques and approaches, as in giving greater detail on how to use learning contracts. Gradually a more trusting atmosphere developed, and there was more open sharing. In their evaluations after each workshop, participants stressed that the informal gathering together of the college's faculty and staff was in itself valuable. There seemed to be an enjoyment and appreciation of the group members' varied skills, experiences, and ideas.

Teaching of the new orientation course began in the spring semester (February–May). (The other Entry Program course taught that semester was "The Adult in Contemporary Life," which had been taught previously.)

Originally the fifth and final workshop was to be held in March 1982. At the fourth workshop, however, the group decided to postpone the final workshop until the beginning of June, after the completion of the spring courses. In this way a whole day could be devoted to a fuller sharing of the teaching outlines and classroom experiences. The plan was to combine progress reports on specific courses, evaluation of the series of workshops, minilessons by Knowles on adult education and by a volunteer faculty member on material from her course, a tape by Patricia Cross on "Working with Adult Students," and planning for the future.

Responsibility for the evaluation of the workshops was undertaken by a volunteer faculty committee from the task force. The evaluation instrument was modeled on an instrument used by Knowles for his courses. In a mailed confidential questionnaire sent out prior to the last workshop, each workshop participant was given both objective rating scales and open-ended questions to answer. The return rate was twelve out of the thirty sent out. The lack of response was not considered significant because the time period involved was the hectic end of the semester. The respondents reported themselves attending a mean of 3.61 workshops (out of four), so it was the involved participants who returned the questionnaire. Only one respondent out of the twelve answered that the workshops had no value in increasing understanding/abilities in any of the objective categories; this respondent reported no change in four of the seventeen objective questions. All the other respondents reported at least some change in recognizing and fulfilling needs of adult students, in such areas as designing learning experiences, involving students in planning, conducting and evaluating learning activities, and using group dynamics and small-group discussion techniques.

In the questions that called for an open-ended write-in response, the general tone was of satisfaction, engagement, and cooperation. Not surprisingly, in describing the most helpful aspects of the workshops, virtually all stated that the exchange of views and sharing of various techniques and methods with other faculty was of greatest value. We had already observed that the workshop setting had provided the faculty with an opportunity to come together in a supportive learning environment, promoting a stimulating esprit de corps. The workshops had served as a model for the classroom climate we were hoping to provide for new adult students, providing validity for the self-directed learner philosophy. Some respondents wrote that they had noticed different student behavior in their classrooms: a more relaxed attitude, greater receptivity and appreciation of the value of the course, better class cohesion and student interaction, and greater student motivation and self-direction. Some participants regretted that the sessions were too short and that time had to be spent on teaching fundamentals and dealing with resistance. However, as the instructors of the new orientation course were discovering, time had to be spent at the beginning of that course in allaying students' fears and insecurities about placing the responsibility for learning in the students and not the instructor. The exchange of power from the knowledge transmitter to the learner can be uncomfortable, given our common background in pedagogical classroom settings. A number of participants wanted to continue or extend the workshops, by organizing groups based on common programs, disciplines, or problems.

The faculty responsible for redesigning course outlines for the Entry Program courses submitted the revised outlines to Continuing Education for publication in the *Adult Entry Program Faculty Handbook.*

Adult Entry Program Students

Most of the students enrolled in "Career and Life Planning: College Orientation for Adults" have not attended college at all or have been away from college for many years. Almost all have experienced a traditional learning process in the past and felt little control over their education prior to the orientation course.

A majority of the students are female, but a growing number of males attend each semester. Age is distributed from twenty-five to sixty-five years of age. Approximately half of the females are employed outside the home, while the majority of the males are employed.

What brings these students together? The unifying thread is the desire to find academic and career direction with the necessary support.

The target group at which the Adult Entry Program, and the orientation course in particular, is aimed is the high-anxiety, lower-skill adult. The students attracted are high in anxiety but, surprisingly, also fairly high in skills, as is demonstrated by the results of the English placement exams taken by each student at the completion of the orientation course. This exam places students in the appropriate level of English and is normally taken by all incoming students before taking classes at the college. Many students taking the orientation course express intense anxiety over test taking and therefore are permitted to wait until completion of the course before taking these exams. Seventy-five percent of orientation students have been placed at freshmen English level, with very few adults requiring remedial work. This is far in excess of the college-wide 25 percent placement at the freshmen English level.

The majority of Adult Entry Program students have families, with children varying in age from newborns to college age. Students indicate some initial concern from family and friends about their decision to return to school, but as school becomes routine family members seem to make the adjustment. Students are encouraged to discuss these adjustment problems in the orientation class and share their experiences and solutions with other class members. Many students do their homework when their children do or discuss their courses with spouses and friends. School then becomes an accepted part of the family situation. As a result of this sharing, families and friends often register for the course themselves.

At the completion of the orientation course, students are asked to complete a questionnaire to evaluate the course. Specifically, students are asked to indicate the value of the course in increasing their understanding/abilities in many different areas on a scale of 0 (not at all) to 4 (a great deal). Selections from the questionnaire follow, and the average of all responses is indicated:

1. I feel more self-confident than I did at the beginning of the semester. (3.22)
2. I have a better understanding of what goes into making a career decision. (3.13)
3. As a student, this course has helped me become more confident about study skills. (2.7)

4. As a result of this course, I am now better able to decide what I want to learn. (2.96)
5. This course has helped me to recognize that I am learning. (3.37)

A goal set forth in the objectives of the orientation course is to help the students become self-directed learners. The following comment by a course participant reflects the feelings of many who complete the course: "What I liked best was the facilitative atmosphere which was introduced rather than the perfunctory lecture. I felt that since I was taking on responsibility for part of my own growth, I wanted to work up to my potential. I felt no pressure to meet deadlines, etc., and so was free to work unharassed to my fullest potential."

Adults taking the orientation course begin to realize that they are capable of taking responsibility for their own learning, just as they take responsibility for events in their own lives outside the classroom. As this realization takes place, students want to take an active, rather than a passive, role in deciding what they want to learn, how they want to learn it, and how they will demonstrate their learning. Taking on an individual learning project as part of the orientation course at first is seen as threatening; yet, as the students progress in the course, it becomes a source of great satisfaction and accomplishment to have taken such control over their learning.

The combination of work, family, and education is a subject dealt with by most orientation students. Time management becomes the vehicle for successfully combining it all. But, as any orientation student will confirm, it is not something that is learned easily. Throughout the course an awareness of the problem is developed, and students begin to see that how they spend their time is really under their control. The trained facilitator works with each student in planning the best method for individuals to include their education in their life plan.

To assist the new adult student in adjusting to the college, the Continuing Education counselors prepared a handbook designed to answer the questions most asked by adult students returning to school. The handbook follows a "question-and-answer" format, taking the most asked questions and responding to them. Also included in the handbook are a dictionary of college terminology, a listing of college procedures for adults, and a detailed building and room map. Quotes from attending adult students are included throughout the handbook to present the student point of view. Pictures of adult students and the Continuing Education staff are printed, to introduce the new adult student to the staff and fellow students. Each Adult Entry Program student is presented with a copy of the handbook on the first day of returning to school.

With the assistance of the Continuing Education staff, Adult Entry Program students have organized to publish a newsletter for adult students at the college. A contest, open to adult students, was held to name the newsletter, and the newsletter became known as the *College Adult Update*. The newsletter includes a variety of fiction and nonfiction articles written by adult students. An editorial board of students and Continuing Education staff selects the material to be included in each issue. Social events at the college of special interest to adults are mentioned in each issue, as well as registration and financial aid information.

Students' attrition and retention were a portion of the grant proposal that are still under study. The findings at this point seem to indicate that students for the most part continue schooling after taking the orientation course. As with the general adult attrition trend, a few students do drop in and out of the college, depending on finances (primary reason), personal problems, or career conflicts. Those students who do drop out generally indicate that they intend to continue their college studies at another time. Most of the students who have decided not to continue with college after taking the orientation course made that decision because they learned from the course that college would not help them reach their personal or career goals and were planning alternate methods (such as work experience or secretarial programs) to reach those goals.

3

An External
Undergraduate Degree Program

Marilou Eldred

External degree programs are one of the most rapidly expanding elements of higher education as colleges and universities become more and more dependent on adults who cannot leave jobs and other responsibilities to live full time on campuses to earn their degrees. Demographic projections assure that this trend will accelerate for a long time in the future; the pool of teenagers, the traditional predominant student body of higher education, is shrinking. External degree programs will work only if their students take a heavy responsibility for their own learning, but adults enter into these programs typically with the self-concept of dependency that they were conditioned to have in their previous schooling. Therefore, they need to be helped to make the transition from dependent to self-directed learners. This selection describes a "Seminar in Process Education," which was designed to give this help to the students of one of the largest external degree programs in the country, the University Without Walls.

Marilou Eldred is a former faculty member at the University of Minnesota and is now Dean of Students at the College of St. Catharine in St. Paul.

Special features:

• Process education defined
• Self-directed learning skills
• Long-term degree plan

Reprinted, with permission, from a paper, "University Without Walls Seminar in Process Education," presented to the Adult Education Research Conference, April 1977.

131

- Components and criteria of a liberal education
- Orientation seminar
- Recognition for prior learning

One of the primary characteristics of the adult students in the University Without Walls program is that they are self-directed. They have clearly defined educational goals, but they need help in planning how to meet their goals and in using appropriate learning resources. Most adult students in UWW want to include experiential learning as part of their degree program. The University Without Walls helps students develop their degree programs through a Seminar in Process Education.

Education derived through UWW differs from a traditional undergraduate program primarily in the design and delivery of learning opportunities available to students. A UWW education includes the traditional concept of liberal education; in addition, the University Without Walls attempts to educate through what we term process education—helping students develop skills in question asking, reflecting, analyzing, and synthesizing for the purpose of integrating their academic education with their experiential education into a baccalaureate degree program.

One of the premises on which the UWW program is based is that students must accept the primary responsibility for the outcomes of their education and must be active participants in charting the most appropriate degree course for achieving their learning goals. The vehicle used by UWW students to design their program is a Long-Term Degree Plan. The Long-Term Degree Plan describes the methods by which students will demonstrate their competence in each of UWW's graduation criteria. It also contains the students' timetable for completing their UWW program. Exhibit 1 is a sample page from a Long-Term Degree Plan. It shows how students combine prior and present learning experiences with formal academic education. Exhibit 2 shows how a degree program is structured. The seven graduation criteria, shown on the left, represent the components of a liberal education. The ways in which students can meet those criteria are shown on the right side of the page. The definition we use for each of the graduation criteria is given in Exhibit 3.

Name __Mary Jones__   Quarter of admission __Fall 1976__

Main study area __Day Care Administration__   Projected quarter of graduation __Spring 1978__

Date __4-77__

Graduation Criterion: Academic Achievement
                        (Identify Specific Criterion)

	Formal Course Work	Comp. Date	Workshops Conferences Seminars	Comp. Date	UWW Directed Study Projects	Comp. Date	Life/Work Experience	Comp. Date
Completed Activities (descriptive titles only)	Introductory child psychology	1975	Curriculum workshop	1974	Setting up a volunteer staff in a day care center	1977	Founded day care center	1975
	Topics in child psychology	1975	Volunteers' workshop	1975			Teacher in day care center	1973-1976
	Infancy	1975						
	Introduction to management	1976						
	Management in human service agencies	1976						
Projected Activities (descriptive titles only)	Behavioral and emotional problems	1977	Seminar in after school care	1977	Codirecting a day care center	1978	Present job experiences	1977-1978
	Socialization of children	1977						
	Developmental psychology	1977						
	Planning and administration of social services	1978						
	Personnel management in human service agencies	1978						

Exhibit 2. University Without Walls Seminar in Process Education: Developing the Long-Term Degree Plan.

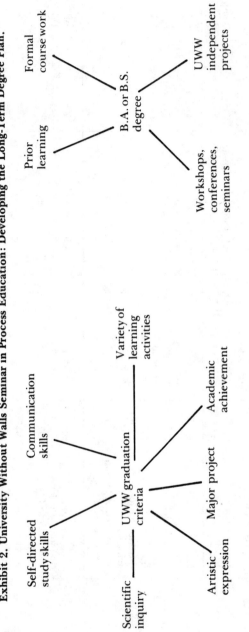

Goals of Process Education Seminar: the development of learning skills (questioning, reflecting, analyzing, synthesizing) for the purpose of integrating various forms of learning (experience, independent projects) into an individualized baccalaureate degree plan.

Exhibit 3. University Without Walls Graduation Criteria.

1. *Self-Directed Study Skills:* You will need to present evidence which demonstrates your ability to design and carry out study projects of your own choosing. In order to meet this requirement, you will need to evidence the following conceptual and practical skills: (a) question-asking ability; (b) appropriate resource identification and use; (c) ability to develop suitable rationales for studies undertaken; (d) willingness and ability to engage in self-evaluation in studies pursued; and (e) an ability to pursue such studies in a self-directed mannner wherein the student is the primary initiator of learning activity.

2. *Communication Skills:* You will be expected to present materials which clearly evidence an ability to write effectively and intelligibly in the English language. This involves, minimally, meeting commonly accepted criteria of organization, grammar, and punctuation used in the evaluation of written materials. In addition, you will, in a general manner, evidence an active pattern of seeking to share your questions and insights with others while at the same time seeking out the communications of others. These more general communication skills may be evidenced through the use of other than written media.

3. *Academic Achievement:* You shall present evidence of learning in your main study area(s) in terms of the following: (a) knowledge of the commonly recognized historical and contemporary core (basic) literature and a consequent understanding of the basic vocabulary of the field; (b) an understanding of main theoretical concepts or perspectives in the field; (c) a demonstrated ability to use the basic methods of investigation required for study in the field; and (d) exploration of the ways the main field of study relates to broader concerns (problems/issues) of contemporary or future society.

4. *Variety of Learning Activities:* You shall present evidence of having pursued learning in a variety of ways and contexts. The formal classroom, a job environment, the library, and the experimental laboratory are some alternative contexts. Reading, field survey, and experimental research are some alternative ways of learning.

5. *Scientific Inquiry:* As a degree candidate, you will need to demonstrate your understanding of the scientific method of inquiry. At minimum, this understanding involves the following:
   a. An understanding of the differences between *objective* and *subjective* knowledge.
   b. An understanding of the *philosophical foundations* of science. This understanding involves knowing about the beliefs and assumptions scientists have regarding the order of the universe and the relationships between phenomena.
   c. An understanding of the basic ingredients of an *experimental paradigm.* This understanding involves knowing what a basic experiment looks like and the factors which must be taken into account in the construction of an experiment.
   d. An understanding of how science relates to your world. What does science mean to you as a person?

(continued on next page)

Exhibit 3. University Without Walls Graduation Criteria, Cont'd.

As a degree candidate, you will *not* be required to have actually used the scientific method in your studies. However, you must demonstrate your clear understanding of the scientific method of inquiry in terms of each of the categories given above.

6. *Artistic Expression:* You shall demonstrate an understanding of the artistic process as it is expressed in the fine arts (for example, painting, sculpture, theatre, architecture, dance, literature, music). You may demonstrate this understanding in one of two ways:
    a. An understanding of the artistic process can be gained through direct experience with a medium.
    b. An understanding of the artistic process can be gained through the investigation of some aspect of the fine arts from the perspective of "critic" (one examining the artistic works of others).
    In both cases, you must evidence, as an end point, an understanding of the artistic process as one mode of inquiry about the world; either your own creative endeavors or examination of the works of others may be used as a "means" to this end.

7. *Major Project:* You shall present a major project in your main study area. The project shall evidence quality work in the main study area toward the goal of demonstrating that you are more than a consumer of what earlier scholars and artists have offered. The form of the major project—be it in the written or another medium—is your choice. The major project shall be your contribution to your main field of study.

We find that students often have difficulty deciding how to incorporate the two parts of the diagram shown in Exhibit 2 into one degree program. The criteria of academic achievement and major project focus on the student's main study area and include a knowledge of content, theory, and application, demonstrated through a major project. The criteria of scientific inquiry and artistic expression are generally demonstrated through a combination of subject matter content in one of the sciences or arts and an appreciation for or personal involvement in those disciplines as a "doer." The remaining criteria (self-directed study skills, communication skills, variety of learning activities) are concerned less with specific content and more with students' ability to organize and recognize relationships, to reflect upon and integrate learning and experience, and to assume primary responsibility for designing plans to meet their learning objectives. UWW students generally have had difficulty, first, in understanding the concepts of process education and, second, in applying those concepts to their degree program in accord with the UWW graduation criteria.

In past years UWW advisers have spent a great deal of time with students on an individual basis discussing the graduation criteria and the integration of various kinds of learning experiences. Advisers have, in the past, relied on their individual abilities and inclinations to assist students in understanding the concepts of process education. Advisers are not equally skilled in conveying those concepts, and we have found that an individualized approach is not the most effective way of helping students understand the components of process education.

Thus, a more systematic orientation to the UWW educational process was introduced through the UWW Process Education Seminar. The seminar was developed through a grant from the Small Grants Program at the University of Minnesota and pilot tested with students admitted to UWW for fall quarter of 1976.

The seminar met for twelve two-hour weekly meetings. Each meeting focused on presenting, discussing, and responding to questions about one of the UWW graduation criteria. The seminar instructors tried to incorporate the process education concepts with the academic content criteria and to give illustrations of how to combine the two elements. Students were given time during seminar meetings to begin developing their Long-Term Degree Plans, to describe their various learning activities, and to explain how they planned to integrate formal and informal learning experiences into their degree programs.

There were at least eight significant variables over which the seminar project had no control: (1) the nature and frequency of contact with students' UWW program adviser; (2) the nature and frequency of contact with their University of Minnesota faculty and community faculty advisers; (3) the amount of prior formal education; (4) the amount of work experience that a student would use as part of his or her UWW program; (5) the amount of time and energy available to students for UWW seminar work, given their job and family responsibilities; (6) the availability of library and personnel resources; (7) the clarity in the student's mind of his or her main study area; (8) the level of students' ability to conceptualize and write in an "academic" context. In the seminar meetings, we tried to handle these variables with students on an individual basis. Undoubtedly other variables also affected the performance of each student.

The weekly seminar meetings approached the graduation criteria from a question-and-answer perspective and asked students to write in class about their learning experiences and how they were to be used in their UWW program. It did not take long for students to begin to question staff about the meaning of the graduation criteria. They wanted to know how to approach the criterion of self-directed study skills. They urged the staff to describe ways a student could demonstrate self-directedness. They asked how a person would relate a main study area, such as day care administration, to a variety of learning activities. The staff questioned students about their learning experiences. The students posed possible ways in which their learning experiences seemed related to one another, but wanted some assurance that their thinking was logical.

We found that the adult students in the seminar were initially quite reluctant to talk specifically about learning experiences that were not related to formal classroom settings. The students would state that they "had done many things for which they should receive credit," but it was often difficult to elicit from them specific learning activities. Seminar students demonstrated the characteristics of security in their intellectual ability but some uncertainty about their academic ability and how to translate various kinds of learning experiences into a degree program. A major difficulty was, and still is, getting students to analyze an experience from the viewpoint of what was *learned*, rather than the perspective of simply going through the experience. An example is the following. A student has worked fifteen years as a personnel administrator in a small company. Undoubtedly he has learned many specific techniques and pieces of information to enable him to perform his job well. But those specific techniques or facts may not comprise a learning activity in an academic sense. The person would need to relate those isolated parts of his job within the theoretical framework of personnel administration, management theory, or organizational management, in order for them to be incorporated into his UWW degree program. In other words, the student needs to identify the parts of the particular experience to be used for his degree program. Then those parts must be examined within the broader context of the academic discipline. Finally, the student needs to draw some conclusions about the learning experience in relation to that broader context. The fact that UWW is a non-credit-based program adds to the difficulty because we are not able to tell students that X experience is worth five credits, while Y experience is worth eight credits. We always return to the necessity of students' integrating theoretical concepts with practical experiences. That is the most difficult task for most UWW adult students. They often tend to take the theory for granted or do not readily see its usefulness to them in their present job situation. We find that adult students want to know that whatever they are studying is of immediate use. For many students that means usefulness in their job situation, since the adult students in UWW tend to choose a main study area that is closely related to their job or career.

The UWW program enables students to make the choice of using job-related learning experiences but also is committed to offering students a liberal education rather than a strictly vocational education. The task of students in UWW is to understand the relationship between theory and practice. They need to demonstrate breadth of knowledge as well as depth in their main study area. The seminar meetings almost always included discussion of those relationships.

In addition to developing a fairly clear understanding of the UWW graduation criteria and how to plan their UWW programs, students derived other benefits from the seminar. One was the opportunity to interact with each other. One of the hardships faced by students in UWW is the "learning in isolation" syndrome. Because the program is individualized, with no required courses or common meeting times, it is not unusual for a student to spend two years in UWW and never meet another UWW student. So the student interaction provided opportunities for students to discuss common study areas, help each other identify resources, and sometimes develop friendships.

UWW staff members also were challenged by the seminar.

Staff enjoyed the process of probing, questioning, drawing out students to talk about and analyze their learning experiences. Students saw staff members in roles other than those of advisers. Staff members shared in presenting many of the sessions, and students became acquainted with staff thinking about the UWW graduation criteria. Staff members clarified their own thinking and learned from students about issues such as new ways of integrating prior learning experiences into a degree program. Students and staff enjoyed learning from each other in a group setting, which is a novel experience in UWW.

In planning to offer the seminar again, we are using more outside reading than we did previously. For example, in discussing the UWW graduation criterion "variety of learning activities," we are asking students to read a short autobiographical sketch, in which the author describes the personal experiences throughout her life that helped her learn new things about herself, her family and work relationships, and her progress in intellectual growth. For the criterion "self-directed study skills," students will read a chapter from Kidd's *How Adults Learn* (1972) and will be able to identify with many of Kidd's descriptions of the adult learner and the "self-learner." Kidd's discussion of factors such as time, educational and work experience, and organization of learning will make a great deal of sense to our students, who find themselves in many of the situations described in that chapter. We will discuss the reading during the seminar meetings. The approach of using a specific reading as a "jumping-off" point for students to examine their own learning experiences has proved to be beneficial. Students seem to be gaining a clear understanding of the UWW graduation criteria and of the process of integrating academic and experiential learning.

The process for many adult students is one of learning to think in new ways, to look for relationships, and to communicate in such a way that each learning experience can be evaluated. The composite of such learning experiences makes the UWW adult student an autonomous, responsible, self-directed learner.

4

Faculty Orientation
and In-Service Development
at a State University System

Maurice Olivier, Frances Mahoney

A universal problem plaguing traditional colleges and universities that are gearing up to serve "the new clientele" of adult learners in nontraditional study programs is how to reprogram faculty—especially part-time faculty—to serve this strange breed of adult learners. One of the more innovative of the new nontraditional programs in higher education is the School of Lifelong Learning of the University System of New Hampshire. It has gone about solving this problem in two ways: (1) producing a special edition of the faculty journal of the School of Lifelong Learning, *The Meeting Place,* which describes the unique characteristics of adults as learners and suggests guidelines for adjusting teaching styles and methods to adult learners; and (2) establishing a Resource Network of Campus and Community Faculty, known as "Project Alliance," to provide a mechanism for a continuous dialogue between campus-based and community-based faculty in exploring better ways to serve adult learners. This selection describes the processes used in Project Alliance.

Maurice Olivier, associate dean of the School for Lifelong

Adapted, with permission, from a paper by Maurice Olivier, project director, and Frances Mahoney, project coordinator, "Project Alliance: A Resource Network of Campus and Community Faculty: Final Report for the Fund for the Improvement of Postsecondary Education," December 10, 1982.

141

Learning, University System of New Hampshire, Durham, New Hampshire, is the director of Project Alliance. Frances Mahoney is the coordinator of the project.
Special features:

- Faculty networking
- Faculty work groups and meetings
- Outcomes

_____

In Fall 1981 the School of Lifelong Learning (SLL), a separate institution in the University System of New Hampshire, received a one-year Fund for the Improvement of Postsecondary Education (FIPSE) grant of $29,700 to create an approach to faculty development which would be workable in an institution serving adults statewide with a "borrowed" faculty. As an initial step toward realizing this goal, the school established a framework, known as Project Alliance, for fostering dialogue among faculty. Four working groups of faculty, each focusing on issues related to adult learning in a particular curriculum area, met over a period of eight months. Each group defined its own purpose and task. As a result of the project, the beginnings of a statewide faculty network/dialogue have been established; and follow-up statewide and regional faculty meetings utilizing the ideas and, in some cases, products of the four working groups have been set up.

Purpose

Building a faculty network is especially important to an institution which has no full-time faculty. The school's mission is to provide adults statewide with the opportunity to pursue both degree and nondegree programs, using the resources of the University System.

The school draws its faculty members from the campus-based institutions of the University System of New Hampshire, from private colleges, and from the professions, business, and industry. They teach for the school in a variety of locations spread across the state. Rarely do they even meet each other, let alone have an opportunity to talk about their teaching, the needs of adult learners, and the ways in which the teaching/learning situation can be improved. The purpose of the project involved a number of closely related objectives:

1. To foster a sense of faculty identity with the school, with its educational mission, and with faculty colleagues and to create the beginnings of a faculty network across the state.
2. To establish a dialogue between campus-based and community-based faculty. Frequently these two groups of faculty have different perspectives on the relationship between the academic disciplines, content, applied dimensions, and the adult's life or work experience.
3. To involve faculty in a model of faculty development which centers on a task inherently interesting to faculty and requiring new learning for its completion, thereby creating the impetus for faculty to seek out special resources.

Background

The school was established in 1972 and in the early years of its existence drew most of its faculty from the full-time faculty of the campus-based University System institutions (the University of New Hampshire, Merrimack Valley College, Keene State College, Plymouth State College). These faculty came from traditionally organized academic departments and taught predominantly younger students. As the school, following its USNH mandate, expanded its outreach to the six major regions of the state, non-campus-based faculty, or community-based faculty, increasingly were employed as instructors, especially in regions where campus-based faculty were not readily available. At the present time, the school draws its faculty (numbering approximately 300 in any given semester) almost equally from the campuses and from the community. What the two groups of faculty have in common is a part-time association with the school, an enthusiasm for working with highly motivated adult students, and a general lack of familiarity with the literature, research, and educational practices related to adult development and learning. What they typically differ in is their approach to the various academic disciplines, with campus-based faculty tending to be more strongly versed in theory and community-based faculty tending to be well grounded in current applications. Project Alliance attempted to build on the respective strengths of the two groups of faculty as well as to address their common need for greater understanding of the school's mission and the nature of adult learning.

Project Description

Before the project began, the school had identified four curriculum areas—Written Communication and Critical Thinking, Humanities/Arts, Behavioral Science, and Management—as being of particular importance in its current degree programming and, therefore, in its faculty development efforts. The first step in setting up the project was to identify campus-based faculty from the various USNH campuses to serve as the major Project Alliance faculty. These five faculty provided leadership in initiating and developing the faculty dialogue in each of the four areas. The school's first statewide faculty meeting was held on February 5, 1982, to explain the project and to recruit voluntary faculty involvement in the four working groups that were to be established. Over the next six months, twenty-six faculty, including twenty-one campus-based and community-based faculty and five Project Alliance faculty leaders, met within their respective groups. The focus of these meetings differed according to the discipline area:

Area	*Focus*
Written Communication and Critical Thinking	Approaches to and materials for teaching written communication and critical thinking skills to adults.
Humanities/Arts	Identification of key elements in humanities/arts general education for adults.

Area	*Focus*
Behavioral Science	Need for an interdisciplinary approach and a balance between theory and application.
Management	A redesign of the existing SLL Management curriculum based on competencies identified for the competent manager.

In September 1982 a second statewide SLL faculty meeting was held. A major purpose of this meeting was to provide a forum for the Project Alliance faculty and members of their working groups to report on the results of their discussions.

Outcomes and Impacts

During the one-year period of its funding, Project Alliance met and in some cases surpassed the expectations of the authors of the project proposal. The impact was primarily on faculty: principally on the major Project Alliance faculty and the participating campus-based and community-based faculty, but also on the other faculty who attended the two statewide faculty meetings and other regional meetings. In addition, there was a significant impact on the school and its staff.

For faculty the outcomes associated with Project Alliance were:

1. A better understanding of the mission, organization, and administrative functioning of the School for Lifelong Learning, an institution committed exclusively to adult learning.
2. An emerging sense of identity as a faculty working with and for the school.
3. The beginnings of a faculty dialogue about issues of teaching and learning, especially in relationship to an adult-oriented curriculum.
4. An initial exposure to some of the theory and research about adult learning and adult development.

5. A better understanding of the school's degree requirements and the major components of the curriculum.
6. The incorporation of some ideas and materials from the project into the teaching/learning process at their home campus.
7. The experience of reexamining some facets of their discipline and rethinking some of their instructional approaches in the light of an adult audience.

For the school the outcomes associated with Project Alliance were:

1. The development of knowledgeable and articulate faculty advocates for the school on the USNH campuses from among participating USNH faculty.
2. The establishment of a direction for future faculty development activities, based on the work of the project.
3. Confirmation of the school's belief that an "organic," task-oriented approach to faculty development has more far-reaching and powerful effects than the conventional workshop approach.

Summary

Through Project Alliance the school has developed a viable model for faculty development for institutions employing part-time faculty only and serving a wide geographical area with an off-campus delivery system. The project demonstrated that a significant number of faculty will involve themselves on a voluntary basis in tasks related to improving the teaching/learning process. The project also demonstrated that interaction between campus-based and community-based faculty can help to increase a sense of colleagueship and faculty identity with an institution to which they have a part-time commitment. A major outcome of Project Alliance was a proposal to establish a faculty assembly as a way of recognizing and involving the permanent and temporary faculty in the educational mission and learning activities of the School for Lifelong Learning.

5

Faculty Development Through Growth Contracts

Harold Heie, David Sweet

An especially effective approach to faculty development is through "growth contracts." This selection describes how Gordon College in Massachusetts put such a system into operation, modified it, and evaluated its results. The selection ends with "Some Modest Suggestions if the Thought of Growth Contracting Has Crossed Your Mind," which are as helpful as they are modest.

Harold Heie is professor of mathematics and chairman of the Division of Natural Sciences and David Sweet was director of computer services, faculty dissemination coordinator, and chairman of the Faculty Development Committee at Gordon College, Wenham, Massachusetts, at the time this selection was written. They were assisted in preparing this document by R. Judson Carlberg, dean of faculty and director of the Faculty Development Program at Gordon College.

Special features:

- Contract learning
- Faculty profiles
- Use of advisory committees
- Individualized approach to faculty development
- Combining personal and professional goals
- Relationship to promotion and tenure
- Evaluation procedures
- Peer helping

Excerpted, with permission, from *Professional Development Through Growth Contracts Handbook*, published by Gordon College in 1979.

In January 1976 Gordon College instituted a program of faculty development by growth contracting, supported by a grant from the W. K. Kellogg Foundation. Gross (1976, p. 74) describes growth contracts as "a systematic approach to defining faculty roles, charting the direction of professional growth, and assessing one's performance."

Program Components

Gordon's growth-contracting program can be briefly described as follows: Each participating faculty member writes a faculty profile that contains an assessment of strengths and weaknesses, a statement of current faculty roles, an assessment of effectiveness in carrying out these roles, and a statement of long-range professional and personal goals, typically for a period of three to five years. This profile then forms the basis for a series of yearly individual development plans (growth contracts) intended to cumulatively implement one's long-range goals. Each growth contract consists of statements of specific goals for the year, with each goal accompanied by a description of intended means of accomplishment and assessment, and a budget request. The participant also chooses an advisory committee, primarily made up of faculty colleagues, whose purpose is to help the participant refine his or her growth contract, to give advice during the year of implementation, and then to write an assessment of goal accomplishment to accompany the participant's self-assessment at the end of the calendar year.

What follows is a progress report of what we have learned in our three years of operation under this program. This will include a description of the general principles that have been the theoretical basis for our program, answers to some difficult questions that arose as we attempted to implement these principles, a consideration of some questions still looking for answers, and some modest suggestions for those who would like to implement growth contracting at other institutions.

Principles for Faculty Growth Contracting

The following broad principles have informed Gordon's growth contracting since its inception. Our efforts to implement these principles led to significant questions, some of which are noted below. Attempts to respond to these questions are given later in the report.

1. Growth contracts should be individualized to reflect the faculty member's own perceived needs for growth in light of individual strengths and weaknesses.

Our program did not start with a preconceived definition of faculty development intended to apply equally to all faculty members. Rather, it started with the assumption that each faculty member has some awareness of his or her professional and personal needs and has a natural desire to address those needs.

As reported by Milley (1977, pp. 7-9), this individualized approach toward faculty development is not as common as the collective approach, often centered around workshops, that deals with such perennial topics as teaching methods and philosophies of teaching, with the implicit assumption being that all faculty members have more or less the same professional needs. Of course, a danger of the individualized approach is that, without proper safeguards, growth contracts can become so idiosyncratic that there will be no assurance of meeting the needs of the institution in terms of its teaching, research, and/or community commitments. Can such safeguards be designed without destroying the emphasis on individual growth?

2. Faculty members are whole persons who need to grow in all areas of professional responsibility as well as in personal areas not directly related to their professions.

Faculty members were encouraged to address themselves to areas of professional responsibility that went beyond their traditional teaching and research roles. For example, the development of counseling and student advising skills or the development of administrative skills for chairing committees or departments were considered legitimate aspects of growth contracts.

More radically, faculty members were encouraged to include goals of a more personal nature that were only indirectly related to professional responsibilities. As might be guessed, this led to some interesting internal debates, such as whether a physics professor might request tickets to the Boston Symphony as a means toward refining his aesthetic sensitivity. Again, the crucial question appears to be: How does one ensure that institutional needs are met while still allowing for some measure of personal growth in areas only remotely related to institutional responsibilities?

    3. Within the context of common responsibilities shared by all faculty, there should be opportunity for individualizing the role of a given faculty member on the basis of particular strengths and weaknesses.

The overall aim of this principle is the development of a strong faculty in which diverse gifts complement each other. For example, all faculty have some instructional responsibility. However, there may be room for individualizing teaching assignments within that common responsibility. Gross (1976, p. 75) notes an ideal case where "faculty with particular strengths in lecturing and administrative organization . . . may be assigned to teach large classes, while others, who may not be good lecturers but who have gifts relative to discussion and tutorial methods of instruction, may be assigned seminar courses, guidance of independent study projects, or supervision of practicum experiences."

This principle also allows for the possibility of fairly radical role redefinition, such as a faculty member building into his profile the long-range goal of moving into an administrative position. Since all faculty profiles are discussed in depth with the dean of the faculty, the possibility of making such a change within the college can be assessed at an early stage. This possibility of radical role redefinition takes into account the not uncommon need for mid-life career transition discussed in some of the recent literature on the stages of adult development.

In practice, some preliminary steps have been taken toward this ideal of individualization of role within the context of common faculty responsibilities. But some difficult questions of implementation arise. To what extent can such an ideal be realized in a small college? Can such an ideal be harmonized with the traditional reward system for promotion and tenure?

    4. The success of individual efforts to achieve growth will be best realized when growth contracts are self-designed and self-imposed.

This principle partially reflects the view that "faculty are a particular breed of professionals and vigorously resist any external attempts to impose restrictions on their mode of functioning" (Gross, 1976, p. 76). More basically, it reflects the prior assumption that each faculty member has some awareness of his or her professional and personal needs and will initiate steps to address those needs. Again, the issue of how one maintains this principle and still ensures that institutional needs are met is crucial and will be discussed later.

In light of this principle, growth contracting at Gordon is strictly voluntary. In 1976, 1977, and 1978, 75 percent (thirty-nine) of the faculty wrote growth contracts. Since the inception of this program in 1976, all but one of the college's fifty-two faculty members have written at least one growth contract.

    5. Successful growth contracting requires that faculty be specific in their statements of goals and in their descriptions of means of accomplishment and assessment.

What we had to learn the hard way in attempting to implement this principle could fill a book. From the beginning we sensed a predisposition on the part of some faculty to rebel against the very idea of committing themselves to specific written goals. For some the disagreement was philosophical; all this talk of specific goals and assessments seemed to buy into an overly quantitative type of mentality that questions the validity of those important qualities that cannot be measured. For others the disagreement was more practical: "It's a waste of time to put all of this down on paper. I know what I want to do; I know how to go about doing it; and I know how well I am doing." But the majority of the faculty were willing to give it a try. The problem now was that almost all of us were totally inexperienced in how to go about it. How does one overcome these dual difficulties without turning off the faculty?

    6. Growth contracting should be viewed as a means for a faculty member to generate positive evidence in support of promotion and tenure consideration; but the emphasis must be on individual development, with institutional evaluation a secondary by-product.

This principle is an expression of the conviction that

"faculty growth contracts should be related to the institutional reward system. The outcomes of individually devised plans should provide an important perspective on such decisions as promotions, tenure, salary increments, and other personnel decisions" (Gross, 1976, p. 76). Because of the nature of promotion and tenure at Gordon, this initial intent was tempered somewhat as the program evolved in the hands of the Faculty Development Committee (FDC) that was given responsibility for implementing this program.

In order to obtain promotion or tenure, the faculty member must provide the Faculty Senate, made up of seven elected full professors, with concrete evidence that he or she measures up to suitably defined "merit" (as opposed to "acceptable") levels of attainment in at least two of the following three categories: ability as a teacher, scholarly and professional attainment, and institutional usefulness. The onus is clearly on the faculty member to provide positive evidence, via student evaluations, faculty activities reports, copies of publications, and any other means he or she sees fit to use.

In light of this evaluation procedure, it was very natural for the Faculty Development Committee to set the policy that faculty members may choose to include in their professional files—for eventual consideration by the Faculty Senate when they come up for promotion or tenure—the results of their self-assessments and the assessments of their advisory committees relative to accomplishment of their contract goals. But such a decision is a voluntary one made solely by the faculty member, thus tempering somewhat the original intention. Of course, if a faculty member does not choose to use this sort of evidence, he or she must generate alternative positive evidence in support of promotion or tenure. In the event that a faculty member is denied promotion or tenure, the Faculty Senate has been given the prerogative of requesting that a growth contract be initiated for the purpose of remedying specific weaknesses.

7. Growth contracting should encourage innovation and experimentation by maximizing the potential for reward for successful attainment of goals while minimizing the penalty of failure.

This principle is consistent with the opinion expressed by the Group for Human Development in Higher Education (1974, p. 61): "Like students, teachers need opportunities to play from uncertainty as well as tested strength, to try new things, and to stumble. Any teacher should be able to get advice about teaching, try out new techniques, monitor his or her own performance, receive information and confidential criticism, observe the work of other teachers, and discuss common problems—all without prejudice to administrative decisions about tenure or salary." The connections established between growth contracting and considerations for promotion and tenure (as described under principle 6) seem to be a workable means for implementing this present principle, especially the policy of giving faculty members the option to choose which, if any, of their goal assessments are to be included in the case they must build for themselves in order to merit promotion or tenure.

8. Growth contracting should seek after the ideal of creating a sense of community wherein persons are helping other persons to grow.

This lofty principle is based on the assumption that each member of the academic community is a potential resource for other members. Although growth contracts are individualized, a faculty member's growth should not take place separate from the shaping force of colleagues. Rather, the program should encourage the individual to seek dialogue with a helpful assessment by peers. This was the rationale behind the establishment of advisory committees. Is such a lofty ideal significantly realizable anywhere, least of all on a college campus?

Answers to Some Thorny Questions

It is one thing to state general principles. It is another to try to implement them. The various questions noted in the above section on principles reflect some of the difficulties of implementation that we encountered. We now share some of the things we learned the hard way as answers to these questions slowly evolved.

1. Faculty development programs that emphasize indi-

vidual growth based on perceived strengths and weaknesses must have safeguards for ensuring that institutional needs are also met.

What about areas of personal growth only remotely related to institutional responsibilities (such as tickets to the Boston Symphony)? The policy eventually evolved that such items were legitimate aspects of personal growth and could be included in growth contracts. However, due to limited funding, such personal goals could not receive monies unless the participant could demonstrate that they made a significant contribution to at least one of the following three areas: strengthening Gordon as an institution for Christian higher education; contributing to the development of students; contributing to disciplinary or interdisciplinary scholarship. This decision was the first of two safeguards intended to ensure that our emphasis on individual growth would not be detrimental to the meeting of institutional needs.

A second safeguard is built into Gordon's present criteria for promotion and tenure, which require evidence of merit in at least two of the three fairly traditional areas of teaching effectiveness, scholarship, and institutional usefulness, with these categories defined so as to meet institutional as well as faculty needs. Faculty members have been given considerable freedom in their choice of contract goals, but if they choose to use growth contracting as a means for building positive evidence for promotion or tenure, it behooves them to pay attention to these categories.

Note the relatively nondirective approach taken in the above safeguards. From the very inception of the program, the faculty pressed the Faculty Development Committee to indicate which types of goal activities were allowable and which types would be deemed most valuable. We now believe that one of the keys to the significant success of our program has been this committee's refusal to establish such prescriptions—at first because we did not have the foggiest idea how to do it but later because we saw the merits of a more nondirective approach. We eventually had to establish some guidelines, like the above safeguards, for weeding out or at least discouraging certain types of "unusual" goal activities. But through it all we seem to have maintained fidelity to the crucial principles that growth contracts are to be self-designed and self-imposed and should be individualized to reflect each faculty member's own perceived needs for growth. Additional negative guidelines gradually evolved. For instance, funding is not available for student assistant activities designed to relieve faculty members of their normal teaching responsibilities so that they can put more time into their growth contracts. Also, funding is not available for remunerating faculty for summer work (not because the idea is not a good one but simply because of limited funding capabilities).

2. In its initial stages, growth contracting requires an unusually heavy time commitment for working one on one with individual faculty members, helping them to design the details of their contracts.

Growth contracting was new to most of us, the faculty-at-large as well as the five of us on the Faculty Development Committee. It soon became apparent that we (the FDC) would have to try to convince some faculty of the importance of being specific in their statements of goals and in their descriptions of means of accomplishment and assessment, and then help them get these statements down on paper. Our first rule was to avoid educational jargon (behavioral objectives, change agents, evaluation assessment feedback cycle). We emphasized the common-sense approach of simply putting down on paper what one is continuously doing mentally when planning, and we pointed out the clarification benefit of trying to be specific in articulating such plans. We then provided the faculty with some simple examples of well-stated and poorly stated goals, means of accomplishment, and means of assessment. Participating faculty were then asked to write first drafts of growth contracts.

Now the work really began. In the first year of the program, largely due to our own inexperience, all five members of the FDC carefully read all thirty-nine first drafts. In general, we found that these first drafts left much to be desired. Goals tended to be vague and too global to be realizable during the contract period, and much too little thought had been given to viable means for assessing the extent of accomplishment. Each reader carefully noted criticisms. Each FDC member was then assigned seven or eight participants, to whom he or she wrote detailed letters summarizing various "suggestions" for improvement (very low key). In a number of cases, this was followed up by considerable discussion with the faculty member. All the work paid off. Many of the final drafts were hardly recognizable, they had improved so significantly.

What seemed so difficult at first, the generating of specific details of a growth contract, has become second nature in a matter of three years. This has enabled the work of the FDC to be somewhat streamlined. But their responsibility is still extremely time consuming.

     3. The extent to which participants in growth contracting are helped by peers on their advisory committee varies significantly from person to person, both in input during the term of the contract and in extent of rigor in assessing goal accomplishment.

One of our lofty dreams was that the use of advisory committees would enhance the sense of community on campus. We hoped that participants would seek dialogue with and helpful assessment from peers. There is evidence of increase in such dialogue, but generally between faculty who already were interacting with each other. There is little evidence that growth contracting has significantly broadened our sense of community by bringing together faculty who seldom interact. However, many would judge that there already was a reasonably strong sense of community on our small campus prior to this program.

In the first year of our program, the role of the advisory committee (then called the evaluation committee) was highly structured. For instance, set meeting times between participants and their full advisory committees were called for. We soon found that participants generally preferred to work one on one with certain individuals on their advisory committees as the need arose rather than at set times. It was not unusual for these individuals to have been chosen for this advisory function because they were already close personal friends with the participants. We soon relaxed our advisory committee structuring to accommodate these preferences, despite the fact that this change does not seem to contribute to a broadening of the sense of community.

Probably our biggest disappointment with the growth-contracting program has been the frequent lack of rigor in the advisory committee assessments of the extent of goal accomplishment of participants. The reasons for this lack of rigor may be varied. Some committee members may fear that to be too critical of a colleague might one day adversely affect his or her evaluations for promotion and/or tenure. Another possible reason is the general belief that a participant is really the only one in a good position to evaluate his or her attainment of individualized goals, and therefore advisory committee evaluations are at best a formal exercise not to be taken too seriously.

Some Modest Suggestions if the Thought of Growth Contracting Has Crossed Your Mind

How transferable is the concept of growth contracting? Diverse institutions—ranging from small liberal arts colleges like Gordon to large universities and even to church organizations concerned about the growth of their ministers—have expressed interest in the idea. Some modest, and possibly obvious, suggestions will be made here for the sake of readers who may be contemplating growth contracting as a means for faculty development at another higher education institution.

1. Create a unique institutional approach to faculty development in light of your institution's character, needs, and value commitments.

Do not equate faculty development with growth contracting. There are a variety of alternative approaches to faculty development that may better suit your institution. (See Smith, 1976, pp. 37-49, for brief descriptions of some alternative programs.)

The place to start is with an analysis of your own institution. It might be helpful to see how certain aspects of such an analysis seemed to suggest the feasibility of growth contracting at Gordon. In the mid-1970s, the institution was experiencing a

low rate of faculty turnover, with a resulting increase in the proportion of tenured full professors. Since this situation could
lead to a lack of the new approaches and fresh perspectives that
might characterize a more mobile faculty, perhaps an internal
program that would encourage attempts at innovation and experimentation was needed. Another factor was the national
trend toward greater emphasis on accountability as applied to
faculty productivity, suggesting the need for creative approaches
for assessing faculty performance. But this theme was tempered
by institutional commitment to the view that faculty, as professionals, should retain the initiative in defining their roles and
developmental needs (Gross, 1976, p. 74). Furthermore, the
college's commitment to the teachings of Christianity suggested
the need for further enhancing a sense of community where persons genuinely care for one another and are concerned about
each other's growth. These factors and others (see Gross, 1976,
pp. 74, 75) suggested the desirability of growth contracting and,
in particular, that version of it embodied in the eight basic principles previously presented.

Your approach to faculty development must reflect the
nature of your institution, not the way you would like it to be
but the way it is, including whatever external constraints are
placed on you.

2. If growth contracting seems applicable to your institution, do not adopt Gordon College's program.

Our eight basic principles for growth contracting reflect
the nature of our institution; aspects of these principles may be
totally inapplicable to your institution. Three brief examples
will suffice to illustrate this statement. First, our principles
suggest the need for a faculty member to frankly share with
colleagues not only his strengths but also his own assessment of
weaknesses and needs for growth. To do so is to make oneself
vulnerable. This procedure presupposes an atmosphere of trust,
where a person will not feel threatened by the thought of hon-
estly disclosing weaknesses. By and large, this type of atmosphere has seemed to be workable, no doubt helped along by
the various buffer layers between such disclosures and eventual
judgments concerning promotion and tenure.

Second, there is some question whether our principle of individualization of faculty role in light of particular strengths can be realized significantly on our own campus. You will have to judge its feasibility on yours.

Finally, our connection between growth contracting and promotion and tenure considerations may be totally inapplicable to your campus due to various internal and external constraints that your institution might have on faculty advancement procedures. There is little doubt that establishing a workable connection of your own will be the most important as well as the most difficult aspect of your design should you decide on faculty growth contracting. We can only repeat the following general recommendations based on our experience:

3. In growth contracting, emphasize development first, with evaluation for advancement as a secondary by-product; eliminate or minimize discrepancies between your expectations for growth contracting and the expectations of your faculty reward system; try to maximize the potential for reward for successful attainment of goals, at the same time that you encourage experimentation by minimizing the penalty of failure.

The primary emphasis should be on helping people, not just judging them. If your program is viewed by faculty as just another clever way for administrators or external agencies to judge faculty performance for salary and/or advancement purposes, then it probably will not get off the ground, and maybe it should not. In our experience it was a wise move to assign the task of implementing a growth contracting program to a new faculty committee (the Faculty Development Committee) rather than assigning it to the existing committee (the Faculty Senate) that had previously been responsible for faculty development, but whose main responsibility was to make promotion and tenure judgments. This separation of responsibilities helped to make credible the claim of the FDC that its main concern was to help fellow faculty to grow.

4. Create a climate of readiness.

The idea of growth contracting can be threatening. It takes a significant amount of getting used to. The benefits often do not become obvious until after you try it, which suggests the desirability of a relatively small pilot project. At Gordon such a trial run was undertaken a full two years before the start of a faculty-wide program. The pilot participants consisted of the academic vice president and four tenured full professors, all respected members of the Faculty Senate. The fact that these academic leaders were the first to be willing to spell out their weaknesses and needs for growth before the entire faculty did much to create the general climate of trust that seems to have characterized the program.

     5. Give your growth-contracting program the freedom to evolve.

     It is important that you initially develop some general principles for your program, principles that reflect the character and needs of your faculty and institution. But do not wait to start until you think you have all the details of implementation worked out on paper. You cannot foresee all the implementation problems that may arise until you actually try out a tentative version of the program. Be flexible as you try to implement your program and allow for a considerable amount of trial and error.

     6. Provide budgetary support for growth contracting.

     The inherent value of clarifying one's goals and ways of getting there, and of drawing on colleague help and advice through growth contracting, will probably not justify in the minds of the faculty the work involved in participating in a structured program—especially in the initial stages, when these values may seem like so much pie in the sky. The faculty need to feel that this program is helping them to do things that they could not do otherwise. And that generally takes money.

     The need for budgetary support does not necessarily demand external funding, although it certainly is a big help. At Gordon institutional funds already being devoted to a diversity of faculty development activities (such as faculty travel and sabbatical leaves) were pooled for redistribution under the more unified growth-contracting program. There may be some similar way for you to combine existing internal monies or, more drastically, to rearrange your institution's funding priorities so as to finance growth contracting from within.

7. Create faculty ownership of the program.

A good way to kill the idea of growth contracting is to impose a full-blown program on the faculty from above, either through the administration or through an external agency. You have the greatest chance of success if your program is developed and run by the faculty, with suitable external input to ensure that institutional needs and requirements will be met.

At Gordon the seed for the program was sown by an academic administrator, who suggested some general principles that could guide growth contracting and initiated the pilot project. But then he very wisely (in our estimation) gave the task of refining and implementing these principles to a Faculty Development Committee. In line with the terms of the Kellogg grant, our program is ultimately administered by the current academic dean, who is expected to devote approximately 20 percent of his time to the program and who is a member (though not chairman) of the FDC. The other members of the FDC consist of one elected faculty representative from each of the five academic divisions. The task assigned to this committee required an unusually heavy commitment of time and energy, especially in the initial years, when we were learning what it was all about. This should be taken into account if and when you form such a committee.

Conclusion

It is our opinion that the faculty growth-contracting program at Gordon has been a noteworthy success. But the purpose of this report has not been to pat ourselves on the back. We have tried to be frank in disclosing the difficulties we have encountered, our responses to some of these difficulties, and the questions we still face at this point in our progress. Our hope is that you the reader may benefit from our experiences.

6

Internships for Improving Academic Administration in Brazilian Universities

Jose Carlos Dantas Merielles,
Margarida Maria Costa Batista,
and Associates

Here is yet another approach to staff development in institutions of higher education—with an administrative internship at the core of a program to develop change agents for Brazilian universities. By planning and carrying out actual change projects at host universities, the interns are helped to gain the skills of change agentry.

Jose Carlos Dantas Merielles and Margarida Maria Costa Batista and their associates are members of the faculty of the Center of Interdisciplinary Studies for the Public Sector, Federal University of Bahia, Salvador, Brazil.

Special features:

- Creating a learning environment
- Internships
- Change projects and consultants
- Networking
- Field visits
- Evaluation

Adapted, with permission, from an internal report, "Training Andragogical Change Agents for the Universities in Brazil," published by the Center for Interdisciplinary Studies for the Public Sector, Federal University of Bahia, 1977.

In 1974 the Brazilian Ministry of Culture and Education contracted with the Center of Interdisciplinary Studies for the Public Sector (ISP) of the Federal University of Bahia to plan, organize, and coordinate an interuniversity technical assistance program. In 1975 a new program—a ten-month course designed to train change agents—was undertaken by ISP, sponsored by the Rockefeller Foundation and the Brazilian Ministry of Culture and Education. Thirty-three university administrators from different regions of the country participated. The main purpose of the program was to contribute to the betterment of the standards of planning and management in Brazilian universities.

Most of the participants, 65 percent, were twenty-five to forty years old; academic background was mostly in the fields of administration and economics (44 percent); 49 percent of the participants had less than five years of experience.

The objectives of the training program were to sensitize the participants to the problems of Brazilian universities and to prepare them as change agents in the university, rather than merely to instruct them in administrative technologies.

To meet these objectives, ISP chose a training strategy and methodology patterned after the approach to adult education called andragogy. Knowles (1970) says that andragogy is premised on certain assumptions about the characteristics of adult learners that are different from the assumptions about child learners, on which traditional pedagogy is premised. The main implication of these assumptions is that the participants—trainees—can and should take responsibility for their own learning.

The training strategy and methodology encompass different kinds of activities, designed to:

1. Create a learning environment adequate to the development of adult learners.
2. Provide the participants with a frame of reference concerning Brazilian universities as a whole and the university where the internship program will be developed (host university).
3. Articulate the program with some current projects and activities being undertaken at the host university.

4. Enable the trainees to meet with top officials of different institutions, including their own universities, in special seminars and workshops.
5. Develop projects, under the responsibility of each participant, related to the interests of their respective universities.
6. Establish a network whereby the participants can exchange experiences and information.

The program may be developed with emphasis in one of the following three areas of university administration: global university planning, academic administration, or business affairs. The activities include:

1. Central activities, involving the use of the methods and techniques of the training program:
   a. Participation by the trainee in selected projects and activities being undertaken by the host university during the time of the program (internship).
   b. Preparation and/or implementation of a project.
2. Complementary activities, which are intended to supplement the development, by the participants, of the central activities. As part of the complementary activities, each trainee should:
   a. Describe his or her own university, including basic data and information about it.
   b. Describe the role and functions of the university administrator.
   c. Collect and analyze basic data and information that might be of interest for his or her project and other activities of the program.
   d. Participate in seminars and other meetings and conduct interviews.
   e. Visit selected units of different universities—particularly the host university.
   f. Write periodic reports during the program and a final report at the end of the program, analyzing and evaluating all the learning experiences developed in the program.

The program is carried out under the responsibility of (1) a general coordinator, (2) one coordinator for each of the optional areas (university planning, academic administration, and business affairs), (3) internship advisers, and (4) project consultants. Project consultants are of three types: (1) those in charge of helping the participants prepare their projects, called "project methodology consultants"; (2) those who assist the trainees in the substantive aspects of the project; and (3) those who are concerned with helping the participants in the process of implementing the project.

Finally, an evaluation system is worked out in such a way that those in charge of each particular group of trainees participate in planning the evaluation procedures for that group. Considering the andragogical approach adopted, self-evaluation by the participants also is emphasized.

7

Training College Lecturers in Africa

Charles Kabuga

This selection is especially interesting for two reasons. In the first place, it demonstrates that the andragogical model is not culture bound. Members of the faculties of African universities responded to an andragogical experience with the same philosophical defensiveness, anxieties, preconceptions, and—eventually—enthusiasms that we have encountered over and over in North America. In the second place, it describes the design of a faculty development seminar that could serve as a model for faculty development in any university system. It provides a practical tool (Appendix A) for engaging teachers in a process of self-diagnosis of their learning needs.

Charles Kabuga is education and training consultant, International Cooperative Alliance, Regional Office for East and Central Africa, Moshi, Tanzania.

Special features:

- Climate setting
- Identifying problems with applying andragogy
- Use of exercises and simulations
- Microteaching
- Analysis of Personal Training Styles inventory

Adapted, with permission, from the *Report on the Regional Seminar for the Cooperative College Lecturers*, Mauritius, November 27–December 14, 1978.

This seminar had five main objectives:

1. To provide the trainees (Cooperative College lecturers) with an opportunity to critically reflect on what successes and failures they have encountered in using the andragogical approach and to plan strategies for overcoming the problems.
2. To develop insight into each trainee's personal philosophy of education and an understanding of the implications of such a philosophy for the management of an adult education program.
3. To help the trainees examine their instructional behavior and reflect on how certain behaviors militate against or facilitate learning.
4. To provide the trainees with an opportunity to construct and demonstrate the use of teaching aids.
5. To provide the trainees with an opportunity to appraise the curriculum.

After the official opening, we plunged into the program. First we had a session on practical matters and climate setting. We then took an inventory of what the participants hoped they would get out of the seminar. Their fears, hopes, and expectations were recorded so that we might incorporate them into our final evaluation questionnaire.

Since this was a follow-up seminar to the ones we had conducted on andragogy, we carried out an inventory of the problems which the Cooperative College lecturers face in using the andragogical approach. The following were the problems which they said they face:

Certain subjects (such as accounting, law, economics, and sociology) do not lend themselves to the approach.

In a setting where a prescribed curriculum has to be covered in a given period, traditional lecture methods are easily resorted to.

Conservative lecturers prefer to teach the way they were taught.

Structured curriculum militates against the andragogical approach.

Colleges lack some facilities necessary for using some of the new techniques.

Habits of teaching/learning inherited from pedagogy are too firmly rooted to unhinge.

The approach is so demanding that lecturers resort to the law of the least effort and lecture.

Role plays, structured exercises, and other techniques used in this approach appear too childish.

Lecturers fear that the students will think they are masking their ignorance by delegating responsibility to the students.

The informal relationship between the lecturers and the students which the approach advocates could backfire in a strongly formal setting.

The rapid turnover of lecturers and an extremely heavy work load at the colleges makes it impossible for every lecturer to use the approach.

After taking both inventories, we never attempted to discuss any of the listed problems, hopes, or fears. Rather, we felt that, if we successfully used the andragogical approach in implementing this program, we would demonstrate practically that the approach works.

We sensed that many of the lecturers had not grasped enough skills and confidence from the previous seminars to make them true andragogues. Accordingly, we administered a simple exercise to help us determine those who were positively inclined to the approach and those who were still amateurs. Appendix A is the instrument we used.

In carrying out the next part of the program, we used structured or simulated exercises or games. Such exercises provided the participants with the experiences which we then analyzed with the participants. From the analyzed experiences, we picked particular items which we wanted them to learn and then generalized these to real-life situations.

Appendix A illustrates how we separated those lecturers who were more inclined to the andragogical approach from those who were still amateurs, with a view to assisting those who still had problems to see why they had problems. As facilitators and resource persons, we assumed that a person's beliefs about learners and learning largely determine his or her teaching style. For example, a lecturer who strongly believes that the heart of education is teaching will teach differently from a lecturer who believes that the heart of education is learning. In the same way, a lecturer who believes that effective learning can take place only in a warm climate of informality will teach differently from a lecturer who believes that effective learning takes place only in a formal and competitive classroom atmosphere.

The instrument shown in Appendix A was adapted from the writings of Malcolm S. Knowles. Ten pairs of statements on beliefs about learning and teaching were formulated along the lines of McGregor's Theory X and Theory Y (McGregor, 1960). The way the participants weighted themselves on each of the ten pairs of statements of the instrument was a useful stimulus for personal reflection and discussion. From this exercise we realized that the beliefs of lecturers about learners and learning had to change first before they could use the andragogical approach successfully.

During sessions on a variety of topics of the program, we used role plays, simulations, and structured exercises to provide the necessary experiences, which we then analyzed and discussed with the participants. Participants liked this approach very much, since it kept everyone active and attentive.

After the learning needs had been determined, each group worked together to develop a lesson and to construct the necessary teaching materials and aids. Together, they also had to think of a strategy for presentation and the techniques to be used. During this exercise the resource persons and secretarial services were put at their disposal.

After this exercise each group was required to teach. During the microteaching, each participant was given a rating form. After each group presentation, participants were asked to express their opinions on the methods or techniques or aids. It was therefore no wonder that many participants felt that microteaching had easily been one of the best experiences at the seminar. They had learned to work as a team, teach as a team, manage their time, use the techniques we had been advocating, and appraise each other's performance.

One of the most rewarding aspects of this exercise was the confirmation that the andragogical approach can work. When an earlier inventory of the problems which lecturers face in using the approach was being taken, many had complained that subjects like accounting and law did not lend themselves to the approach. It was gratifying when the accounting group successfully used a role play to analyze and teach the concepts contained in their lesson.

Appendix A. An Analysis of Personal Training Styles.

This instrument is designed to help you better understand your beliefs about "learners" and "learning." There are ten pairs of statements. Assign a weight from 0 to 10 to each statement, to show the relative strength of your belief in the statements in each pair. The points assigned to each pair must, in each case, total 10. Be as honest with yourself as you can and resist the natural tendency to respond as you would "like to think things are" or "ought to be." This instrument is not a "test," and since you are being asked to weigh your beliefs, there are no right or wrong answers. The instrument is merely designed to be a stimulus for personal reflection and discussion.

1. The heart of education is teaching.   (a) _____
   The heart of education is learning.   (b) _____
2. Learners are dependent personalities and as
   such they have to depend on teachers for their
   learning.   (c) _____
   Learners are self-directing human beings.   (d) _____
3. A teacher is a transmitter of content and by
   controlling rewards and punishments he makes
   it possible for the learners to learn the content.   (e) _____
   A teacher merely facilitates and serves as a re-
   source person to otherwise self-directed learners.   (f) _____
4. As the function of the teacher is "to teach," he
   has to take responsibility for what happens in
   the teaching/learning transaction.   (g) _____
   As the teaching/learning transaction is a mutual
   responsibility of learners and teachers, the responsibility for what happens in the teaching/
   learning situation has to be shared between
   teachers and learners.   (h) _____
5. Effective learning will take place in a climate of
   warmth, respect, and informality.   (i) _____
   Effective learning takes place only in a formal
   and competitive classroom atmosphere.   (j) _____

6. Training is a process whereby trainers transmit
content to the trainees.   (k) ____
Training is a process of self-development
through collaborative inquiry.   (l) ____
7. What is to be learned should always be deter-
mined by those "who know better" rather than
by "learners," who are after all ignorant.   (m)____
Learners should always be engaged in the deter-
mination of those things they see the need to
learn.   (n) ____
8. Learning goals for the learners must always be
formulated in terms of terminal behavior.   (o) ____
Learning experiences ought to be developed in a
sequence that takes into consideration both
group similarities and individual differences.   (p) ____
9. Adults will not learn except under pressure.
Consequently, learning for them will not occur
in the absence of motivations from the teachers
(extrinsic motivations).   (q) ____
Since adults always wish to improve themselves,
learning will be greatly enhanced when it is
self-willed—that is, when learning is propelled
by intrinsic motivations.   (r) ____
10. Learners should be helped to get evidence for
themselves about the progress they are making
toward their educational goals.   (s) ____
It is the responsibility of the teacher to inform
learners how well or poorly they are progressing
toward their educational goals.   (t) ____

To get your scores, add up the points you assigned to the following:

Score Y: sum of (a) (c) (e) (g) (j) (k) (m) (o) (q) (t) =
Score Z: sum of (b) (d) (f) (h) (i) (l) (n) (p) (r) (s) =

8

Sharing Responsibility
for Learning
in a Science Course —
Staff-Student Cooperation

David J. Boud, M. T. Prosser

A comment I frequently hear in my workshops is "But you can't teach science using the andragogical model." This selection describes how a course in science education for experienced science teachers was conducted according to the assumptions of andragogy. The course was designed jointly by staff and students. A collaboratively designed course cannot be undertaken lightly, for not only does it violate some of the norms of teaching in traditional higher education, but it places peculiar demands on both staff and students. These demands are both of an interpersonal, group interaction kind and of a structural, organizational type. The aim of this selection was to describe the main features of the course, to examine some of the demands it makes, and to explore the applicability of its concepts to other areas of higher education.

David Boud is a member of the staff of the Tertiary Education Research Centre, University of New South Wales, Australia, and M. T. Prosser is on the staff of the Centre for the Advancement of Learning and Teaching, Griffith University, England.

Reprinted, by permission of the Council for Educational Technology for the United Kingdom, from "Sharing Responsibility: Staff-Student Cooperation in Learning," *British Journal of Educational Technology*, 1980, *11* (1), 24-35.

Special features:

- Course rationale
- Self-directed learning
- Climate setting
- Student-set goals
- Content vs. process
- Collaborative planning through subgroups
- Resource identification
- Assessment and grading
- Human factors
- Role of facilitator
- Role of student
- A different power relationship
- Student reactions
- Problems and issues

The course is based upon an explicit rationale. The rationale defines certain characteristics of an educated professional in any field and is at once both a definition which can be aspired to by students and one which they can identify as already being partly achieved.

It is assumed that among the characteristics of an educated person who operates as a full professional in any area of activity are the following: They are self-directing and self-motivating; that is, they are able to specify clear goals for their activities, they can design a program of learning activities drawing upon all the necessary resources to pursue their goals, and they are able to evaluate their performance of the tasks they have established and judge the extent to which their goals have been met. Such people do not act in isolation but can draw upon the resources they need wherever they may be found both within and outside educational institutions. This rationale is open to challenge. It is not presented as a well-accepted statement of educational philosophy but as a working hypothesis which is subject to testing through the experience of the course (Heron, 1971, describes this process in some detail). Unlike many educational goals or statements of intent, this is not solely an end point. It is also a starting point.

Such an assumption has two implications. Firstly, there is the Rosenthal effect—namely, that the achievement of students is directly related to the expectation of their teachers; that, in general, low expectations will make for low achievement, and high expectations, all other things being equal, will make for high achievement. Secondly, it is necessary for opportunities to be provided, and a climate established, in which it is possible for students to practice the skills of self-directed and independent learning. Thus, a tutor in a course based on these principles must believe that students will be able to define their own goals, design their own program, and assess their own achievement. And this he must believe without reservation. For, if not, the limiting dependency relationship of students on staff will inhibit the growth of these attributes.

How can these principles be translated into practice? We wish to describe some of the main features of the core elements of a Graduate Diploma course in science education for experienced science teachers. This will enable us to illustrate how in one particular situation a course may be constructed which both fulfills the function of developing the necessary learning skills and addresses the substantive content of the subject area.

In the Graduate Diploma half, the course is devoted to science education, the remainder to further studies in various sciences and education. It is on this first half we wish to focus. This comprises both group and individual study units and gives students the opportunity to pursue the learning goals we have discussed both in consort with their peers and individually.

For this paper we wish to concentrate on the group-based units, particularly the first two, called "Science Education 501" and "Science Education 502." These are taken for a total of four hours per week, in one evening throughout the academic year. Thus, for part-time students, they would comprise half of their total contact hours in the first year of a two-year course. This account is based upon experience with the two intakes of the 501 unit (four and fourteen students) and one intake to 502 (thirteen students), and represents a composite description of the conduct of these units.

We will examine the course design and execution in terms

of two closely related aspects. The first of these is the structural features which comprise the main components of the course, and the second aspect consists of the personal and interpersonal factors which, although of equal importance to the structural features, are less easy to describe analytically.

Structural Features

The first session of the course begins with the participants introducing themselves and outlining their interests in attending the course. The tutor discusses the rationale on which the course is based and presents the distinction between collaborative and unilateral course design. The implications for individual learning and the ways in which the group operates are examined.

Once the rationale is accepted, and so far it always has been, the group establishes the goals for the course. This process is somewhat time consuming, but it is central to the theme of students sharing responsibility for their learning. It turns out that time invested at this stage is amply rewarded by enhanced productivity and commitment to the course later. Students generate their own goals and rank these in terms of their own priorities. The goals are then pooled in order of importance to the individual. Thus, the group is not swamped by multiple goals from one person, but each student in turn states one goal until all goals are exhausted. The set of goals is then classified into a number of categories representing either subject areas (for example, psychology of science learning) or types of goal (for example, research and evaluation skills). Some of these categories are agreed to be unsuited for the present unit because they require preknowledge or because they might more suitably be pursued in an individual project; other categories receive insufficient support from the group; and yet others are further elaborated and selected for study. Decisions about the acceptance or otherwise of goals for the course are always made by consensus. In keeping with the second principle of Heron (1974), all students are expected and encouraged to make their views known and have them heard by the rest of the group. The

views of an individual are not always accepted, but it is important that each person feels that his or her opinion has been recognized by the group.

At this stage it is usually appropriate to talk about the
distinction between the substantive content of the course and
the process of learning in the course. In a course unilaterally designed and conducted by staff, there is no need to use class time
for planning—that is something which forms part of teacher's
preparation. However, in a collaboratively planned course, the
process is no longer controlled by the teacher and it therefore
becomes necessary for all the participants to be aware of process issues and take part in planning. Parts of the program will
need to be modified in the light of experience and the timetable rearranged.

To facilitate the planning process, participants form subgroups to take responsibility for various parts of the program in
accordance with their particular interests. The subgroups are
charged with making sure that the part of the program for
which they are responsible forms a coherent section of the
course, draws upon the range of resources which are available,
and is in accord with the identified goals. It is up to them either
to present learning activities of their own design or to coordinate others. These subgroups meet on their own or with the
tutor to discuss the content of the course and to identify the
material and manpower resources which are needed.

These planning subgroups need to consult with the rest of
the total group from time to time, and the group as a whole
needs to keep a check on the progress of the course. A regular
period of time each week is set aside for this, called process
analysis, normally consisting of thirty minutes out of a four-
hour session. The process analysis time is used for activities
which fall under a general heading of group building and for the
important aim of enabling students to become fully committed
to the goals and the program. Participants are encouraged to
voice their concerns and to raise issues which they feel have not
been resolved. Early in the course, the tutor took responsibility
for facilitating this session; but as the course progressed, the tutor's role diminished as members of the group gained confi-

dence and recognized the worth of this activity. (For further discussion of group-building activities, see Bradford, 1976.)

Resource identification also takes place in one of the early sessions. If an effective program is to be constructed, it is necessary to determine the resources which are available, both material and human, both within and outside the group. At this stage all participants, including the tutor, present a summary of the experience, expertise, and special interests that they individually bring to the group. The resources of the institution and of other local institutions are also discussed, and the planning subgroups for each area then continue this preliminary determination at greater depth. To give an example of human resources used, in 1977 contributions were made by the tutor, the students, Western Australian Institute of Technology (WAIT) staff, State Education Department and Examining Board personnel, staff from other local institutions, interstate visitors, and visitors from the United Kingdom and the United States of America. These figures do not include all the other people who assisted individual students or planning subgroups.

Finally, no account of the structure would be complete without consideration of assessment. In a course based upon principles of self-direction and collaboration, the normal mode of unilateral assessment of students by staff obviously needs to be rejected. We are faced with assessment for two purposes. The first is to satisfy institutional requirements, and this places on us the constraint of producing a numerical grade. The second is assessment to help in the learning process. The first of these constrains the second, and the mechanism for arriving at the institutionally validated grade must be consistent with the process of the course. The solution to this problem was reached by a decision to allocate a minimal passing grade (50 percent) for full participation in the activities of the course: taking part in sessions, planning activities, presentations, and allocated study. If students wished to obtain more than a pass, they had to complete a self-assessment procedure in which they were required to identify their goals and objectives, detail all their contributions, judge the extent to which they had achieved their objectives, and justify a numerical grade between 50 percent and 100 percent. This self-assessment was influenced by a peer assessment process in which students received comments from their peers to assist their own judgment. (It is still being debated whether it is necessary for peers to allocate grades. Some people argue that grading does have a divisive influence on the group and could be disruptive of the climate of trust and cooperation.) The last element of the assessment, mainly to satisfy institute regulations, is the assessment by staff, which takes the form of a post hoc moderation of the self-assessment by the tutor.

Assessment is, however, not solely a terminal activity. Peer assessment—that is, the giving of constructive feedback to other members of the group—is an ongoing process and occurs during the time allocated for process analysis.

Personal and Interpersonal Factors

It has long been recognized that productive groups have concern both for the task and for the well-being of group members (Rice, 1965). It is therefore important to focus on the personal and interpersonal factors which are the most potent influence on the conduct of the entire course. The structure described above can be easily applied to any course. However, as our reading—and, more significantly, our experience—has shown, it cannot be applied with success unless there is commensurate emphasis on the more subtle human factors. A climate of trust and cooperativeness has to be established, and the initiative for this must come from the tutor. Unless students perceive the commitment of the tutor to this form of learning, and unless the tutor can demonstrate his confidence in the process, the course will grind uncomfortably to a halt or the tutor will be faced with an embarrassed return to the unilateral model. The comments which follow are a result of our reflection on some of the personal and interpersonal factors identified in the process of the course.

The tutor must feel at ease in a situation in which he does not have complete control. His control is shared with students for all elements of the course: setting of goals, design of learning experiences, selection of content, and methods of assessment. Subject matter may be included in which he is not an expert. The tutor must be prepared to admit his lack of expertise in certain areas and not pretend to knowledge which is not his.

The tutor has to be comfortable in his multifaceted role of peer, facilitator, expert, and exemplar. He must forgo his traditional dominance in the group and present his goals when students are presenting theirs and make his special contribution in the same way that other people in the group make their special contributions. He needs to be able to facilitate the process of the course by suggesting frameworks for planning, helping students present their efforts most effectively, and building the supportive climate of the group through his interventions. He is an expert and is normally in his position of tutor by virtue of his subject matter expertise; as such he must be prepared to conduct workshops, prepare study guides, give inputs, and provide access to his special skills. Finally, his most potent influence is through his role as exemplar; his conduct should, as far as is possible, model the behavior of a self-directing person and demonstrate his commitment to the peer learning community.

As well as the tutor, the student needs to accept new roles. No longer is he a somewhat passive recipient of courses designed by others. In the same way that many of the problems for the tutor arise as a result of the relinquishment of total responsibility, much of the uncertainty and tentativeness of approach of students is due to their having to accept greater responsibility. The success or failure of the course is undeniably in their hands.

Some students have difficulty adjusting to their role in formulating their objectives. They are unsure of their ability to identify all the objectives which such a course should fulfill: they are used to deferring to the expertise of staff. Confidence in their own abilities does, however, quickly emerge. As they see their course develop and see their efforts producing stimulating and effective learning, they recognize their own role in this and learn how to appreciate their own powers. It is striking to see students who have had one experience of this kind of learning embark on a subsequent unit.

The student faces the same set of roles which face the tutor, although with a different emphasis. As the tutor needs to limit overt expressions of his expertise, the student has to manifest his own learning which has occurred in preparation and planning subgroups. Just as the tutor needs to be facilitative, the student also has to respect the contributions of colleagues, suggest useful structures, and contribute to building the climate of the group. The interactions in the group need to move from the normative-competitive relationships in which students are continually judging their performance against that of others and striving for success over others to a criterion-cooperative relationship, in which students judge their performance against their own established goals and strive for success as part of a team. Each student must be able to accept the right of others to intervene in the course, to attempt to change the course in the direction of their own needs just as he would expect to be listened to in turn.

Finally, the concept of a peer learning community requires that the usual differential power relationship between student and tutor must be modified. While the tutor faces the burden of being the representative of the institution, a role which he cannot in practice deny, the students have to be able to take their share of responsibility in achieving more equitable distribution of power in ways that are more congruent with high levels of learning. If this final requirement cannot be met, then not only will the subject matter learning be restricted but the fundamental rationale of the course will be abused.

Evaluation

Most reports of teaching innovations have a section on evaluation. It is usually described as formative (ongoing during the course) and summative (end of course). These two forms of evaluation are usually done by resort to comments by students or responses to a questionnaire. While we can do this, of course, we have to point out the irrelevance of most of this kind of evaluation to collaboratively designed and conducted courses. Students in such courses are not commenting on something which has been performed on them; they are discussing their own endeavors. It is impossible to separate self-assessment from course evaluation if the rationale we have described has been successfully pursued. If students have invested themselves in the course and come to own the course, then their comments need to be interpreted in a different light from the situation in which they are consumers of a predetermined service.

The essence of the course as we have described it is that it is self-regulating. The regular process analysis is a type of formative evaluation and as such has a self-correcting function. This type of course evaluation is in effect an ongoing process. Modifications and adaptations are made as a matter of routine. Many of the problems and issues that arise from this formative evaluation are discussed in the next section. But while the products of the course cannot be evaluated from an uninvolved stance, it is possible to comment on the process itself. Did it succeed in involving students? Were students committed to the tasks? All students completed a summative questionnaire and engaged in an end-of-course discussion.

The following comments have been chosen because they reflect the overall reaction to the course. When asked to comment on what they would say to a colleague thinking of enrolling in the unit, a selection of student replies were: "Go ahead, it is the most interesting educational experience I have had." "Urge him to do so—a very worthwhile experience."

Students perceived some of the strengths of the course to be as follows: "Experience in organization and planning. Mutual growth through discussion sessions. Participating in setting goals and having your say on goals set is satisfying." "Noncompetitive climate." "Commitment of individuals to the course as a result of giving them responsibility in planning."

On initial contact with the rationale, many students were apprehensive, but after some experience in the unit, the rationale was accepted enthusiastically: "Though having doubts about the rationale early in 501, am now quite happy with this type of course." "Entirely appropriate. . . . It would lead to greater learner independence. . . . Having students assess resources and determine appropriate goals is unfortunately a seriously neglected part of education."

The comments on planning indicated some student concern with the amount of time devoted to these tasks, but they nevertheless felt that it was important. "Slow, frustrating, but essential to self/group-directed learning." "Necessary and effective. Everyone seemed prepared to accept responsibility. . . . The planning maintained the good atmosphere."

Peer and self-assessment were seen to be difficult but certainly worthwhile tasks. Some comments were as follows: "This [peer assessment] I found to be a difficult task. . . . I don't have much confidence in my ability to make perceptive, constructive comments—all the more reason to keep trying." "What surprised me was a growing commitment to the view that I was quite capable of specifying the level to which I should perform, and measuring myself against the resulting objectives."

What, then, are the problems and issues resulting from the experiences of the tutor and student during the conduct of the course?

Problems and Issues

Many of the issues that arise can be traced to the extent of experience and skills of the participants, particularly the tutor. However, we have selected some problems which we think may have wider ramifications for anyone contemplating embarking on a course of this kind.

1. Students were committed to the course without a doubt. No dropouts occurred after the second week, in marked contrast to some other Graduate Diploma courses at WAIT. They also demonstrated this commitment in their summative evaluation comments. The criticisms did not relate to the model of the course but the extent to which certain elements were underdeveloped. In particular, they felt that in the process analysis sessions insufficient emphasis was placed on consideration of the ways in which the course operated, and that peer assessment was not fully an ongoing activity. The problem is that it becomes very easy to use the process analysis time for mundane timetabling issues at the expense of a more profound analysis. Suggestions were made that the purely administrative

time should be reduced and specific sessions devoted to purely process *analysis*. The degeneration of process sessions into announcements is something to be guarded against.

2. Students experienced most difficulty in peer and self-assessment. There are two aspects to this. Firstly, such assessments are personally challenging. They require that a person expresses his or her attitudes and judgments and be prepared to back them with good arguments. This can only occur in a climate of trust and support. It is our view that without this climate the notions of peer and self-assessment will be easily corrupted into superficial and meaningless forms. Secondly, these assessments are one of the most novel features for university students. The literature on them is extremely limited and it is almost impossible to find well-tried procedures of conducting peer and self-assessment.

3. An unresolved issue is the amount of time that should be spent on initial planning. On one occasion this was more or less complete at the end of the first meeting—this was too rapid and left some participants in a state of academic shell-shock. On another occasion it was spread over more than three weeks, while other workshops were being conducted concurrently, and a clear sense of direction was lost. It is necessary to balance the need for closure on the part of the participants against the gaining of commitment to the task.

4. Transferability of the approach taken by this course to other subject areas is a question we have often discussed with our colleagues. We have seen applications of the philosophy we adopted from the primary school (Howe and Howe, 1975) to adult education (Knowles, 1975), but to our knowledge there have been few applications in higher education, particularly in the sciences and engineering (a major exception to this in the United States is Romey, 1976). Where applications have occurred, only parts of the rationale of self-directed learning have been adopted. For example, Cowan (1978) developed a first-year course in civil engineering in which students had freedom to determine the syllabus. However, he concluded, as our thinking has led us to conclude, that the change from dependence to independence should be a gradual one. In our case, with a group

of postgraduate students, we could assume that they already possessed to some extent skill in independent learning. Groups with members with experience limited to only didactic and unilateral educational experiences, as is common in most undergraduates, would need more preliminaries before embarking on the type of course we have described. These preliminaries would include activities to orient students to new approaches and to set a different climate for learning and would include opportunities to practice, on a limited time scale, goal setting, cooperative planning, and self-assessment. One of us has grasped the nettle and, in conjunction with another student from the course, has been applying our principles to the difficult area of a first-year undergraduate course in physics for home and consumer studies students (Thorley and Prosser, 1978). Other graduates from the course have reported to us that they are applying aspects of this approach to their own teaching in high school science and technical education.

9

Instruction in Public Speaking at a Community College

Michael A. Kerwin

As the author of this selection points out, "Community college instructors often react to andragogy by saying that it may be appropriate for continuing education programs but not for curriculum programs." Here he describes how he designed and conducted a credit course in the regular program of a community college in North Carolina.

Michael Kerwin is coordinator of faculty and program development for the University of Kentucky's community college system.

The "Educational Description Questionnaire" mentioned in this selection may be obtained from Michael A. Kerwin, Office of Vice President, University of Kentucky Community College System, Breckenridge Hall 00561, Lexington, Kentucky 40506.

Special features:

- Student perception of instructor behavior
- Orientation
- Learning/teaching groups
- Performance objectives and assessment
- Performance contracts
- Evaluation

Reprinted, with permission, from "Using Andragogy in an Oral Communication Course," *Community College Review*, Winter 1981–82, 9 (3), 12–14.

Community college instructors often react to andragogy by saying that it may be appropriate for continuing education programs but not for curriculum programs. Unlike the students in
continuing education programs, these instructors will often say,
curriculum students want or need instructors to direct their
learning. Other community college instructors will say that their
institutions demand that they exert a high degree of control
over the instructional process. Otherwise, how can instructors
maintain adequate standards in their classes? Many community
college instructors reject andragogy, therefore, as being impractical or inappropriate for a community college curriculum
course.

The preceding concerns are very real in the community
college setting. Many students who enroll in vocational and
technical programs are academically underprepared for many of
these programs. Most community college students expect teachers to tell them what to do. Many community colleges require
each instructor to follow a competency-based outline that prescribes how he or she will teach. Nevertheless, andragogy can be
an effective instructional strategy in some community college
curriculum courses. The following case study describes how andragogy was used in an oral communication course in a community college. The course not only motivated students to learn
and meet high standards of performance but also conformed to
the guidelines of a competency-based outline of instruction.

As stated in the course syllabus, the major goal of oral
communication was to help the student develop poise and confidence in his or her ability to speak in civic groups and job-
related situations. The thirty-three-hour course was organized
around four major topics: the basic elements of oral communication, interviewing, group meetings, and small-group presentations. Two, three, or four one-and-a-half-hour sessions were
allocated to each of these topics.

The instructor began the course by administering the
Educational Description Questionnaire, an instrument designed
to measure the students' perception of an instructor's behavior.
He told the students to use this questionnaire to describe the
average teacher at the college or the way that students expect

teachers to behave. After these forms were completed, he reviewed the course syllabus and had the students introduce themselves to the group. He explained that he would be the teacher for the first several class sessions but that each of them must become a member of a group responsible for teaching the class about one of the three other topics. They would have two weeks to decide which topic—interviewing, group meetings, or small-group presentations—they preferred to teach and to organize themselves into three groups. The participation in these group activities was required to pass the course and would constitute one fourth of their grade.

The goals of the first part of the course were to (1) introduce instructional strategies, (2) create a comfortable learning climate in the class, and (3) introduce the basic elements of oral communication. The students' grades on the first part of the course were based on a test, and at the next class meeting the instructor distributed the test and began helping the students answer the questions on it. During this and the next class sessions, he used group activities, videotapes, and tape recordings to help the students answer the test questions for themselves.

During the class session following the test, each student met with his or her teaching group. The instructor visited each group and explained that students would be graded on their participation in their teaching group. Basically, each student identified one, two, or three performance objectives for his or her contribution to the group. One performance objective, for example, would be to conduct an effective employment interview; another would be to introduce a film and lead a ten-minute group discussion after the film. Satisfactory completion of one objective was a "C," two was a "B," and three was an "A." To be judged as satisfactory, each performance had to be validated by certain criteria that the student and the instructor agreed on before the activity was undertaken by the student. For an employment interview to be conducted satisfactorily, for example, student observers used a rating sheet to evaluate the interview, and the interviewer had to receive a preestablished minimum average rating to be judged as satisfactory.

Four class sessions were used by the groups to develop

these performance contracts and to prepare their presentations. The instructor reviewed each group's presentation plan and each student's performance contract before the first group taught the class. Students who were not in the teaching group took a test developed and scored by the teaching group for their grade on that part of the class. Group presentations continued until the final class session.

At the final class session, the instructor administered the Educational Description Questionnaire along with a seven-question class evaluation form.

A comparison of student ratings on the Educational Description Questionnaire administered at the first class session and the one administered at the final class session indicated that they perceived themselves to have a much higher level of involvement in the class than they expected. The summary of student ratings on the evaluation form also indicated that students learned a great deal about oral communication and had a positive attitude toward the instructor and toward oral communication.

Community college students seem to like being involved in planning, conducting, and evaluating their own learning; and the instructor's use of a performance contract as a part of a course seems to increase student involvement in a course. Community college students need help from the instructor, however, in developing their performance contracts. They will work diligently to achieve high performance standards if they are involved in setting these standards. Using a performance contract for a part of a student's grade seems to be an effective way of introducing andragogy into a community college curriculum course.

10
Environmental Education at Kansas State University

Robert K. James

One of the sharpest criticisms of the adult education movement in this country is that it does little to educate our citizens about the really important social issues facing our society. Here is an imaginative application of the andragogical model to one of the most pressing of these issues—environmental protection. It describes the Eco-Action Project at Kansas State University, in which adults are engaged in a self-directed experiential investigation of environmental problems with which they are concerned.

Robert K. James is professor of science and environmental education in the Department of Curriculum and Instruction at Kansas State University.

Special features:

- A case for environmental education
- Selection of problems by learners
- Action projects
- Experiential learning
- Inducing readiness to learn
- Problem-centered learning
- The environment as a learning resource

Reprinted, with permission, from "Environmental Learning for Adults at Kansas State University," *Media Adult Learning*, Winter 1982, *10* (1), 25–28.

The formal education of many adults predates the environmental education efforts of the 1970s. These same adults will continue to make environmentally related decisions well past the year 2000. They will decide how to use much of the economically recoverable petroleum supplies of the world. They will cast ballots in support of, or against, a variety of environmental issues. The need to attend to the environmental education of this large segment of our population is great. The literature reports little regarding what adults know about environmental education. What are the unique needs of adults in this area? Is environmental education relevant for adults? This paper explores some of the dimensions and potentials of environmental education for adults.

Knowles (1978) has attempted to clarify some differences between the learning of adults and the learning of children. He also points out that much of what is known about teaching and learning has assumed that adults can and should be taught like children. He suggests that our word "pedagogy" is, in fact, limited to "youth learning" and that a new word, "andragogy," be used for adult learning.

It is possible to consider environmental education in the light of Knowles's assumptions about the nature of adult learning and thus to make some estimates as to the appropriateness of environmental education for adults. Beginning with Knowles's first assumption, that maturation brings with it a degree of self-directedness, environmental education provides an ideal opportunity for adults to practice self-directed learning. They can examine an environmental condition and direct their interests in that area. They can identify an environmental problem and pursue as much or as little of it as is of interest to them.

The Eco-Action Project has been especially valuable in allowing adults to direct their own learning. They work in a group to identify local problems. After a careful examination of a variety of local problems, they decide which problem is of greatest interest to them. They are then asked to do three things: (1) prepare a carefully written statement of the problem they wish to investigate; (2) substantiate the existence of the problem by collecting data (for example, scientific measurements, such as in the existence of pollutants; or photographs, for substantiating illegal dumping; or a simple count, for establishing how many showers have flow restricters; or observation or questionnaire techniques, for gaining other types of information; (3) describe an action they have taken to resolve the problem. They consider a wide variety of possible environmental actions. Letters to the editor or to legislators and meetings with administrators or county supervisors have been common actions that adult learners have taken in the successful completion of this project. Participants gain skills in identifying and specifying environmental problems, collecting and analyzing data, and acting through some problem-solving strategy.

Knowles's second assumption calls for experiential techniques which tap the experience of the learners and involve them in analyzing their experience. He suggests that "canned" media—such as lectures, audiovisuals, and print media—be avoided in favor of laboratory sessions, simulations, field experiences, team projects, and other action-learning techniques. One strategy for doing this successfully has been the use of a set of materials produced by the U.S. Forest Service (Warpinski, 1975). Participants are involved in several four-hour "investigations" in which they work in small groups with a facilitator. They become involved in developing and using their skills of observation in outdoor settings. These investigations include studies in forestry, soil, water, animal habitats, and natural resources and their use. Other activities involve environmental simulations and a major group problem-solving project centered about a local environmental problem. In short, they bring their experiences to bear in explaining the experiences they have during the workshop. They learn from the experiences of the other participants.

Readiness to learn is related to adults' need for the learning in their roles in life. Adults can be asked to apply environmental content to their "situation." Teachers, 4-H leaders, and agency personnel build strategies for implementing environmental concepts into their educational "situations." They are encouraged to draw teaching ideas from a review of environmental curricula such as *Teaching Environmental Education*

(Hungerford and Peyton, 1976), or the Forest Service materials. All adults are asked to confront their values and the values of their peers in relation to environmental quality.

In his fourth assumption, Knowles states that adults tend to be problem centered in relation to learning. Adults face numerous problems today which are environmentally related. Paying their monthly energy bills is one of them. Adults are excited about learning ways to conserve energy. In a recent in-service class, teachers were asked to estimate how much the class was costing them and to plan conservation actions which over the next twelve months would save enough money to pay the cost. Though it was not an easy task, it was one which caught their attention and involved them in conservation practices. Adults face other problems related to environment. Included are deregulation of natural gas, depletion of water resources, the anti-nuclear debate, unwise use of pesticides, waste disposal of hazardous substances, the mining of natural resources on federal lands, and a host of other problems of local, national, or international scope. Not all adults are equally interested in the same topics, but the number of problems seems almost endless.

Another area in which the author has noted needs among adults is in regard to their effective response to the environment. Most adults seem to rush through daily tasks without having stopped to observe, appreciate, and value the natural environment. An amazingly effective strategy has been to involve adults in a regular out-of-doors observation. Participants choose a "natural" setting where they go alone and record their observations, feelings, and experiences in a journal. In semester-long courses, teachers have been asked to spend a minimum of twenty minutes per week in this site. One example of an outcome involved an elementary teacher who chose her back yard as a "natural site." While her choice is questionable, her testimony was that prior to this time she had been afraid to venture into her own back yard! Only after being forced to complete the assignment did she learn to enjoy her back yard.

Environmental education provides avenues to learning which appeal to the unique nature of adult learning. The environment provides a locale for lifelong learning; in fact, it demands that we learn as we live and by the way we live. We hear much about how learners are inundated with sophisticated mass media, but the environment is much more stimulating and sophisticated; all that is required is that learners be directed into that arena.

11
Delivering Adult Education to Distant Communities: A Cost-Effective Model

David B. Phillips

A growing concern of adult educators, as this selection well documents, is reaching people in isolated locations—"distance education." This selection does not address the andragogical model of learning directly, but it does describe how one key concept of andragogy—learner involvement—was applied to establishing learning groups in distant locations.

David Phillips was director of community services and the Summer School of the Arts at the Georgian College of Applied Arts and Technology in Barrie, Ontario, at the time this selection was written.

Special features:

- Identifying and using "catalytic persons" in local communities
- Selecting and training liaison staff
- Gearing program promotion to local communities
- Developmental sequence in implementing a distance education program

The Summer School of the Arts commenced in 1970 with the offering of courses in painting, ceramics, and drama during a two-week period in Barrie and in the Owen Sound area. In the fall of 1970, a director was assigned the summer school as one of his responsibilities in the Continuing Education Division. Successful summer schools in both the United States and Canada counted on residential accommodation, which greatly enhanced the learning.

From its inception the summer school adopted a policy of taking the courses to the people rather than just concentrating on a main center. No apparent precedent had been set for this arrangement, and Georgian performed some pioneer tasks. In 1971 summer school courses were successful in Barrie, Orillia, Owen Sound, Midland, and Gravenhurst. From whom did this concept derive?

The Key Concept

In 1970 Malcolm Knowles shared his experiences at a continuing education conference in Toronto. By way of an apt illustration, he showed how a new concept could be introduced into a community, not by publicizing it to public gatherings or any large groups but rather by ferreting out and selecting an innovative and respected community leader and sharing the new concept with such a catalytic person. If that person accepted the concept, then close followers would observe and follow the leader. The new concept, now visible and being practiced by leaders, would inevitably reach the multitude, perhaps a year or so later. The "new way" then would become an integral part of the life of the community—from within—*from one of its own!* The innovative leader could be found by asking leading citizens in the area, such as the school principal, clergy, bankers, and town officials, "Who makes this town move ahead?"

This key concept was adopted by the summer school director as a means of mounting courses and programs in several centers for which Georgian College was responsible in the 11,000-square-mile Georgian Bay region. Malcolm Knowles's idea of the selection of key local people was extended to a search for key liaison officers, who would act as the *ears* of the college, to listen for the community needs; to act as the *voice* of the college, to speak to the community about opportunities the college had to offer. Communication could be frequent, personal, and direct—by a neighbor within the community rather than once-in-a-while visits by a distant traveler. When these liaison officers learned the skills necessary to mount, monitor, and evaluate courses, the college extended its outreach in an efficient and organized manner.

Growth of Programs

The growth pattern began to emerge. In 1972 the Huntsville area came under the inspired leadership of a husband and wife team who served as part-time program supervisors. The husband was technical director of the high school; the wife was closely associated with the arts. Seventeen courses were held in Huntsville alone. That year also recorded ecology-oriented sessions with wildlife studies at Wyemarsh and with one-day trips to Beausoleil Island. The summer school operated during most of July and a part of August in Penetanguishene, Midland, Stayner, Waubaushene, Orillia, Owen Sound, and Barrie.

Mounting and monitoring off-campus courses posed numerous administration problems. Suitable local personnel had to be selected to provide local leadership and to work in cooperation with the central clerical support group, located at the Barrie campus. This staff provided coordination and control of the regional activities by preparing brochures, registering students, and processing all relevant documentation. Publicity and promotion had to be geared to residents and cottagers, to make them aware of the opportunities available through the college. New promotional and distribution techniques were established.

In 1973 the boundaries were broadened to include Bracebridge, Parry Sound, and Collingwood, and courses were offered as early as May and June as well as during the strictly holiday months of July and August. It was becoming clear that management of courses over such an extended area necessitated further emphasis on local supervision and control.

A community-spirited couple residing in Parry Sound, and esteemed by the town folk, took on the challenge as part-time program supervisors for the district of Parry Sound. They provided Georgian College with a presence in that more northerly region some eighty miles from Barrie. In the same manner, the Collingwood/Blue Mountain courses were developed under the capable leadership of a local active resident catalyst. Malcolm Knowles's principle of relying on an innovator/catalyst was working.

From 1973 to 1975, the summer school distributed a booklet which identified all locations and all courses under one cover. While this was good for promotional purposes and for the dissemination of information, it proved to be costly to print and mail. A better method had to be devised. The utilization of separate local-area brochures enabled a remarkable cost reduction and highlighted community activities better. Having the communities' name on the brochure proved most effective and is still the method in use to date. Selected household mailing is used by most of the centers.

In 1976 enrollment reached almost three thousand in the six established centers supervised by part-time personnel. For the second year in succession, the college became involved in music courses with a Toronto college at the Blue Mountain Resorts. The project, however, was later abandoned, due in part to excessive costs. A program supervisor in Midland developed courses in the northerly region of Simcoe County.

In its eighth year, 1977, the summer school recorded an increase in enrollment of 23 percent over the previous year. Regional program supervisors operated courses on a breakeven basis. Log Construction, Horsemanship, Disco Dancing, Tennis, and Stained Glass proved very popular.

In 1978 statistics showed a further 23 percent increase in enrollment over the previous year. Area program supervisors developed further satellite centers where courses were mounted. Small office/information centers were opened in Huntsville, Parry Sound, Collingwood, and Lafontaine. These centers, along with the three main campuses, served as registration points and gave a sense of permanence to the college extension work in each area. Up to this time, program supervisors worked out of their homes. Programs in both crafts and French were developed in cooperation with the Ontario Teachers' Federation.

Organization and Administration

The evolution of the Summer School of the Arts required a progressively changing organizational structure and administrative procedure to respond to the growth of the system. The development sequence presented in Figure 1 identifies twelve

Figure 1. The Regional System, with Central Coordination and Control.

Development Sequence		Area 2	Area 1	Area 3
I	Identify need	(L)	(L)	(L)
II	Define requirements	(L)	(L)	(L)
III	Approve the proposal		(C)	
IV	Plan the program	(L)	(L)	(L)
V	Promote the courses	(L)	(L)	(L)
VI	Receive student applications	(L)	(L)	(L)
VII	Register the students		(C)	
VIII	Prepare the premises	(L)	(L)	(L)
IX	Present the courses	(L)	(L)	(L)
X	Pay the expenses		(C)	
XI	Evaluate the results		(C)	
XII	Recommend revisions	(L)	(L)	(L)

Code: (L) Local involvement (C) Central coordination and control

specific tasks to be performed during the implementation of the program and, in fact, for each course. Initially, all support staff tasks—preparation of brochures, registration, and reports—were done by the "core" group at Barrie campus. As clerical staff were employed at regional offices, from 1978 onward, detailed duties were assigned to them, and completed documentation was channeled through the central office for coordination and control of activities. Close cooperation and team effort are required to complete the sequence of scheduled events and still meet the various time deadlines that prevail.

Appraisal of the System

Experience has established that communities can be served efficiently and effectively by this extension service system. The college is in continuous contact with the community through the involvement of the resident program supervisor. Travel costs are less than they would be for nonresident college representatives. The local information center provides a physical college presence in the region. It should be noted that this delivery system was only one of many methods Georgian College utilized for its outreach into the region.

Further developments of Malcolm Knowles's key idea are already emerging as area program supervisors select further local liaison personnel to help give a more immediate response to local adult education requirements. It is an ongoing process always associated with local leadership.

FOUR

❖◆◆ ◆◆ ◆◆ ◆◆ ◆◆ ◆◆ ◆◆ ◆◆ ◆◆ ◆◆ ◆◆ ◆◆ ◆◆ ◆◆ ◆◆ ◆

Applications
in Education
for the Professions

People preparing for professional careers are adult learners—by virtue of having made one of the most adult decisions possible, choosing a career. It is therefore especially critical that programs of professional education be based on principles of adult learning. Fortunately, leaders in many of the professions—medicine, nursing, law, social work, education—got this insight over a decade ago. Accordingly, some of the most thoroughly tested applications of the andragogical model are in professional schools.

This chapter opens with a description of one of the pioneer programs of medical education built around concepts and principles of adult learning—the program at the McMaster University Faculty of Health Sciences in Hamilton, Ontario. Selection 2 describes the application of these principles to clinical legal education at Vanderbilt University. Applications to social work education at the University of Georgia and at the University of Victoria are presented in selections 3 and 4. Selection 5 discusses an incremental series of learning experiences designed to help nursing students become increasingly self-directed at Franklin University School of Nursing, and an andragogical course in school administration at Cleveland State University is presented in selection 6.

The designs and techniques portrayed in these selections could easily be adapted to a variety of educational programs.

1

Preparing Medical Students
for Lifelong Learning

Victor R. Neufeld, Howard S. Barrows

As a result of the knowledge explosion and technological revolution in the last half of this century, the rate of obsolescence of human beings has been increasing exponentially. In few areas of life has this obsolescence been more pronounced than in the medical profession. Doctors who know only what they knew when they got their M.D.s are obsolete within a few years; they must be skillful lifelong learners if they are to keep up to date. Accordingly, medical schools have been reevaluating the philosophy, curriculum, and techniques of medical education. They have been realizing that doctors must be taught as self-directed learners in medical school if they are to be lifelong learners.

One of the pioneers in this revolution has been the McMaster University Faculty of Health Sciences in Hamilton, Ontario. This selection describes the innovative program of medical education that was designed at the founding of the school in 1966 and the revisions in the program that were planned in 1982 on the basis of fourteen years of experience. Although the program was not self-consciously based on the andragogical model, its assumptions about adult learners and its strategies for facilitating learning are totally congruent with this model, and the faculty later discovered that they also had invented andragogy.

Excerpted, with permission, from "The 'McMaster Philosophy': An Approach to Medical Education," *Journal of Medical Education*, 1974, *49*, 1040–1048, and Charles P. Friedman and Elizabeth F. Purcell (Eds.), *The Now Biology and Medical Education: Merging the Biological, Information and Cognitive Sciences*, The Josiah Macy, Jr., Foundation, New York, 1983.

Victor R. Neufeld is chairman of the M.D. program, Faculty of Health Sciences, and Howard S. Barrows is a member of the founding faculty at McMaster University.
Special features:

- Goals in terms of student outcomes
- Self-directed learning
- Problem-based curriculum
- Basic sciences learned in clinical context
- Utilization of prior learning
- Small-group learning
- Peer evaluation
- Individualized learning
- "Problem boxes" (modules)
- A variety of learning resources
- Diagnostic, performance-based, evaluation
- Integrated learning
- Five faculty roles
- Selection of students
- Program evaluation and revision

In 1965 a young, relatively unknown cardiologist-researcher, John Evans, was asked to be the dean of Ontario's fifth (and Canada's fifteenth) medical school at McMaster University in Hamilton. The founders of the program made an early fundamental decision—to try something different. By 1969, when the first students arrived, the key elements of this adventure in medical education were defined, and faculty members had been recruited who were committed to try an alternate approach to medical education. The M.D. Program was just one component of a multifaceted collaborative set of educational and research programs and a range of patient care activities involving the university, the community, and the provincial government.

The M.D. program has as its key features the analysis of problems as the main method of acquiring and applying information, the fostering of independent learning by students, and the use of small groups as the main educational forum (Neufeld, 1973). The thirty-three-month program consists of a series of interdisciplinary curriculum units, several elective blocks, and a year-long clerkship. There are no discipline-specific courses. The "basic sciences" are learned in the context of clinical cases. There are no examinations; evaluation of student progress occurs informally and continuously in the tutorial groups, supplemented by performance in a variety of individual problem-based exercises. An intensive selection process admits students from a variety of academic and experiential backgrounds, whose learning habits are compatible with the style of the program and who demonstrate both academic ability and desirable personal qualities (Ferrier, McAuley, and Roberts, 1978). The M.D. program is seen as the responsibility of the faculty as a whole. Its operation is entrusted to a program committee, rather than to departments or disciplines. Departments supply the human resources for several defined educational roles within the program.

The goals of the M.D. program focus on the individual student-physician. The emphasis is placed on specific capabilities and characteristics rather than a store of knowledge. The faculty recognizes that the body of factual knowledge in the program is inevitably both incomplete and redundant; because of this, a high value is placed on the student's ability to manipulate data, to recognize and define problems, and to evaluate their solutions. Rather than a commitment to "streaming" (that is, to prepare students for specific careers), the program prepares "undifferentiated" physicians, who, at graduation, will be able to select more specific postgraduate training programs.

Goals as Student Outcomes

The general goals of the program, stated in terms of outcomes for the student, are as follows:

1. To identify and define health problems and to search for information in order to resolve or manage these problems.
2. Given a health problem, to examine the underlying physical or behavioral mechanisms. A spectrum of phenomena might be included, from molecular events to those involving the patient's family and community.
3. To recognize, maintain, and develop personal characteristics and attitudes required for professional life.
4. To develop the clinical skills and to learn the methods re-

quired to define and manage the health problems of patients, including their physical, emotional, and social aspects.
5. To become a self-directed learner, recognizing personal educational needs, selecting appropriate learning resources, and
evaluating progress.
6. To be able to assess critically professional activity related
to patient care, health care delivery, and medical research.
7. To be able to function as a productive member of a small
group which is engaged in learning, research, or health care.
8. To be aware of and able to work in a variety of health care
settings.

The three-year program consists of four phases; the first
two are ten weeks each, and the last two are one year each.
Phase I is an introduction to the community—its facilities and
its people; to the learning strategies of problem solving, independent study, and small-group tutorials; to universal concepts
in structure, function, and behavior; and to basic clinical skills.
Phase II concentrates on the body's response to stimuli, using
pathophysiological models such as ischemia, inflammation, and
reactive depression. Phase III consists of four ten-week combined organ system units, using more specific disease entities in
a problem-based approach. The clinical clerkship, Phase IV,
comprises three major blocks: hospital based, ambulatory, and
elective. Throughout the program there are additional extensive
elective opportunities, both concurrent with ongoing phases and
in two blocks between phases.

The following components of the educational program,
while stated separately, are interrelated. None of these ideas is
entirely novel in education. What is perhaps more unusual is the
combination of these ideas into a single and unified approach
and the creation of an administrative arrangement that allows
these ideas to flourish.

Self-Directed Learning

If physicians are to be lifelong learners and able to assess
changing health care needs, to keep up with changing concepts
and new knowledge, and to adapt their own performance ac-

cordingly, they must develop the requisite skills during the formative years of medical school training. Therefore, in the McMaster program, the student is assumed to be a responsible and motivated adult. He is encouraged, with appropriate guidance, to define his own learning goals, to select appropriate experiences to achieve these goals, and to be responsible for assessing his own learning progress. In defining his learning goals, the student is encouraged to review his previous experiences in academic training, his future career plans, and the current learning opportunities at McMaster. The student is helped by a tutor or an adviser in defining these personal goals and in seeing their relationship to the goals of the tutorial group as well as to the overall program goals. It is important that these personal objectives are clear, assessable, and realistic.

The student is responsible for the design of his own program, bearing in mind his responsibilities to the tutorial group. (Students are assigned randomly to tutorial groups of five or six upon entrance; each group has a carefully selected faculty adviser.) The schedule facilitates this independence, with a maximum of one optional class-wide event per day. A large range of learning resources is available to the student to help him achieve his objectives. Self-directed learning also involves the learning of methods for managing information; included are such basic abilities as efficient reading and the effective use of practical personal information retrieval (filing) systems, study outlines and notes, medical journals and texts, and the medical library.

Approximately twenty-five weeks in the three-year program are designated for electives. "Elective" time in the McMaster program means individual time when the student does not need to consider concurrent responsibilities to the tutorial group. Most students use these periods for pursuing individual interests, shoring up areas of deficiency, or studying in other centers.

Just as the determination of goals and the selection of learning experiences are the student's responsibility, so self-evaluation is a component of self-directed learning. The prerequisites for this are a willingness to do it, an understanding of what the goals are, and some idea of performance criteria (that is, the desired or expected level of performance or learning).

How does this self-evaluation actually happen? It is a constant and informal process. The student has feedback about his own performance and makes value judgments about it in discussions with his peers, in tutorial discussions, and more formally in reviewing a write-up of a problem with his tutor or engaging in self-assessment exercises of various kinds. At the end of each unit, he also reviews his progress comprehensively with his tutor.

Problem-Based Learning

Learning based on problems represents an alternative to studying blocks of classified knowledge in a strictly organized sequence. In problem-based learning, the learner focuses on a problem that he has identified and that involves genuine intellectual effort. The learner brings to the problem all of his previous information and expertise as well as his ability to think rationally about it. As he begins to ask questions, certain issues become defined that will require a further information search. After assembling the appropriate information, he synthesizes a problem solution. The student learns to recognize that few problems in medicine are totally "solved" and that wrestling with any one problem opens up many other questions, which can be pursued either at that time or at some future date.

Since the problems encountered in medicine are primarily those of individual patients, most problem situations presented to the student relate to an individual clinical case. In this way the learning is highly relevant and similar to the method by which many health professionals learn in real life. There are many advantages to this kind of learning: it contributes to the student's motivation; it encourages active intellectual processes at the higher cognitive levels; it probably enhances the retention and transfer of information; it can be modified to meet individual student needs; and it encourages curiosity and systematic thinking.

Problem-based learning can occur in both individual and in small-group learning situations. In the tutorial group, critical thinking can be encouraged and arguments developed; one idea can be constructively built on another; information can be pooled and strategies laid out for obtaining information from external sources as required.

A form of problem-based learning frequently utilized at McMaster is called "biomedical problem solving." It has been defined in the following terms. Given a description of a patient or other clinical situation, the tutorial group or individual student should carry out the following sequence of activities. A series of questions, which may be stated in lay terms, will be listed as they arise from the biomedical problem; these questions will be translated into issues in structure, function, behavior, and response to stimuli; acting singly or in a group, students will identify and study in depth educational resources which provide information relevant to issues previously identified; the students will then synthesize this information into a cogent explanation of the clinical situation, either during a group tutorial session or individually; the development of additional questions, suggestions, and hypotheses for further steps in the evaluation and/or management of the clinical situation follows logically from this synthesis and emphasizes the fact that biomedical problems can be pursued in a number of directions and tend to be open-ended; the tutorial group will complete the process by evaluating individual and group performances, the biomedical problem itself, and the related learning resources.

The assumption of sequential learning is challenged by this approach. Sequences are based on arbitrary decisions, which are frequently unrelated to real-life situations. It is commonly assumed that normal structure and function should be learned prior to the abnormal, and yet only by comparing the abnormal with the normal can the range of normal become clear to the student.

The sequence myth includes the idea that basic science must be learned prior to clinical science. In the McMaster program, basic science and clinical science are interwoven. The central focus is on the series of biomedical problems. When tackling a clinical problem, the student asks questions about basic mechanisms, both physical and behavioral. The student spirals through the same content area several times in the program, each time at a more sophisticated or broadly applied level. For example, he has an introduction to "puffing and pumping" in Phase I, studies the model of myocardial ischemia in Phase II, delves more deeply into mechanisms of cardiac and respiratory dysfunction in Phase III, and learns directly from patients with heart and lung problems in Phase IV.

Also challenged is the assumption that information is required before problem solving can begin. In general, we tend to forget the fact that students bring a wide variety of expertise to the program; that, to some extent, they can think logically (based on many years of problem-solving experiences in their personal lives and possibly in their schooling); and that, at the very least, they possess an intelligent "lay public" baseline of information. Thus, with the recognition of an appropriate level of activity, problem-based learning can start at the beginning of the program.

Is problem solving a legitimate goal in itself, or is it a vehicle to "get at the content"? The acquiring of a problem-solving approach is a stated goal of the school. It is useless to have a stockpile of information without a method of handling it. On the other hand, given a good approach to problem solving, students will be able to define the information they require to handle encountered problems, not only during their medical school experience but also in medical practice. There is some evidence that the information learned in this way will be retained longer. Implicit in this philosophy is the recognition that no attempt will be made to "cover" particular content areas; instead, the student samples them in relevant problem situations. Rather than knowledge acquisition per se, it is the use of information in the solution of problems that is encouraged.

When problems are used effectively by a tutorial group or individual student, not only are the "process goals" reinforced but also specific "content goals" are tackled. The content focus is determined in the selection of the problem and in the specific issues defined when the problem is discussed.

Problem-based learning includes more than simply learning around clinical problems. It represents a fundamental intellectual process, which can be applied to physiological problems in a research laboratory, to a problem of family dysfunction, or to problems of health care in the community.

Small-Group Learning

The small-group tutorial represents a laboratory of learning about human interaction, where students can develop interpersonal skills and become aware of their own emotional reactions. It is an opportunity to learn how to listen, to receive criticism, and in turn to offer constructive criticism. It is a forum for group problem solving, where the pooled resources of the group members—in terms of academic training, experience, personality, and perspective—are more effective than the sum of individual abilities. A small-group tutorial provides an opportunity for self-evaluation by which a student can compare informally his own learning progress with that of his peers. The small-group tutorial setting also facilitates the processes of peer evaluation. Many groups develop a sense of responsibility for the learning progress of each member, and students learn how to give accurate and candid feedback to each other. This process is often difficult because it represents a stark contrast to previous competitive educational systems from which some students have come. In addition, students learn about educational planning because they are free to design their own group program within the general framework of a larger learning unit.

The faculty tutor has a key role in this learning group. Although he will be an "expert" or content area specialist in some branch of medical science, his role as a tutor is primarily that of a generalist and a facilitator. The tutor must understand the general goals and methods of the program. He must be skilled in managing small-group interaction. While a participating member of the group, he must help the group become gradually more responsible for its own activity and more mature as a learning resource. He must coordinate effective and meaningful evaluation. He should himself be an example of self-directed learning and problem solving.

The tutorial role is relatively new for most faculty persons who come to McMaster. Particular concerns are the tutor's role as an evaluator and the tutor's "nonexpertise" in an integrated curriculum. The facilitator role is difficult for the faculty to learn and for the students to appreciate ("Why won't he just tell me?"). Using the facilitating approach, as contrasted with the didactic, the tutor attempts to assist the student in his learning progress. This includes encouraging, reinforcing, shaping, and hinting and may involve the use of parallel examples, of schema, of diagrams, and of logical approaches. The facilitator utilizes the principle of "guided discovery," allowing the student to learn from his own mistakes but not letting him become totally frustrated by lack of progress. There is an obvious need for an adequate orientation to the tutor role for both students and faculty. Increasing efforts are being made toward tutorial orientation both before and during a unit.

While the need for defining the tutor role is recognized, each tutor brings his own individual approach to the tutorial. The group must recognize and use this individuality to the optimum, just as the individuality of each student member can be used for the benefit of the group. The tutor's role definition need not crimp the style of any individual tutor; rather, it should help to clarify relationships within the tutorial group and allow the group to function better.

Just as tutors evaluate students as colleagues, so students are asked to assess the contribution of faculty tutors to their learning. This process, when successful, helps to prevent faculty members from developing grand images of themselves. It is admittedly difficult for students and tutors to shape a learning climate where reciprocal assessments are offered and received in a constructive fashion. But with growing experience, the assessments of tutor contributions by students are becoming more useful.

Many tutors find that, by functioning as nonexpert tutors, they can update their knowledge in an area while working with students, thus maintaining an appropriate perspective on problems in the health field and on new knowledge that is available. Furthermore, they can share the excitement of exploring and discovering new ideas.

Learning Resources

The discriminating and effective use of learning resources is itself a learning objective, particularly in Phase I, where a student may be confronting a wide range of resources for the first time. The student is expected to learn which resources are most appropriate for his particular need and his individual learning style. As he moves through the program, the student will learn which resources are most useful for specific purposes. He has the opportunity, for example, of developing a personal library of notes, outlines, diagrams, reprints, handouts, card files, and textbooks—all "extensions" of his memory, readily available, familiar, and adaptable for his continuing learning in the future. This personal library will be used in conjunction with additional resources in the main library or in designated study areas.

Two broad categories of learning resources are provided in the program. There are learning resources that are designed to stimulate problem solving. These include actual patients, simulated patients (healthy individuals who have been specifically trained to mimic the history and physical signs of an actual patient), some computer-based physiological models, and "problem boxes." A problem box is a McMaster term for a patient who has been "captured" in an appropriate audiovisual format. For example, if the medical history is an important feature of the case, an audiotape of an actual or simulated patient is provided. If certain external physical features are important, these are provided in color photographs or slides. If there is a movement disorder, appropriate film cassettes or videotapes are made of the patient and are included in the box. Instead of descriptions of certain laboratory investigations or X rays, the actual X rays in reduced size or actual blood films or pathology slides are included in the box as well. All of these bits of information about the patient are available in the box, and the student works through the case, following a guidebook.

A second type of learning resource provides information; such resources usually include selected readings, various audiovisual aids, and resource people. There are specialists or experts in a field who are available at the call of a tutorial group or individual student, much as a consultant specialist in medical practice is available to another practitioner when a particular problem arises.

Diagnostic Evaluation

Diagnostic or "formative" evaluation refers to frequent assessments with feedback made during the course of a learning experience. The term implies that each assessment provides the opportunity for modifying or "forming" the student's learning progress. This evaluation is conceived of as a constructive and integral component of the learning process rather than a detached, anxiety-provoking activity. The purpose of such an evaluation system is primarily to facilitate student learning and to modify the learning program. The main evaluator is the student himself, and this is consistent with the emphasis on self-directed learning. Participating with him are his peers and his tutor. The student or his tutor may request additional help in this evaluation process from resource people or from appropriate self-assessment sources of various kinds. It should be noted that individual student learning progress is not the responsibility of the unit planner but remains in the hands of the student and his tutor.

At the beginning of a unit, a student and tutor commonly work out the objectives most appropriate for that student. They have available to them the overall goals of the phase and program and the unit-specific goals suggested by the unit-planning group. More specific personal objectives should then be defined by the student; and, based on these, decisions are made about appropriate learning experiences. This occurs both in individual discussions and in the small-group tutorial setting. During such discussions the student(s) and tutor can decide on the methods of progress assessment, make judgments about actual progress, and modify the student's program accordingly. Toward the end of the unit, the student and tutor meet to summarize the progress achieved, as this relates to the student's statement of objectives and the general goals of the unit. The methods of assessment are selected to match the objectives. Critical thinking (problem-solving) ability can be observed in tutorial or individual discussions and in "problem write-ups." Included in the various self-assessment methods, which are available to help the student determine whether the knowledge he has acquired is accurate, are multiple-choice exercises, criterion problem write-ups, and some computer-based programs. Clinical skills are assessed by direct observation. These and other methods are used during a learning unit; there are no end-of-course examinations.

How is agreement achieved in this rather open system of evaluation? Several approaches have been used, the first of which is the continuous effort to clarify learning goals. Discussions involving both students and faculty occur in many places: in open discussions with the faculty, in meetings of the unit-planning group, in orientation sessions for tutors, in group tutorials, and in individual discussions between the student and tutor.

Once agreement about objectives has been reached, the choice of methods of assessment often becomes fairly obvious, and few major disagreements occur in the actual observations of the student's progress.

At the end of a unit, a summary statement prepared by the tutor includes a satisfactory or unsatisfactory progress report. Hopefully, indications about unsatisfactory progress will have been detected early in the unit and appropriate modifications in the student's program made. Precise definitions of criteria for satisfactory or unsatisfactory levels of performance of all students have not been stressed. Although there are methods for specifying acceptable performance levels with respect to knowledge objectives, and to some extent to problem-solving and clinical skills, establishing performance criteria for learning objectives other than these is more difficult. Rather, the emphasis has been on a descriptive profile of strong and weak aspects of learning achievement, with the identification of learning problems to be resolved in the next unit.

Integrated Learning

Integration occurs at various levels. At the planning level, faculty members from a broad range of disciplines, along with students, form planning committees and are responsible for each learning unit. An educational program is, therefore, not a department-based responsibility, and members of the planning group are not specifically representatives of their departments or disciplines. They are, however, selected because of their educational planning ability.

This method of program responsibility exemplifies the "matrix management" approach, which is being used within the Faculty of Health Sciences. In this system departmental administrators are responsible for manpower deployment, career development of each faculty member, and logistics (for example, salary and administrative personnel). Programs are the responsibility of functional groups made up of individuals from many departments. A program group is responsible for determining goals, requesting and managing resources, and evaluating program activity. Also, programs are individually budgeted.

On another level each student is responsible for integrating his own learning. He has an opportunity at every point to look at a problem from all points of view, from the molecular to the social. In addition to exploring several areas within a single problem situation, a student also has an opportunity to develop an overview of a single discipline, organ system, or mechanism. It can be seen that, by such an integrated approach, certain concepts are encountered repeatedly in the student's learning experience.

Faculty Responsibilities

When a full-time faculty member joins the McMaster adventure, there is an explicit commitment of a minimum of 20 percent of his time to be devoted to educational activity; and the undergraduate M.D. program is considered to have a first priority in this commitment.

There are several specific roles that any single faculty member can play in the education program. One of these, the faculty tutor role, has already been described. Four other roles will be described briefly.

1. The function of a resource person is primarily to facilitate in-depth learning in a special discipline. In terms of pro-

viding information, he is the "last in the line" of resources utilized, following the student's individual thinking and reading, discussion in a tutorial group, and the exploration of audiovisual material. The resource person is warned against the "nickelodeon effect," where a coin is plugged in and information spouts out. He is advised to adopt a facilitating approach in the same way as the tutor but within a particular content area. His contribution might include referring the student to an appropriate review article or producing a learning resource such as a paper handout or a slide-tape show or problem box. It may also involve evaluating the learning achievement of a student or of a tutorial group at the request of the tutor, the group, or a student. Resource persons should be no less aware of the general goals of the program and the approaches used than a faculty tutor. The resource person can also help a student become a more critical thinker. He can explore his specific frontier area of research with a student group, demonstrating how certain broad issues become defined and how scientific exploration occurs. Clinicians can be viewed as resource persons as well, their contribution being to provide access to patients and to help students in the acquisition of clinical skills.

2. The unit planner is the person administratively responsible for a learning unit; he coordinates the efforts of the students and faculty members who are members of his planning group. The unit planner is usually an experienced tutor and resource person and should understand that such functions as program evaluation and tutorial monitoring are also the responsibilities of the planning group. Unit planners are responsible for presenting a preview of a unit to the M.D. education committee (this committee is responsible for planning, implementing, and evaluating the undergraduate M.D. education program and is accountable through the associate dean (education) to the Faculty Council), as well as a detailed postunit evaluation review, with clear suggestions for the subsequent modification of the particular unit.

3. The role of the faculty adviser is that of an advocate, career counselor, and sounding board over the course of a three-year association with the student. He receives student learning

progress reports as they become available. Of crucial importance is his awareness of learning problems that arise in more than one evaluation statement, and it is his responsibility to discuss such issues with the student. He also helps the student to decide on individual elective experiences. In addition, he is responsible for letters of reference, which may be required.

4. Discipline consultants from several specialties contribute to the program in various ways: by preparing documents for unit planners that outline the important concepts in their disciplines, by participating as members of the unit-planning groups, and by developing learning resources for student use. The intent in the M.D. program is to consider principles from all disciplines relevant to the practice of medicine. These include physical (biological), behavioral, social, ethical, epidemiological, and clinical areas—all of which are considered to be basic to the understanding of problems of human health and disease.

An unusual feature of the McMaster system is the assessment of faculty, not only for their contributions in research and service but also for their contributions to education. The quality of the contribution of each individual serves as a basis for recommendations of salary increases, promotion, or tenure. In the educational area, the sources of information are the faculty member himself and the perceptions of students and faculty peers with whom the individual is associated. These considerations are undertaken on an institutional and program basis rather than departmentally.

Selection of Students

It is the overall goal of the admissions committee to select students who are most likely to fulfill all of the goals of the program and who will thrive in a relatively unstructured learning environment. Two general policies apply to this process. The first is the principle of heterogeneity: given that applicants have the basic qualifications of a three-year university experience and a "B" average minimum, students are then selected from a wide variety of academic backgrounds. Close to half of the students have undergraduate specialization in fields other than the biological sciences.

The second policy involves the selection of students not only on the basis of academic credentials but also on the basis of personal characteristics and abilities. Included are demonstrated abilities for independent learning, for imaginative problem solving, and for productive contributions to various small groups. Additionally, the committee members look for emotional stability, responsibility, motivation for a medical career, and the capacity for self-appraisal. These academic and personal characteristics are then weighed in a series of decision-making steps leading to an offer of a place in the program.

A review of the selection process in 1973-74 will illustrate some of the specific features. All the 2,352 applicants who met the basic requirements were initially assessed using two methods: an academic assessment of grade point averages, which resulted in a rank-ordered list, and an assessment of an autobiographical letter with a biographical sketch, including a list of extraacademic activities. Each letter was reviewed by a team of three readers, one each from the faculty, the student body, and the community. The specific items that were rated emphasized the personal characteristics reflected in the goals of the program. A training program preceded this review process. Since three "control" letters were included in each batch and the data were computerized, it was possible to conduct such analyses as interrater agreement. Applicants scoring high on the autobiographical letter were also rank-ordered.

On the basis of reference letters and a geographical region formula, 430 applicants (an equal number from both lists, with some double qualifiers) were invited to a set of interviews. Two methods were employed. A forty-five-minute interview with each applicant was conducted by a team of three interviewers, the team again consisting of one faculty member, one student, and one community person. Each team had attended an interview-training workshop in which "simulated applicants" were used. Again, items rated reflected the goals of the M.D. program. Interview teams were monitored through one-way glass audio systems by experienced interviewers, as one method of quality control. A second method was the simulated tutorial, in which groups of six applicants were observed through one-way glass discussing standard health problems. Applicants were assessed primarily for group skills and contributions to group problem solving.

Finally, all the information in the files of the 160 applicants ranking highest on a composite interview score were thoroughly reviewed by a collating committee, leading to the offer of places to 80 applicants, 40 each from the rank-order lists.

Program Evaluation and Revision

In general terms, the program has been successful. More than 800 graduates have acquired postgraduate training and entered professional practice. It appears that McMaster graduates are going into academic or research positions at a rate higher than the national average. The attrition rate is low (less than 1 percent). Reports from supervisors of McMaster graduates in postgraduate training across the country are very favorable. Graduates surveyed at two and five years after graduation are generally supportive of the program's approach to learning (Woodward and McAuley, 1981). The program has attracted considerable national and international attention (Fraenkel, 1978). Several new medical schools in various parts of the world have adopted a similar approach. One Canadian school, making a major curriculum change, has been considerably influenced by McMaster's experience.

Despite the generally favorable experience of the program over more than a decade, however, there were persistent suggestions from various sources that not all was well and that changes were desirable and necessary. With some turnover of program leadership in the summer of 1981, the time seemed appropriate to consider whether changes were required and, if so, what these should be and how they could be implemented. From the summer of 1981 to the summer of 1982, as a product of widespread discussion among students, faculty, and program graduates, a set of proposals were developed. These are currently at various stages of refinement and approval.

During the initial discussions, several reasons for change were clarified:

1. There was much new knowledge in human biology, health care, and health-related aspects of society.
2. There was a continuing criticism that the objectives of the program and of its component parts were not sufficiently clear; this contributed to imprecision in the student evaluation system.
3. Like any institution, it was realized that the M.D. program could become trapped in its own neo-orthodoxy; we felt that the exercise of reviewing our goals in the light of current opportunities could promote institutional renewal.
4. A recurrent observation was that students in our thirty-three-month program were excessively busy and that in some areas the faculty required an infusion of energy and interest.
5. While the follow-up studies of our graduates showed that their performance was comparable to graduates of other institutions, there was a sense that we should be seeing more of such distinctive abilities as efficient continuing learning, the use of conceptual and integrative models in patient care, and the critical appraisal of clinical literature.
6. Many of our learning resources were outdated, and new technological developments needed to be explored.

In all of the discussions, it was clear that there was a desire to retain the original basic elements of the learning approach: integrated learning based on problems, independent learning by students, and the use of tutorials as the central learning event.

Several specific proposals for program revision have been developed. These include:

1. The preparation of an objectives document: This will be a statement of the overall goals and expected achievement by students at points in the program. It will describe the key concepts to be learned through the study of problems, the fundamental skills to be acquired, and the professional attributes to be demonstrated. This "road map" is intended to serve as a guide for learning by students and for educational planning by faculty.

2. The modification of curriculum units: This is being done to introduce new and revised concepts and case studies. Of particular interest will be a new integration unit located just before the clerkship. This unit will use "the life cycle" as a theme.

3. Flexibility in the duration and scope of studies: It is proposed that a small number of students have the opportunity to study certain topics more broadly and intensively; this would extend the duration of their studies by up to twelve months. The indications for this extension will include academic and enrichment reasons, based on specific criteria.

Other proposals are at earlier stages of development. These include revisions within the clerkship, a revamping of the evaluation system, and the development of new learning resources.

As could be predicted, these proposals have provoked a variety of responses. For the most part, the reactions have been favorable. There is the predictable concern by students and some faculty planners that some of the curricular structures that are now comfortably in place will be changed. There is widespread acceptance of the preparation of a clearer, more coordinated set of objectives. These initiatives taken by the M.D. committee have evoked a general sense of direction and adventure among students, graduates, and faculty.

2

Clinical Legal Education
at Vanderbilt University

Frank S. Bloch

Here is one of the most comprehensive, systematic, and detailed expositions on the application of the andragogical model to graduate professional education that I have seen. Although this particular application is to legal education, it has rich implications for professional education of all sorts.

Frank S. Bloch is associate professor of law and director of clinical education at the Vanderbilt University School of Law, Nashville, Tennessee.

Special features:

- Andragogical aspects of the case method
- Law students as adult learners
- Mutual teacher/student inquiry and co-counseling
- Overcoming resistance to self-directed learning
- Experiential learning
- Gearing instruction to readiness to learn
- Problem-centered learning
- An andragogical model of clinical legal education
- Mutual evaluation
- Case selection

___

As with any general theory based largely on a single idea, a danger of tautology exists when one attempts to explain and apply the theory of andragogy at a practical level through numerous

Adapted, with permission, from "The Andragogical Basis of Clinical Legal Education," *Vanderbilt Law Review,* 1982, *35* (2), 321-353.

examples. Although Knowles and those following him have elaborated upon and expanded the four basic assumptions of andragogy and the methodological implications based on those assumptions, the important elements of each andragogical assumption can be reduced to a single set of methodological points. These points can be presented, in declining order of importance, as follows: (1) Learning should be through mutual inquiry by teacher and student (adults' self-concept as self-directing). (2) Emphasis should be on active, experiential learning (role of experience in adult learning). (3) Learning should relate to concurrent changes in the students' social roles (readiness to learn). (4) Learning should be presented in the context of problems that students are likely to face (orientation to learning).

These four central elements of andragogy and their related methodological implications provide a theoretical framework for examining the appropriateness of the methods by which law is taught to adult law students both in clinical programs and throughout legal education. This theoretical framework offers legal educators the opportunity to plan a course of law study that is fully consistent with the capabilities and aspirations of adult law students. Although the purpose of this article is to consider andragogy as it applies to clinical programs, a few observations about andragogy and legal education in general will help put in context the subsequent discussions of the andragogical basis of and a proposal andragogically based model for clinical legal education.

Andragogy and Traditional Legal Education

The application of the methodological implications of Knowles's andragogy to legal education does not lead to a wholesale indictment of the traditional case method of instruction as hopelessly nonandragogical. Indeed, although Knowles was primarily concerned with developing theories about the means of adult learning, he recognized that case method parables and Socratic dialogue are examples of useful techniques of adult education that have existed since ancient times. Moreover, some aspects of traditional law-teaching methods not only are fully consistent with andragogical theory but also are premised —at least to some extent—on a recognition that law students are adult learners.

One example—the act of really listening to what the student says—is a technique of the case method of instruction which is necessitated by its reliance on Socratic dialogue. This technique requires mutual respect between teacher and student and is central to the andragogical notion of deferring to the self-concept of adults. In addition, the traditional dialogue between law teacher and student that requires the student to analyze a case and explore legal doctrine is itself an experiential learning technique, since the process of case analysis is not taught in the abstract but instead takes place with student participation at the time of learning. The exchange between teacher and student in the classroom does not reach the andragogical standard of true mutual inquiry, however, at least to the extent that the teacher plans the dialogue in advance and waits for certain answers, which are used, together with assigned case materials, to convey a particular mode of analysis or point of law. Moreover, law students, particularly in the second and third years, can choose not to participate in class and thus adopt a passive role for most, if not all, of a course.

At least in a general sense, traditional legal education also meets the andragogical concern that the content of law study should match law students' readiness to learn and their orientation to learning. By its very nature as professional training, legal education takes into account the students' approaching changes in social roles and orients learning to problems they are likely to encounter in law practice. After all, law schools exist to enable law students to become lawyers. After the first year, however, law students often view traditional methods of legal instruction and the preparation required for traditional law classes to be far removed from the type of professional education that they are ready to receive.

In sum, the basic elements of andragogy are found—at least to some extent—in the traditional methods of legal instruction. As Reich (1965, p. 1402) has observed, however, law students "are not really treated as adults. They are made to feel that they are beginning their education all over again, and the classes put very little emphasis upon individual work and thinking." This brief discussion, therefore, indicates that even traditional law teachers could improve their teaching with a careful reading of Knowles's work. For example, teachers could establish a greater sense of mutual inquiry with students by presenting at least a few new hypotheticals in each class that they had not worked through beforehand and letting the students know that they would be analyzing the issues together with the teacher for the first time. Another change that andragogical theory suggests—the use of problem-oriented materials—has already begun to take place in the traditional curriculum.

Andragogy and Clinical Legal Education

The clinical method is now an accepted technique for teaching law, notwithstanding the absence of either any empirical evidence of its effectiveness or any accepted educational basis for clinical programs. Andragogical theory provides a new and more substantial reason for welcoming this success because it shows how and why clinical legal education meets the educational needs of adult law students at the threshold of their professional careers.

Law students, of course, are a varied group. At a minimum, they are college graduates, and in many cases they have worked or have participated in some form of nonlaw, postgraduate education. Law students, therefore, clearly are adults, and the concerns that led to Knowles's andragogy thus are undoubtedly relevant to the field of legal education. Moreover, the first year of law school is uniformly perceived to be a unique experience for all law students—at least to the extent that they must be introduced to new areas of study and new methods of inquiry. As a result, the second and third years of law school must be designed to take into account that second- and third-year law students are different from those who first enter law school. Often by their second year, and almost certainly by their third year, law students have spent a summer working in a law office and may be working part time during the year; thus, the line between approaching entry and actual entry into the profession becomes blurred. How clinical legal education can meet the requirements of an andragogically based program of instruction for such experienced, adult law students is the subject of the following subsections.

Learning Through Mutual Inquiry by Teacher and Student. The recognition of adults as self-directing learners is the most important source of the departures from traditional pedagogy that are contained in Knowles's andragogy. The key methodological implication that follows from this recognition is the creation of a learning climate which includes what Knowles calls "a spirit of mutuality between teachers and students as joint inquirers." The idea is that teachers and their adult students, by working together, can create a setting in which the students are both acting consistently with their self-concept and benefiting from a teaching of their co-inquirer/teacher.

The clinical method of legal instruction applies this aspect of andragogical methodology in a way that is otherwise unavailable in the traditional law school curriculum. Bellow and Johnson (1971, p. 664) describe the unique "two-way street" of the clinical experience and its contrast with traditional law teaching as follows: "While the combative nature of the Socratic method tends to substitute sparring for learning, in a setting in which faculty and students find themselves in a shared enterprise, and in which inquiry is concerned with emotional reaction as well as analysis, the classroom, although rigorous, becomes a mutual search for solutions and knowledge. The instructor receives direct feedback indicating the relevance of his conceptual approach and is thereby forced to rethink his approaches and perceptions in light of the experiences of those whom he is teaching. If such a dynamic is implicit in the clinical methodology, this may be its most pervasive contribution to legal education."

The sharing of responsibility for clinic cases creates the proper atmosphere for an optimum andragogical learning experience, which takes place when the teacher uses a shared experience to point out and convey to the student points of law, methods of practice, and elements of the legal process. In this setting all learning does not have to come directly from the teacher; indeed, when a case is so novel or complex that the clinical teacher really must struggle together with the student, the answer may be that there is no answer, and the student both experiences and learns this limit of the rules of law.

Knowles and other educators working in the field of andragogy have found that the adult students for whom a self-directed learning setting is designed do not necessarily welcome this type of environment. When first placed in the position of having to participate actively in the planning and execution of a learning experience, students can be skeptical and even resentful before coming to realize the benefits of this aspect of andragogical methodology. Meltsner and Schrag (1976) also noted this problem in general terms when they experimented with various clinical models at Columbia Law School and moved toward a policy of requiring students to assume a more active role in representing clients. They noted that this change in approach affected both students and faculty: "Students and faculty had to come to terms with the passivity of the student role and the implicit assumption of much legal education that the faculty is solely responsible for whether learning takes place" (p. 584). Writing a few years later on their experiences with the clinical program that they eventually developed following earlier experimentation with various clinical models, Meltsner and Schrag (1978) reported instances in which students initially would be confused and even actively hostile when given responsibility for handling and administering their cases—that is, for planning and executing their clinical experience.

Active, Experiential Learning. Experiential learning has been promoted, of course, outside of the context of andragogical theory. In fact, experiential learning is a part of any professional education program that has a clinical component. An obvious example is medical training, which often is cited as a model for law schools to consider when designing a program of clinical legal education. The use of experiential learning in clinical programs ties the clinical method of legal instruction into the second key element of andragogical theory.

Clinical legal education is experiential learning both in terms of what the students bring to the learning setting and in terms of the experiences that the students work through in the clinical program itself. Law students, like any other adults, have their experiences in life to draw upon in learning. Perhaps more important, second-year and particularly third-year students often have law-related experience that they can use—and that they expect to use—in their last two years in law school. Finally, the experience of actual representation is available to the law student in the clinic. In sum, there is a role for experience in law teaching, and that role is best developed through the clinical method.

The range of experiences that are available to students in clinical education programs encompasses more than the normal lawyering skills of interviewing, counseling, negotiation, and trial and appellate advocacy. To the extent that broader human relations skills are a desirable subject of learning in law school, clinical legal education—with its emphasis on experiential learning—offers the opportunity to teach those skills. As Stone (1971, p. 392) stated, "The student's experience with human problems in the legal clinic always has the potential of being emotionally real. The student is directly involved in a case and can explore its social and psychological implications in as great a depth as his motivation allows."

Since clinical legal education provides law students with the opportunity to relate their own experiences, as well as their new lawyering experiences presented to them in clinical practice, to whatever is being taught in the clinical program, supervised practice can achieve the optimal level of educational meaning and impact. Stolz (1970, p. 138) perhaps summarized this notion best when he stated that "attitudes toward the world—morals, to use an older term—especially insofar as they influence behavior, probably come more from classmates and experience than anything that happens in the classroom. Perhaps including clinical exposure in legal education will improve the law school's capacity to reach the deeper motivations of its students and thus to influence their careers." Bellow and Johnson (1971, p. 693) found that students handling cases in their clinic "began to be far more interested in their own experiences as a source of theoretical generalization, and far more concerned with theory as a tool for defining and understanding experience, than they were when they first started." When students use the experiences that they obtain in the clinic as a tool for learning, "the clinical process radically alters the usual relationship of faculty to student. The students have, at last, a body of their own experience which they can compare to the faculty's assertions and statements" (p. 693).

   Learning, Students' Social Roles, and Problem Solving. The final two elements of Knowles's andragogy—students' changing social roles and their readiness to learn, and students' focus on problem solving and their orientation to learning—also fit the clinical method of legal instruction. These elements, however, are perhaps less uniquely suited to clinical legal education than learning through mutual inquiry and active experiential learning. Since law students are about to make one of the major social role changes of their lives—becoming a lawyer— they are naturally ready to learn about law and lawyering. Regardless of the method of instruction, they will view whatever they learn as some form of preparation for solving problems that they will face in their professional careers. One need not enter into the debate over the quality and relevance of every part of the law school curriculum to recognize that—at least to some extent—legal education generally is andragogically sound in the categories of readiness to learn and orientation to learning.

   Nevertheless, the clinical method of legal instruction does apply andragogical methodology in these areas more directly and regularly than does traditional legal education. When a student who is about to become a lawyer enters a clinical learning environment and is taught through actual representation of a client in a legal dispute, optimal compliance with the andragogically dictated sensitivity to the student's readiness to learn is attained. Clinical legal education epitomizes andragogy's problem-centered methodology. Not only are issues and material presented as problems, but also "legal training is immediately useful. The student must learn or he will be embarrassed before real clients, lawyers, and judges" (Meltsner and Schrag, 1976, p. 584).

Toward an Andragogically Based Model
for Clinical Legal Education

As previously discussed, proponents of clinical legal education usually have supported their case by emphasizing the new areas of study that can be introduced into the law school curriculum. Most critics of the clinical method also have focused on the substantive content, arguing that what is taught in clinical programs need not or should not be taught in law school at all. Only recently have clinicians begun to go beyond the debate over the value of the substantive content of clinical programs to look critically at their own methodology and its implementation. These efforts differ fundamentally from the literature on effective models for clinical instruction, which are concerned primarily with questions of technique, and from guidelines for clinical legal education, which seek to establish the characteristics that clinical programs should have without any particular reference to a theory of learning.

Andragogy can be extremely useful in this critical examination of clinical methodology because it can provide the coherent, theoretical framework of a methodology-based justification for clinical education that has been missing in the attempts to establish various content-based justifications. As discussed above, andragogy has become established as a significant theory of instruction for adult learners, and its methodology is consistent with the general methods used to implement clinical programs. When viewed as an educational basis for clinical legal education, andragogy can be useful to clinicians in their attempts to improve the clinical method of law teaching, to take full advantage of a clinical setting for legal instruction, and to establish clinical legal education as an essential element of professional legal education.

Andragogical theory need not provide a single, definitive model for clinical legal education to be useful. Indeed, uncritical reliance on the principles of andragogy is unwarranted if for no other reason than because andragogy is still a developing field. Nonetheless, the four central elements of andragogy suggest the beginnings of a model for clinical legal education that addresses the three major issues which legal educators have debated in this field: the use of actual clients rather than simulations, the method and extent of supervision by clinical faculty, and the types of cases to be handled in a clinical program.

Actual Client Representation. An andragogically based model for clinical legal education should rely heavily on actual client representation. A relationship based on shared, mutual inquiry simply cannot be established through the alternative technique of simulation. An effective, competent simulation must be preplanned so that, even if the instructor participates in the simulation, the law student knows that there is not a completely shared inquiry or a co-counsel relationship between student and teacher. In fact, it is likely that the instructor would not participate at all in the simulation and instead let the student work through the problem alone. In an actual client setting, on the other hand, the student and teacher are forced to work together at every step in the case because crucial decisions may have to be made at any time that could be critical to the client's claim or defense. As a result, a co-counsel relationship develops between the student and the teacher that continues throughout the student's involvement in the case and offers the student opportunities for valuable learning experiences both at expected and unexpected moments during representation. The differences between the use of actual clients and the use of simulations in establishing an atmosphere of mutual inquiry can be seen perhaps most clearly in the area of decisions on case strategy. Such decisions are so important in actual client representation that the clinical instructor must examine and participate in the student's analysis and judgments. In a simulation setting, it is most likely that the instructor would not participate in any case strategy at all, and the advantages of such an experience would be lost.

Although an actual client representation setting makes it possible for the student and the teacher to establish a continuous co-counsel relationship, the proposition does not follow that the teacher and the student should work together on every aspect of all the student's cases. The optimal andragogical setting is one in which students are given the opportunity to learn through their own initiative by working together with—rather than being dominated by—the teacher. When students and teachers work together on actual cases, a true "climate of adultness" consistent with the self-concept of law students is maintained because the students practice together with their instructors in a setting in which their participation means something not only to themselves but also to the instructors with whom they work. A teacher representing an actual client in conjunction with a student relies heavily on the student's work and, therefore, is deeply concerned with how the student performs during the representation. In such a setting, even though the instructors are set apart because of the knowledge that they can convey to students who are working with them, they are not removed entirely from the process of learning, as tends to be the case with simulations. Instructors thus are far less likely to engage in the type of one-way transmittal of knowledge that is antithetical to andragogy.

Actual client representation is also necessary to involve law students in andragogically sound, active, experiential learning. Although role playing is a type of experiential learning, law students must be allowed to practice law on behalf of real clients if a clinical program is to take full advantage of the role of experience in adult learning. Actual client representation is real and, therefore, andragogically effective. Simulations, on the other hand, are recognized as imaginary and thus are less effective as learning experiences, since law students may not be willing to relate what they were taught in simulations to other lawyering experiences that they have had or will have outside of law school.

Similarly, while clinical legal education possesses the potential to take full advantage of law students' readiness to learn, the lack of reality inherent in simulations can undermine that potential. When representing actual clients, law students are in fact lawyers; accordingly, they are fully aware that what they are learning relates to what they came to law school to learn. In a simulation setting, however, students can become unsure about the relationship between the simulation and actual practice of law, and, consequently, they can become less interested in what the teacher is trying to teach.

Close Supervision by Clinical Faculty. Proper implementation of andragogical methodology in a law school clinical setting requires that clinical faculty supervise students closely and directly. Probably the most important element of an andragogically sound model for clinical supervision is the establishment of a co-counsel relationship between the student and the teacher. This method of supervision allows students to learn through mutual inquiry, which is consistent with andragogical theory, and to make the most of the learning opportunities that are available through actual client representation. Placing students outside of a law school–controlled setting in which they are likely either to work unattended or to be limited to observing the "real lawyers" in the office would dilute the educational value of having students represent actual clients. Both of these circumstances are totally at odds with the type of shared responsibility for learning that andragogical theory envisions.

Clinical faculty, however, must do more than just work together with students on cases. Clinical instructors must be willing and able to teach their students once a proper andragogical setting is established. Although the teacher and the student working together as co-counsel create Knowles's "spirit of mutuality," the teacher is largely responsible for taking advantage of this setting and turning it into an effective learning opportunity. A law teacher working on a case with a law student must be able to guide the student toward learning whatever lawyering skills or substantive material the student needs to know to participate effectively in handling the case. This guidance can be provided without undermining the co-counsel relationship between the teacher and the student or sacrificing the teacher's responsibility to teach, particularly if the teacher follows the andragogical prescriptions of being sensitive to the student's role as a self-directed learner in planning the learning experience and of giving the student the opportunity to choose how to make the most of the learning opportunity. Thus, the teacher and student should share the assignment of responsibilities in a particular case.

Since clinical teachers are still teachers and their co-counsel are still their students, the possibility always exists that mutual inquiry will be forsaken and that the teacher will take control of the representation by lecturing to the student and directing him or her to do what the teacher knows—or has determined—must be done. An andragogical model would specifically discourage this type of supervision, except to the extent that it is necessary to ensure competent representation in a particular case. Instead of extensive lecturing and excessive direction, students should be encouraged to decide when to ask questions and when to explore for answers on their own. In other words, the student should help the teacher decide when the teacher needs to direct and teach and when the student can be left alone. Close supervision, therefore, does not mean a constant faculty presence.

Evaluation, of course, is an important element of any educational program, and students in a clinical setting must be evaluated as well. Although traditional grading methods usually are based on the one-sided evaluation of students by teachers—which is disfavored in andragogical theory—the solution is not necessarily to eliminate grades or to reduce the rigor of the evaluation process by means of a pass/fail system. Instead, the student, together with the instructor, should assess the student's performance at critical points during representation in order to evaluate the work in the case, to determine the student's learning needs and to measure the student's overall progress. Just how students finally are graded or evaluated at the end of the course is not so important, since the positive, andragogically based process of shared evaluation between the student and the teacher already will have taken place.

Cases Selected for Educational Value. Although the use of actual client representation and close, direct supervision by clinical faculty are the most important elements of an andragogically based model for clinical legal education, andragogical theory can be implemented most effectively in a law school clinic if the cases that are selected for law students maximize the educational value of their clinical experience. This does not mean that by adopting this approach law school clinics must forgo representing groups of clients that traditionally have been underrepresented or providing a socially valuable by-product of legal services to the community. Indeed, cases arguably should be chosen that demonstrate the positive role which the legal profession can play in society in order to instill in law students a responsible professional attitude at a time when they are particularly receptive to learning about the profession.

One goal in an andragogical case selection process should be to choose from among all the types of cases that are available the ones that are the most likely to appear to students to be relevant both to their changing roles as student lawyers and to their upcoming entry into the legal profession. In other words, to maximize law students' readiness to learn from a clinical experience, the cases must present real legal disputes and must require the use of lawyering skills. Thus, an andragogical model would include a case selection process that would favor cases such as administrative appeals from denials of various public benefits and contested eviction proceedings in which law students can act as lawyers, rather than cases such as multiple debt actions without viable defenses that require financial counseling and cases involving routine applications for benefits that can be resolved by a case worker or a social worker. For similar reasons, students should be able to choose to the extent possible those cases that appear most interesting to them.

This application of andragogical theory does not mean that cases would be selected to teach students how to handle a particular type of problem or how to practice in a particular court; instead, cases would be chosen because they emphasize the fundamental elements of law practice. In this way the maximum number of students will be motivated to learn, and what they learn will have the broadest impact on their future practice. The use of a limited range of cases that allow the instruction to concentrate on general principles of trial practice, the lawyering process, or professional responsibility will make the absence of certain other types of cases that are not usually represented in the clinical case load irrelevant. The important point from an andragogical perspective is that students must be able to relate what they are learning from the clinic experience to their own projected future careers. Clinical programs operating under this type of case selection process will capitalize on law students' particular readiness to learn and their orientation toward learning; they will also avoid the danger of becoming a narrow, mechanical course in how to file a divorce or how to defend against a public housing eviction in the local trial court.

Finally, case selection can be important both in the establishment of an atmosphere of mutuality between the student and the teacher and in the creation of a setting for active, experiential learning. The most routine types of cases, such as uncontested, no-fault divorces, should be excluded because a meaningful co-counsel relationship cannot be established when students are handling cases that are too simple to require any serious work by the faculty. On the other hand, other relatively routine matters, such as certain tort cases, can be valuable learning experiences because there will be genuine mutual inquiry between the student and the teacher whenever they work together preparing a particular case or handling that particular case on behalf of a client. Extremely complex cases can present similar problems if students are unable to assume any significant responsibility in the client's representation. In such a case, students effectively would be removed from the active experience of representing a client, or they would be limited to performing such simple tasks that the establishment of a co-counsel relationship would be impossible. This problem can be avoided, of course, by assigning students manageable portions of complex cases and by choosing cases that are challenging but still within law students' capabilities.

Conclusion

Clinical legal education offers law students the opportunity to work together with faculty on cases that present the types of problems which law students want to learn how to solve. Andragogical theory holds that adult learners such as law students should be taught through mutual inquiry between teacher and student, through the use of actual experience, and with the recognition that students are ready and oriented to learn about that which they perceive to be relevant to their current social roles and professional goals. The clinical method of law teaching adds an important andragogical component to professional legal education; at the same time, andragogy provides both a theoretical basis for clinical legal education and some suggestions about a model for implementing the clinical method. Clinical legal education works in large part because it is andragogically sound. Legal education in general can benefit from andragogical theory, and the recognition of the andragogical basis of clinical legal education perhaps can hasten the integration of the clinical method into the mainstream of legal education.

3

Social Work Education
at the University of Georgia

Allie C. Kilpatrick, Kathryn H. Thompson,
Herbert H. Jarrett, Jr., Richard J. Anderson

An early and comprehensive attempt to apply the andragogical model to social work education was undertaken by the University of Georgia School of Social Work. This selection provides a clear description of the process used in helping students and faculty move from a pedagogical model to an andragogical model. It closes with a thoughtful presentation of "principles" and "pitfalls" gleaned from the authors' experience.

Allie Kilpatrick, Kathryn Thompson, Herbert Jarrett, and Richard Anderson are members of the faculty of the School of Social Work at the University of Georgia, Athens, Georgia.

Special features:

- Events leading to the application of the andragogical model
- The pedagogical legacy in social work education
- Movement from pedagogy to andragogy in the program sequence
- Gearing learning experiences to learning styles
- Use of learning contracts in courses and field placements
- The student advisement process
- Evaluation of learning outcomes
- Faculty roles
- An experimental andragogical course
- Constructing competency models
- Student-developed course designs
- Orientation of students to self-directed learning
- Suggestions and pitfalls

The University of Georgia School of Social Work has a rich history of experimenting with educational models designed to maximize student learning. Before andragogy became a well-known term, the School of Social Work offered a "Living Learning Institute" in the summer of 1970. Baccalaureate social work educators from all over the southeastern United States, along with some of their students, were invited to join us. Various teaching styles were utilized in a creative atmosphere. This institute, sponsored by the Southern Regional Education Board (SREB), was led by the late Paul Deutschberger, assistant dean and chairman of the School of Social Work's curriculum committee. Because of his ability to provide curricular leadership, several faculty members, in examining the nature of the learning climate, were pulled toward this new approach called "andragogy." Malcolm Knowles provided leadership in a 1974 retreat for the entire faculty and some field instructors and students. This retreat led to presented papers and published articles in the area, and to our presentation here.

After a brief overview of the historical development of social work education, we provide several illustrations of how we implement andragogy into the undergraduate social work (BSW) and graduate social work (MSW) programs at the University of Georgia. We believe that the examples used demonstrate a continuum approach, culminating in the most independent learning in the later stages of the MSW program. Naturally, the most elementary forms of andragogy are introduced at the baccalaureate level. Finally, we present guiding principles, drawn from our experience, which we hope will be helpful to others who are applying the principles of andragogy. Some pitfalls to be avoided are also discussed.

Historical Development of Social Work Education

Social work education developed during the latter part of the nineteenth century (Bernard, 1977; Levy, 1981), when the recently created social agencies began employing and training staff members. Soon, training schools were established to provide instruction in job responsibilities selected by the employer;

and the partnership of social welfare services and social work education began. Early in the twentieth century, the training schools started affiliating with colleges and universities, evolving into graduate education programs with practical training in the agencies. This practical training is now called "fieldwork" or "field instruction." While this partnership of social agencies and universities has continued, at various times one partner has exerted more influence than the other. Even today, social agency leadership and the faculties of schools of social work must continually mediate this partnership.

The agency-school partnership is a great strength to social work education, but a tension-filled relationship. In general, the social agency personnel seek to have students learn practical, applied skills and knowledge that will support doing a particular job. Faculties in the schools of social work have tended to move over time from the early training approach to a greater emphasis on theory, research, and knowledge generation. Mature social workers still have a tendency to remark, "He was 'trained' at a certain school" or "She is a 'trained' social worker." The focus of social work training has been pedagogical and control oriented. The andragogical approach to independence and self-direction is more common in the programs heavily influenced by the university model of graduate education.

As a result of this dynamic and tension-filled partnership, the emphasis of graduate programs has moved back and forth, depending on which partner was currently holding the greater power. When public bureaucracies became employers of social workers, the values of these organizations were imposed on the ethics of social work. Sentiments were expressed about the need for social work students to be "good" employees first, and professionals second. A large component of the preferred behavior was an ability to follow the rules, to accept direction (usually dignified by calling it "supervision"), and to be humble and compliant.

These preferred behaviors are, of course, distinctly not andragogical. Because social work faculty are themselves socialized into the behaviors of the typical bureaucratic system, they are usually unaware of the issues involved. Hence, efforts to have students take more responsibility for their own education not only result in problems of credibility from students as they struggle with new educational expectations, but faculty and agency personnel often fail to provide the supports needed for growth and mastery. The traditional words and phrases of social work education illustrate this issue:

The applicant is "judgmental" (nonjudgmental is valued).

Students are "assigned" advisers.

Students are to be "assigned" (or to be placed in) field-work.

The curriculum is composed of "required" courses, since students do not know enough to make good choices.

Students are "supervised," rather than "instructed," in the practicum.

With the legacy of social work education arising from the "training" of good employees for a particular job, there has been inertia among social workers in general to allow for individual learning, curricular adaptations, and student choices, or to recognize student competency acquired outside of the educational program. This combination of tradition and circumstance has tended to devalue students as individuals with capacity to direct their own lives. It has produced unneeded stress in students as learners. Faculty have noted this stress and—demonstrating a lack of awareness of their own part in it—have suggested that certain students would benefit from treatment.

However, as the professionalization of the occupation occurred, a greater proportion of faculty have pushed to trust social work students as partners in the learning process, rather than as subjects to be trained. For example, application interviews are typically no longer required for checking up on the applicant but offered as a source of program information. Students are no longer "counseled out" for improper attitudes. If they are to be dismissed from the program, it must be because of failure in academic standards. Students may elect and change their academic adviser. Perhaps most important of all, many social agency personnel seek to have social work students come to their agency for their practicum because they realize that they can learn from students, as well as having students learn from them.

Application of the Andragogical Model

BSW Program. A conceptual drawing of the scheme of andragogy in the baccalaureate program at the University of Georgia School of Social Work might be depicted in a bell-like structure (see Figure 1). At the top of the bell, the student is

Figure 1. Movement Toward Andragogy.

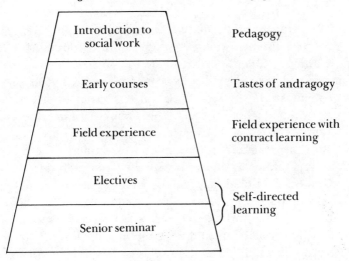

being introduced to the profession, and much basic information needs to be digested. Hence, the format is largely that of pedagogy. As the student matriculates through those early courses, a gentle introduction to andragogy is planned.

In the sophomore year, students take a second introductory course. At this point we introduce them to formulating their own educational outcomes for this course. This is usually the first time that students have been asked to think for themselves about what direction their learning might take. The new experience usually results in some tentativeness about speaking up for what they really want out of the course. Instructor openness and support will usually help as the group of students involved are asked to come to some consensus about the final state of their objectives or educational outcomes. The instructor's role is to facilitate this andragogical process and to indicate what is possible within the time frame and scope of the course.

During the junior year, as the students approach their first field placement, they are asked by their educational adviser to examine their own learning styles (experiential or conceptual or some other style). The adviser helps the student make this evaluation. This information is passed on to the agency field instructor, who then can structure learning experiences to "fit" the learning style of the particular student.

As students matriculate through the BSW program, they are expected to exercise increasingly more autonomy for their own learning. Students are expected to select topics and style for individual term papers plus other research reports or even independent studies. After these various tastes of self-directed learning, students finally reach the senior seminar, the course taken during the last quarter that students are on campus for their BSW program. In this final course, students are asked to critique and evaluate their entire college curriculum: the adequacy of instructional design, the instructors' teaching skills, and the students' own acceptance of responsibility for the learning process that has just taken place. This process is accomplished through class discussion and a paper in which students assess their learning and indicate why it was or was not significant. Later in the course, students are asked to assess their post-BSW learning needs—a look at lifelong learning, with the recognition that most of it from now on will truly be self-directed.

MSW Program. The bell-shaped drawing is also applicable to the graduate program. For example, in the beginning phases of the MSW program, instruction is more narrow and hence pedagogical. At this stage the student is getting fundamental information and orientation to the profession and is deciding on a specialization. However, as the students select their specialization, the bell-like figure gets wider and they have more opportunity for andragogy.

Because the practicum comes early in the MSW program and exemplifies the application of the andragogical model, this part of the program is presented in detail. Following this presentation an example of the application of andragogy to course work is given.

The Practicum: BSW and MSW Field Instruction. The most consistent application of andragogy in the BSW and MSW programs of the University of Georgia School of Social Work may be seen in the practicum. From the initial selection of the practicum site in a social service program through the evaluation of student learning, the philosophy and principles of andragogy are manifest.

In social work education, the practicum or internship has traditionally been termed the "field *placement*." As mentioned earlier, the terminology reflects the customary process by which the professional school "places" the students into a social service program selected *by* the school *for* the student. This traditional model for field education emphasizes the relatively passive and dependent role of the student and conveys the assumption that the "school knows best what is 'good' for the student." In contrast, at the University of Georgia, the selection of the practicum begins with the educational advisement process, whereby the student and adviser identify educational objectives for the student's practicum experience. These individualized objectives incorporate the student and adviser judgment of gaps in the student's current competencies and the student's own personal/professional goals and objectives with those objectives established by the school for each practicum course in the sequence.

Meanwhile, the school has administratively maintained a bank of practicum resources from which it can draw to "match up" with the learning needs identified through this advising process. To facilitate this "match," students are then referred to faculty who serve in the liaison capacity with several practicum sites previously evaluated and approved by the school to provide field instruction. From consultation with the liaison faculty, students identify several programs most likely to provide the kind of practicum experience that will meet their objectives and are most compatible with their learning style. They are then referred to these agencies to interview for a practicum. The appropriate agency personnel are alerted by the faculty liaison to expect a call from the student for an appointment to explore the potential internship. These agency personnel are also provided with copies of the student's résumé of previous experience and education, information about performance in the academic program to date, and the individualized practicum objectives identified by the student and educational adviser. Students are simultaneously provided with information about the experience of potential field instructors and, whenever possible, the names and phone numbers of students who have previously completed practica in the selected sites.

The interview between the student and the agency is arranged by the student and is not attended by any faculty member. Moreover, the interview is considered to be exploratory on both sides, in no way obligating either the student or the agency to contract for the student's internship. Utilizing whatever consultation may be appropriate from the educational adviser, the faculty liaison, former students, and others in the community, both the student and the agency make a determination about the "rightness of fit," based on the information about the student's learning needs, the in-person interview, and assessment of the agency's current potential for providing a relevant learning experience. Unless a student's interests are so specialized that the actual resources are limited to only one program setting, students typically interview in two to three programs, quite frequently interviewing agency administrators and other staff as well as the staff social worker who will provide the field instruction in the practicum.

While the process is administratively more complicated than the traditional method of "slotting" students into the agency "placement" selected by the professional school, it takes advantage of the basic principles of andragogy. The students' learning needs and interests are the starting point for selection of the practicum site; the school and its faculty are utilized as knowledgeable "consultants" for providing a range of resources (alternative practicum sites), rather than as the "experts" in control. "Placement failures" are rare in our school, justifying the initial cost in time and personnel through savings in both time and human anguish which result from a bad match between the student intern and the practicum setting.

What happens after the selection of a practicum site for a student varies greatly among professional schools. Some turn the student over to the agency, trusting in the agency's ability to teach the desired competencies. Others specify not only the objectives of the practicum but the specific task assignments to be provided by the agency for each student. As with the practicum selection process, our school begins this component of the practicum with the practicum objectives, including overall objectives established by the school for each practicum and individualized objectives of the student. A learning plan is developed to portray the learning strategies (in the form of task assignments) to be provided by the agency for implementing these objectives. The learning plan also specifies what the evidence of accomplishment will be (including the processes and the evaluators to be used as well as the criteria for evaluation) on each objective. Exhibit 1 is a sample of a learning plan covering one of the objectives in the first-quarter practicum of our MSW program.

Within the first two weeks of each quarter's practicum, the student develops and submits the learning plan to the school's faculty practicum liaison. Accomplishing this task is one objective of the first-quarter practicum and requires that the student make proactive use of the field instructor's knowledge of potential task assignments in the agency. The plan is signed by both the student and the field instructor and, when ratified by the faculty liaison, becomes the contract between the student and agency for the student's learning in the practicum. Liaison faculty usually contribute most to recommendations about appropriate evaluation processes and criteria; they also assess the overall plan for the "fit" of task assignments and the evaluation of learning outcomes to the objectives and may recommend changes in the proposed plan to enhance those connections.

Exhibit 1. Learning Plan Used at University of Georgia School of Social Work.

Student: _____   Dates Covered by Plan: _____

Agency: _____

Learning Objectives	Learning Strategies/Resources	Evidence of Accomplishment (Criteria, Processes, Judged by Whom)
The student will demonstrate social work practice competencies in interpersonal skills.		
a. With staff	a. Attend and actively participate when appropriate in staff meetings and committees, clinical or planning conferences; interact informally with staff outside of structured meetings; seek out staff as appropriate to expertise and/or organization role.	a. Feedback from field instructor and other staff indicate that student attends to others' communications; shows empathy and respect for others, their concerns, needs, viewpoints; responds undefensively to appropriate criticism or differences in opinion; expresses self directly, with clarity and focus; is appropriately sensitive to informal structure as well as formal structure in organization.
b. With clients/client system	b. Interpersonal interaction with clients through case assignments, including intake interviews, crisis calls or walk-ins, evaluations, and ongoing clinical interventions with individuals, couples, families, and groups. Tape-record interactions with clients (audio and audiovisual whenever possible).	b. In field instruction sessions, student reviews interactions with clients, giving examples of different interpersonal communications in varying situations, identifying patterns in responses to clients, assessing impact of communication on client(s) and the social work relationship. Feedback from cotherapist, field instructor, and other staff verifies that student demon-

Serve as cotherapist with other staff in: group treatment; family treatment.

Interview clients in a room with a one-way window through which field instructor (or other staff) view interactions with clients.

Interview clients in the presence of field instructor or other staff.

strates interpersonal skills of active listening; attends to affective as well as content components of client's communication; responds empathetically; attends to nonverbal as well as verbal communication; clarifies client's communication when appropriate; manifests appropriate use of exploratory responses; states information clearly and in language that is easily understandable to client(s); is appropriately assertive and presents own role in relationship with clarity.

c. With others in the community

c. Case assignments which require case management activities—brokering and linking, mobilizing resources, and involvement of other service providers.

Assignment to represent agency at community meetings (either alone or with other staff).

Design and implement (either alone or with other staff as assigned) needs assessment, program plan, or program evaluation which necessitates contact with others in the community.

c. In field instruction sessions, student reviews interactions with others in the community. Evidence demonstrates the student's ability to clearly convey information; advocate for the client; undefensively receive feedback from collateral personnel on own performance; accurately analyze barriers to effective communication with others in the community; and represent the agency in a way that engenders respect for the agency within the community.

Student's Signature —————— Field Instructor's Signature —————— Date ——————

Practicum objectives specified by the school for each of the practica require a progression of *increasing self-direction* in the student's demonstration of professional competencies. Hence, in the final practicum the student performs with considerable autonomy and discretion, requiring minimal direction from field instructors in the execution of core practice competencies.

The evaluation of the student's accomplishments during the practicum is focused on the *learning* (instead of just the performance) outcomes of the practicum. For example, in the evaluation of the MSW student's accomplishments in the practicum, the student cites "critical incidents" to portray the way in which specified objectives were engaged; generalizations about those incidents related to the criteria specified on the learning plan are provided by the field instructor. Together, these form the "evidence" for the evaluation and recommended practicum grade arising from the student's activity in the agency.

The expectation that the student will be proactive and assertive throughout is inherent in the school's practicum design. Students not only participate actively in the presentation of their individualized practicum goals and interests; they also carry primary responsibility for assessing the "rightness of fit" between those objectives and the alternative practicum resources provided by the school. Once the practicum site is selected, they must continue to identify and contribute to the assessment of alternative task assignments that will facilitate learning outcomes to meet the practicum objectives. The expectation for increasing self-direction is specifically incorporated into the objectives of the practicum sequence.

In contrast, the school's responsibilities are facilitative rather than controlling or directive. Faculty responsibilities (and expertise) are in the provision, maintenance, and monitoring of (1) the processes by which students may diagnose learning needs and engage in practicum experiences that promote relevant learning outcomes; (2) alternative practicum sites and personnel capable of implementing practicum components of the school's curriculum; and (3) the processes by which students and their agency-based field instructor may present evidence of the students' achievements on the practicum objectives for evaluation and educational planning.

Course Work: An Example. The following example was selected as a peak experience in andragogical teaching/learning. The course was an elective seminar in the final quarter of the MSW program of study. One of the authors implemented a design for this seminar, "Supervision and Teaching in Social Work Practice," a major objective of which is for students to learn the philosophy and principles of andragogy. Extraordinary efforts were made in this seminar to actualize our commitment to the educational philosophy and principles of andragogy.

Several key features contributed to the instructor's ability to introduce andragogical innovation in this particular course and at this particular moment.

1. The course was offered as a "seminar," indicating an expectation that participants would contribute substantially to the content and direction of the course; and it is an elective course, stimulating enrollment of persons with more than the customary level of commitment to the learning by virtue of their own choice.

2. Participants were to be students the instructor had known very well over the previous year, both as a course instructor and as the liaison faculty member responsible for their three-quarter practica. Therefore, the instructor knew what to expect from the seminar members and—because of the particular group of students on this occasion—she knew that their engagement in learning would be substantial. She also knew from her association with them that most had well-developed capacities for self-direction. In fact, most of the seminar members had participated in the use of learning contracts and andragogical methods in a seminar with another of the authors during the previous quarter, and all had developed the learning plans/contracts described earlier for the three previous quarters in practica.

3. Because the seminar was a course offered at the *end* of the MSW program, it did not bear the burden of quality con-

trol carried by courses scheduled early in the program of study and therefore was not expected to serve as a student screening device.

4. The instructor had taught this seminar approximately twice a year for the past two years and had taught modules in the seminar for the past eight years to a wide range of constituencies. She was therefore very comfortable with the content areas and had a well-developed bank of teaching/learning resources.

Two decisions were made by the course instructor prior to the convening of participants: (1) Only the agenda for the first two class meetings was to be prepared in advance. These two meetings would be used to provide the processes and relevant information out of which participants would be assisted in planning the seminar design and content. (2) All students would receive an "A" grade. The purpose of this decision was to remove one of the major impediments to the implementation of the philosophy of andragogy in the academic setting. The instructor wanted to test the consequences of removing the grading power from the dynamics of the student/teacher relationship and to determine whether energies customarily bound up in preoccupation with grade-conscious production would be freed for learning. The instructor also wanted to free her own time and energy from validating the separation of the "A" products from the "B" products (no greater range was expected in the group), so that she could more creatively and productively facilitate student learning. Both of these decisions were dependent on the four factors previously cited as the "experimental conditions" under which the innovations could be responsibly considered.

In the first class session, the grading decision was announced, along with its rationale and educational justification, and a syllabus describing activities for only two class meetings was distributed. The intent to teach course design by "doing" the design for this seminar was presented and explicated. The remainder of the session was devoted to engaging students in alternative methods of course design. Teaching/learning activities developed to "experience" the various methods were led by the instructor to generate data about desired competencies for the practice of supervision and teaching, the students' learning needs and interests, and the resources available for learning. By the end of the four-hour session, students had the following resources available for planning the seminar:

1. The priorities for learning among the class members; these had been developed in the session through Nominal Group Process (Delbeque and Van de Ven, 1971).
2. Several competency profiles related to the practice of supervision and teaching. The class had generated one of a "model" supervisor; the instructor provided a profile she had developed for field instruction of students in the practicum (Thompson, 1978); the instructor also provided a recent listing of supervisory competencies developed by the National Association of Social Workers (1981).
3. The syllabi for the seminar as it had been taught in previous years, including resources and descriptions of learning projects.
4. A list of the human resources in the group. This had been developed in the session through student introductions of themselves, in an exercise similar to Knowles's (1975) Human Resources Exercise, and their listing of experiences relevant to the course. A list of the instructor's resources—modules on specific content, bibliographies, films and other teaching materials, and other human resources and knowledge/skills relevant to design and content—was given to the participants.
5. Basic information about the principles of andragogy and references for study (Knowles, 1975, 1978).

The initial assignment, then, in the first week of the seminar was for students—either singly or in small groups of their own choosing—to design the seminar and be prepared to critique the design on the basis of andragogy.

In the second session of the seminar, members considered and critiqued proposals that had been developed during the week by participants. Two of the proposals were quite extensive, one having been developed by a group of five class members, and encompassed the entire time frame for the quarter. Since the various proposals were in many ways similar, the group members realized that much of their learning could be undertaken together rather than in separate independent study by individuals.

At the end of this session, the students were somewhat overwhelmed by the amount of information and array of options. The instructor then proposed the group's adoption of three teaching/learning strategies to meet several common objectives emerging from the various proposals. The instructor further suggested that she reconcile the various proposals and present a plan for the remainder of the seminar design at the next session. Not only did the group ratify these recommendations but almost half of the class expressed interest in "watching" the instructor "at work" to consolidate the various proposals. The instructor scheduled a half-day session convenient to the members. Over one third of the class attended and observed the instructor "at the work of design"; the instructor explained her thinking on various judgments about appropriate resources, sequencing of activities and content, and other aspects of the seminar. Thus, a plan was developed to match learning resources with the key areas of interest expressed by the group members. The entire seminar plan and schedule were reviewed and adopted by the group at its third meeting.

At the quarter's end, the instructor and the students considered the seminar to have been a peak educational experience. The final seminar meeting was utilized to critique various teaching/learning modules and projects as well as the overall seminar design and process from the perspective of andragogy. The instructor and students shared the anxieties they had felt early in the experience as well as the excitement of discovering new and unanticipated possibilities for learning in this emergent design based on andragogy. They recalled that students had "tested" the instructor, individually and in the group, from time to time, almost as if to say: "Do you *really* mean it? We really *are* in charge of our learning?" Most felt strongly that the removal of the grading from the course dynamics had freed them to engage in more meaningful and creative learning, as had been hoped. One member felt that he was less productive since he wasn't "working for a grade," and another commented on the "loss" she felt over not having that as a measure of the instructor's assessment of her.

One of the most interesting aspects of this experiment was that students extended themselves far beyond the "course requirements." Not only did the students attend and contribute enthusiastically to the planned group sessions, but they also attended "extra" sessions offering relevant content. Moreover, they generated additional meetings with the instructor related to learning interests. In fact, at times the instructor felt that students were willing to commit more time than she had available. They clearly made more of a commitment to their learning than any previous group of students the instructor had taught in seminars using a more traditional format and design. That this commitment and level of enthusiasm were generated at the end of the students' arduous program of study and with the assumed incentive of the grade removed is telling testimony to the power of andragogy in action.

Principles and Pitfalls

Some overall guiding principles can be drawn from the experiences of this School of Social Work for the benefit of other schools that would apply the andragogical model to social work education. There are also, however, certain pitfalls that could militate against the effectiveness of this model. These principles and pitfalls have been gleaned from almost twenty years of school history, the last ten of which all four authors have shared together.

Suggestions. The following suggestions are especially relevant for the application of the andragogical model to social work education.

1. *Consider external constraints.* The setting of a college or university imposes constraints that must be taken into consideration. Most students are accustomed to a pedagogical model, where the instructor gives them a syllabus with objectives,

assigned readings, and course outline already formulated. Indeed, faculty are required to have their syllabi approved by curriculum committees and their textbooks ordered well in advance of the beginning of the course. A certain number of contact hours are required. The instructor must give grades, which specify the level at which the student has met the objectives. The size of the class, the level of the learner (basic or advanced courses, baccalaureate or master's level), and the hours scheduled for class sessions are factors over which individual instructors have no control. Also, final exams are scheduled by the university and assumed to be appropriate as a teaching/learning strategy.

Efforts must be made to work within this imposed structure in order to allow students to be increasingly self-directed. Within basic university and accreditation requirements, schools or departments have some flexibility in structuring their programs. Instructors also have much freedom in their own classrooms. Learning contracts, projects, and experiential techniques *can* be designed to promote self-directed learning and to make use of students as learning resources for one another.

Grading is one of the most difficult issues. Individualized contract learning, criterion-referenced evaluation, and evidence that is validated in various ways by many people may be anxiety producing for instructors—and for students—at first. Care must be taken to ensure that the student's verification plan is specific, measurable, and achievable. Evaluation criteria in the learning contract must be clear, specific, and objective. When the criteria are ambiguous, general, and subjective, then grading is difficult. Students may think they can say (as happened in our experience), "I did it and I deserve an 'A.' You must trust me." The use of only subjective evaluation from students themselves must be avoided.

2. *Be aware of internal conditions.* The phase of the program that students are in contributes to their receptivity of the andragogical model. Social work students who have been together since entering the program will likely have developed subgroupings, cliques, and various norms and may tend to use

only their subgroup as a learning resource. Furthermore, since the stress level is higher at some phases than at others, students may resist the introduction of different learning methods during high-stress periods. Finally, if previous experiences with faculty and staff have tended to encourage dependency, students may become angered by experiential techniques and believe that faculty are not really teaching unless they transmit information through lectures. Previous experiences of the students must be taken into consideration when one is initiating an andragogical model.

3. *Utilize andragogy in the most appropriate areas first.* Beginning courses in both baccalaureate and master's programs are generally more structured. Social work is a new content area for many students. Therefore, they will likely be dependent on the teacher until they have acquired enough content to engage in self-directed learning. Professors with a more pedagogical style would be best utilized in the early phases of the program. The andragogical approach can best be introduced in the advising process, then in the practicum experiences, and finally in the elective seminars during the final quarters. Faculty who are committed to the andragogical method of teaching/ learning would be best utilized in these areas.

4. *Develop faculty commitment to andragogy.* Student learning seems to be more effective when the faculty as a whole is committed to andragogical assumptions as an overall model and to the use of specific techniques in appropriate and selected areas. Various strategies can be utilized to operationalize this principle.

a. Use faculty workshops or a series of faculty meetings to familiarize all faculty with the andragogical model and with research findings concerning its use in social work education and training (see Gelfand and others, 1975; Foeckler and Boynton, 1976).

b. Obtain the commitment of administrative and curricular leaders to the assumptions, principles, and processes of andragogy.

c. Field-test the model in the most appropriate areas of the curriculum and with faculty who have the most relevant teaching styles.
d. Provide collegial support for faculty who try out the model.
e. Evaluate results. If the results are positive, then implement the model in other parts of the program.
f. Institutionalize the model as much as possible. Build the assumptions and process of andragogy into manuals, handbooks, policies, and procedures.

5. *Develop the necessary climate.* The educational climate is more conducive to learning if the assumptions and processes used by administration, faculty, and staff are consistent throughout the program; if conscious decisions are made to use pedagogy in certain areas and andragogy in others; and if students are informed of these decisions. In individual courses it is the instructor's role to set the stage, serve as a role model, provide resources, and be a consultant. The instructor must be willing to face the constraints, take risks, and allow the process to occur.

6. *Obtain collegial support.* Without the active and ongoing support of colleagues, there is a tendency to revert to traditional methods. Instructors must be assertive in obtaining and maintaining this support.

7. *Allocate faculty resources.* Time must be given in faculty schedules for sharing, peer reviews, and planning for the implementation of andragogical methods if collegial support is to become a reality.

8. *Build in rewards.* Administrative and organizational rewards must be built into the system and institutionalized as reinforcers for excellence and creativity in teaching.

Pitfalls. Care should be taken to avoid certain pitfalls that could undermine the effectiveness of enabling students to become more self-directing.

1. *Administration/faculty/staff assuming dependency-producing roles.* This issue should not be confused with nurturing. The goal is to promote a relaxed, trusting, mutually respectful, warm, collaborative, and supportive atmosphere.

2. *Transition from pedagogy to andragogy.* Students should be prepared in advance for the change and know when, where, and why the transition takes place.

3. *Subjectiveness in grading/evaluation.* Trust-producing subjectivity should not be allowed to take the place of objectivity in the grading process. Verification must be provided.

4. *Lack of orientation for new faculty.* Failure to familiarize new faculty with the andragogy model will gradually lead to its demise as a primary teaching/learning philosophy.

5. *Lack of unity.* As programs become specialized (with continuing education, research, work-study, part-time study, grants, baccalaureate and master's programs, and career specializations), there is a tendency for these programs to go their separate ways. A unity in educational philosophy needs to be maintained.

Conclusion

It is the consensus of the authors that Knowles's (1972, p. 39) hypothesis was accurate: "Significant ... innovations will come when social work educators shift their thinking from transmitting the knowledge and skills they think social workers ought to possess to creating educational environments in which maturing professions can build ever improving models of the competencies required for their professional roles and in which they can develop these competencies through mutually self-directing inquiry."

4

Learning Through Teaching Among Undergraduate Social Work Students

Andy Farquharson

One of the epigrams in educational mythology is "If you want to be sure to learn something, teach it." This selection describes an imaginative approach to designing learning experiences and evaluating learning outcomes by undergraduate social work students.

Andy Farquharson is a member of the faculty of the School of Social Work, University of Victoria, British Columbia, Canada.

Special features:

- Teaching as learning
- Learning kits as a form of assignment
- Preparation of learning kits
- Overcoming resistance to self-directed learning
- Learning kits as resources for the learning of others
- Evaluation

In many college and university programs, the student assignment in the form of a project or term paper is a conventional way of promoting and evaluating student learning. The design, completion, and appraisal of these projects consume a good deal

Reprinted, with permission, from "Learning Through Teaching-Learning Kit Assignments," *Canadian Journal of Social Work Education,* 1978, *4* (1), 120–125.

of student and faculty energy. In spite of this there is only a very sparse literature dealing with appropriate instructional strategies in this area (Adderley and others, 1975). The following discussion explores one way in which contemporary knowledge about adults as learners can be used to design a learning project that maximizes student involvement and the dissemination of learning.

Facilitation of Learning—Some Adult
Education Concepts

Several key assumptions about the way in which the learning of adults can be facilitated may be used to inform the design of student assignments. Foremost among these is the notion of teaching as learning, the idea that the opportunity to teach others may be a preferred way of facilitating one's own learning. Reissman (1965) has produced a seminal article in which he summarizes the research on this proposition.

Knowles (1970) and others have stressed that in considering the adult student the following factors are of paramount importance: the adult self-concept requires that such people be regarded as being capable of self-direction; the adult has a fund of life experience, which can contribute to the learning enterprise; the adult is susceptible to new learning at certain "teachable moments" (Havighurst, 1953); and the adult has a problem-centered orientation to learning, which places a value on ideas that have immediate utility. A more general trend within the field of adult education is a shift in emphasis from teaching and toward learning, and learner-centered approaches may now be found throughout the adult education literature (Knowles, 1975).

Learning Kits

The foregoing principles of adult education have been used in a form of assignment that has been refined over a period of five years working with groups of students at three different universities and at one teaching hospital. The assignment has been termed a *learning kit,* and in simple terms the students are required to research topics related to the focus of a course and then to prepare a learning kit that would help others to learn what students themselves have learned about their chosen topic. This program outline, including all necessary resource materials, is the basis upon which a grade is assigned.

This concept of a learning kit may best be understood by providing one or two descriptions of instructional programs produced by students in courses offered in a social work program. One such learning resource was directed to the problems of elderly people living alone in urban areas. The student conducted both community and library research to develop a typical profile of the kinds of personal services required by such people and then designed a simulation game in which the player assumed the role of an elderly, single person. The probability of the player being unable to secure needed services, such as meals-on-wheels or assistance with the costs of medication, was designed to correspond with such probabilities in the local community. The kit was accompanied by questions for group discussion, an annotated bibliography, and a collection of key articles. Another student prepared a learning kit focused on a project in urban renewal, which involved a carefully produced slide-tape presentation and included supplementary written resource materials and a reference list. Other kits have dealt with topics as varied as abortion, play therapy, the influence of waiting room atmosphere upon prospective social service clients, and the social impact of offshore oil exploration upon the lifestyle of the Labrador Innuit.

In planning a learning kit, the student is required to confront such issues as the needs and motivation of those who may use the kit, the identification of learning objectives, the design of a strategy to accomplish these goals, and the development of an evaluation scheme for the change effort. In seeking to clarify these issues, the kit designers are forced to examine their own learning activities as they attempt to design a kit that is appropriate for a specified group of learners. This process of reflection often seems to result in the students becoming more active partners in the design and management of their formal learning activities and more aware of educational strategies that may be used to promote social change (Connor, Searly, and Bradley, 1970). This kind of assignment also results in a sharper understanding of course content, which must be clarified before it can be communicated to others in a learning program. A number of other benefits seem to be derived from this form of assignment. The students must achieve a solid understanding of their own material if they are to promote learning in others, and the novelty of this undertaking tends to inspire considerable effort from the kit designers. The completed assignments become an important and accessible learning resource. For example, learning kits can be designed to meet specific staff training or development objectives, to support the learning activities of other social work students, and to serve as a resource to workers employed in areas that are remote from other kinds of continuing learning opportunities. Finally, students who have had experience with the development of a learning kit appear to develop a fresh approach to some of their other assignments and seem more likely to contract to reach specified assignment objectives by alternative means where this is possible and appropriate.

Introduction of the Assignment

Many students are uncomfortable with the requirement that they communicate evidence of their learning in a new way, and it is frequently those students who have been more successful in achieving satisfactory grades with term papers who are most reluctant to abandon this more conventional format. Such people tend to voice objections related to the amount of time that it will take to complete the learning kit, their inability to identify a suitable topic, the inconsequential nature of the undertaking, or their perception that they lack the creativity and skill required to complete the assignment. A key to overcoming this resistance is the amount of conviction that the teacher has about the merits of this approach. The teacher must feel, and be able to communicate, a strong sense that students will discover latent abilities as they complete their learning kits and that many will feel a sense of accomplishment in the final product. Students who have already completed kits are also able to allay some of the concerns of those who are tackling this kind of project for the first time. But it seems counterproductive to provide examples of completed kits, as this may tend to overwhelm the new students with the scope of the task or with their perceived lack of necessary resources, and it may restrict these people in their search for ways to promote learning for others.

A common difficulty for some kit designers is that they become preoccupied with the form of their project to the exclusion of sound content. It is therefore important in introducing this assignment to emphasize that students should thoroughly research their selected topic and distill these findings into a few major themes before they begin to direct their attention to the ways in which they will communicate these ideas. This preferred sequence of activities can be promoted by requiring students to develop a contractual outline of the topic and a planning sequence that they will follow in assembling their kit. The early submission of such an outline makes it possible for the instructor to ensure that this assignment is clearly understood and will be approached in an appropriate way. Additional benefits may be derived from this assignment if students are required to maintain a journal of their personal learning activities associated with development of their learning kit. Students typically draw on a variety of learning resources as they carry out their institutional and noninstitutional (Tough, 1971) learning projects; these resources include past experience, advice from peers and teachers, visits to community resources, and the library. All these play a part in shaping the learning outcome. In developing their learning kits, students should monitor not only what they are learning but also how they are learning it and what resources they are using. Such reflection upon the learning process not only has intrinsic benefits for the student-as-learner but can provide ideas to the student-as-teacher about teaching strategies to employ in their kit. A final consideration in introducing this assignment is that students evidence greater enthusiasm for the project when they assemble a kit that will actually be utilized by a known group of learners. It is then possible to field-test the learning program and a resource can be developed to meet the needs of people who do not have access to particular kinds of learning opportunities. In instances where materials are prepared for a hypothetical target group, it is often more difficult to estimate the needs of the learners and their entry-level skills with reference to the subject matter of the kit.

Evaluation

One of the most problematical aspects of this type of assignment is centered on the question of evaluation. Hunt's (1970) work on matching models of teaching and learning emphasizes that there is a range of learning styles. In appraising learning kit assignments, evaluators must guard against measuring the product solely against their personal view of priority learning needs and optimal learning strategies. The subjectivity that may thus influence the evaluation of learning assignments may be partly offset by distributing an outline of the evaluation criteria and procedure when the project is assigned. An outline of this nature serves to make the teacher's objectives explicit and may serve as a program-planning guide for the kit designer. The evaluation form in current use consists of a series of sentence-completion items that cover the following issues:

1. The extent to which the topic selected by the student is relevant to the course objectives.
2. Evidence of thorough research to underpin the concepts included in the kit.
3. The degree to which this research has been integrated into a number of distinct viewpoints which the student wishes to communicate.
4. The amount of care with which the individual has identified the learner(s) to whom the kit is directed; and his or her assumptions about the motivation of these learners and their existing level of knowledge or skill regarding the topic in question.
5. The clarity with which learning objectives have been identi-

fied, together with a rationale to support the selection and sequencing of learning materials.

6. The inclusion of a way for kit users to evaluate their learning progress.

7. The range and value of pathways to further learning that are provided for users who wish to pursue their learning beyond the confines of the kit per se.

The evaluator may base an overall grade on these items, or each item may be graded separately and given differential weights in arriving at an overall grade. In either instance a discussion of the way their kits will be evaluated is an opportunity for students to explore some of the more specific factors that they should consider in planning this assignment. The learning kits that have been produced thus far are generally of good quality, but there appear to be some common shortcomings in those that are less well constructed. As mentioned earlier, the areas in which students seem to have the greatest difficulty are in the design of ways to assess the knowledge base and motivation of potential kit users and, similarly, in the development of ways to assess learning achievements. In addition, learning kits often do not include a range of guidelines for ongoing learning by the kit user (annotated bibliographies, list of resource persons, media, training opportunities, or experiential exercises). Frequently there is no built-in mechanism by which the kit user can participate in the revision or amplification of the kit. This latter consideration is particularly important because the students do not usually have sufficient time to do an extensive testing of their kit prior to its submission to the instructor.

Conclusion

There has been no structured evaluation of the merits of the learning kit in facilitating the learning process, but there have been numerous positive references to this assignment in student evaluations of courses in which it has been used. An overriding impression based on a range of student feedback is that this kind of assignment calls forth considerable effort and mobilizes creative capacities which the student may not have previously recognized. Students are generally very positive about the value of this assignment and report that they achieved beyond their expectations. However, it may be necessary to temper some of this enthusiasm because there is a tendency for students to devote an excessive amount of time to researching and developing their learning kit with detrimental effect upon their other responsibilities. In spite of this cautionary concern, the learning kit approach does appear to be a useful way to practically apply some of the assumptions about the effective promotion of adult learning to the design of undergraduate student assignments.

5

A Baccalaureate Degree Program
in Nursing for Adult Students

Deborah Arms, Bonnie Chenevey,
Carol Karrer, Carol Hawthorne Rumpler

Schools of nursing have a higher proportion of adult students than many other undergraduate programs because of the pressure on practicing nurses to acquire a baccalaureate degree. In the Franklin University School of Nursing, for example, the median age is twenty-seven, 50 percent of the students are married, 29 percent have children, 82 percent work full time, and 67 percent have more than five years of experience. This selection describes a baccalaureate degree program that is based on the andragogical model. The program is especially noteworthy because it takes care to meet the dependency needs and expectations of entering students and provides them with a sequence of experiences that enable them to become increasingly self-directed.

Deborah Arms, Bonnie Chenevey, Carol Karrer, and Carol Rumpler are members of the faculty of Franklin University School of Nursing.

Special features:

- Special problems of reentry students
- Progression toward self-directed learning
- Contract learning in courses and clinical placements
- Credit for prior learning
- Using student resources in learning
- Flexible scheduling
- Problem-centered curriculum
- Use of intrinsic motivation

273

- A climate conducive to learning
- Evaluation of learning
- A sample learning contract

In 1965 the American Nurses' Association (ANA) stated in "A Position Paper" that "the education for all those who are licensed to practice nursing should take place in institutions of higher education." One of the tenets of this position was that "minimum preparation for beginning professional nursing practice should be baccalaureate degree education in nursing." The position taken by the ANA in 1965 remains a source of conflict in the profession of nursing today. Although many professional nursing organizations have since adopted similar position statements regarding entry into practice, the nursing community continues to be divided on this issue. Schools of nursing continue to prepare nurses for practice at associate degree (two-year program), diploma (three-year program), and baccalaureate degree (four-year program) levels.

The Bachelor of Science in Nursing (BSN) degree is not required in any state for licensure as a registered nurse (RN); however, many positions in nursing are now requiring a minimum of a BSN as a job qualification, especially for supervisory and administrative positions and jobs in public health agencies. The BSN is also a first step for those considering research, consulting, teaching, or clinical specialization. In the very near future, a BSN will be required for entry into professional nursing practice. Many RNs who have either a diploma or an associate degree in nursing are returning to school to obtain the BSN. Unfortunately, many have encountered the following problems in the world of academia, which act as barriers to the obtainment of the degree: (1) lowered self-esteem resulting from required repetition of previously mastered nursing experiences; (2) altered life-styles due to the time commitment necessary to complete the degree and to accomplish daily preparation for classes; (3) expenses related to pursuit of the degree; (4) geographical inaccessibility and insufficient number of baccalaureate degree nursing programs; (5) limited nontraditional baccalaureate degree programs; (6) lack of standard criteria in assigning academic credit for previously completed course work, clinical experience, and challenge examinations; and (7) conflicting work and school schedules.

Nursing educators must realize that RNs returning to school for advanced degrees are unique as adult learners. Their learning needs and expectations are very different from those of the traditional generic nursing student. If these differences are not recognized, the educational process is quickly impeded.

The purpose of this selection is to describe a nontraditional baccalaureate degree nursing program that strives to provide students with educational opportunities based on principles of adult learning theory. When these principles are applied and the characteristics of the adult learner recognized, the anxiety and frustration felt by the RN returning to school can be lessened, thereby fostering a climate of collegiality and professionalism during this learning process.

Description of Program

Franklin University—located in Columbus, Ohio—is an urban commuter college with 5,000 students. It is known for its student-centered approach to meeting individual educational needs by providing educational experiences that positively influence job skills and intellectual ability.

In concert with the overall goal of the university, a completion program, offering the BSN, was designed to expand the educational base of licensed registered nurses holding either the associate degree or diploma in nursing. Building on the students' previous education and work experience, the nursing curriculum emphasizes the development of analytical and judgment skills. Through a self-directed, goal-oriented approach to education, the program encourages nurses to assume more autonomy and accountability in practice and to apply creativity in patient care. Management theory is also incorporated into the curriculum to prepare nurses for their increasing role in decision making.

The nursing program is based on the assumption that the adult learner has completed specific lower-division requirements that would be the equivalent to the freshman and sophomore years of college. Many required lower-division credits may be transferred to the university or awarded through proficiency examinations. During lower division studies, the nursing students acquire a base knowledge in the sciences, communication, and the humanities. Thus, the student comes to the upper-division nursing program (junior and senior years) with a wide variety of educational preparation, work experience, and professional interests.

The upper-division nursing program includes the professional core of five clinical nursing courses and two lecture-format courses. Seven additional courses from the humanities and the social, behavioral, physical, and management sciences supplement this core. The upper-division courses are structured for flexibility and individuality.

Description of Student Population

Of the 181 RN students enrolled in the School of Nursing, the majority are married women who are employed full time in traditional nursing roles. Sixty-one percent of the students have six or more years of nursing experience. Because most students are employed full time, the majority attend school on a part-time basis. Although a large majority of the students (approximately 75 percent) have taken college courses other than their initial nursing preparation, an average of five years has elapsed since they have been in a student role.

Application of the Andragogical Model

Knowles (1978) presents five underlying assumptions that are crucial to an andragogical model of education: (1) The learner is increasingly self-directing. (2) The learner's experience is a rich resource for learning. (3) The learner's readiness to learn stems from his or her life tasks or problems. (4) Learning itself focuses on tasks, or is problem centered. (5) The learner's motivation is derived from internal incentives or curiosity. These assumptions are applicable to our nursing program. Students who enter the program are typically registered nurses who have been working for several years. They are viewed as self-directing, and they become progressively more accountable for their learning throughout the program. The first-level courses, "Nursing Transitions" and "Public Health," offer more structure and instructor guidance than the upper-level nursing courses. In one of the upper-level courses, "Nursing Management," the student determines clinical learning activities that are personally relevant and selects a clinical mentor who has demonstrated clinical expertise in that area. Using course guidelines, the student and the clinical mentor agree on the proposed learning activities and establish a contract between them. The faculty member, at all times, is responsible for the clinical experiences of students and is ready to intervene if problems arise. The final clinical nursing course, "Theoretical Applications," places the focus, direction, and type of learning entirely on the student. In addition to selecting a clinical mentor, the student develops a more elaborate learning contract, which encompasses nursing theory and practice. The purpose of this course is to provide the learner with an opportunity to diagnose "gaps" or "holes" in his or her learning and to develop strategies to resolve those learning needs prior to completion of the nursing program.

The assumption that learners are rich resources of knowledge is evident in our program's belief that sharing knowledge fosters growth and accountability. Each clinical nursing course has a seminar, which is the primary vehicle for the sharing of knowledge by students. These seminars are student directed; faculty members serve as facilitators of the group process. The nursing lecture courses also have small-group activities and time for discussion built into them. These activities encourage a sharing of knowledge among small-group members, with individuals acting as rich resources of experience for their peers and the instructors.

In accordance with the assumption that students are rich resources of knowledge, Franklin believes that, through the use of proficiency testing, course credit can be awarded for prior knowledge. The university recognizes that individuals sometimes learn material equivalent to that taught in college courses through on-the-job training, reading, and related endeavors. Proficiency examinations are a method of demonstrating learning gained from these experiences. Nursing students entering our completion program have had basic nursing education, and many have completed college courses beyond those basic educational requirements. Therefore, many of the lower-division nursing requirements may be either transferred or awarded through standardized proficiency examinations. Instructor-developed examinations to award course credit are also available in selected subjects that are not part of the core content.

Knowles states in his third assumption that readiness to learn is developed from the learner's life tasks and problems. Houle (1982) further describes three kinds of lifelong learners: (1) those who are "goal oriented," using education as a means of accomplishing clear-cut objectives; (2) "activity-oriented" learners, taking part in education for reasons unrelated to the purpose of learning (for instance, to meet new people); (3) "learning-oriented" individuals, who are involved in learning in order to achieve personal growth and enlightenment. In our nursing program, most of the students are "goal oriented," which fits nicely with Knowles's assumption that readiness to learn is developed from life tasks and problems. The "goal orientation" of most nursing students coincides with the developmental task of career development. The clear-cut objective for most nurses seeking a baccalaureate degree is promotion within the profession. Houle also indicates that "goal-oriented" learners pursue their education in episodes. Since the students in our program work full time and many have families, they often must pursue their education episodically, taking only as many courses as their social and economic responsibilities permit. Franklin University respects the episodic nature of education for the adult learner by scheduling early morning, evening, and weekend classes as well as making courses available during the summer months. If the students request a new or more convenient class time, every effort is made to offer the course at the time requested.

Knowles's fourth assumption is that the focus of learning is task or problem centered. The relevance of the learning is continually being challenged by our nursing students. The expected outcomes listed for each lecture and clinical activity are problem centered and delineate the behaviors that will resolve the learning problem or accomplish the task. "Nursing Transitions," our introductory lecture course, has been developed as a reentry, "survival" course that covers the characteristics of the adult learner and deals with specific problems or tasks, such as test anxiety and time management, that confront the adult learner pursuing a baccalaureate degree in nursing. Considerable time is devoted to examining issues currently affecting the nursing profession. Students select a problem or issue in nursing that is particularly pertinent to their clinical nursing experiences and write a position paper examining both sides of the issue and proposing solutions to the problem they have identified.

The final assumption of adult learning, as Knowles indicates, is that the motivation for learning is guided by internal incentives or curiosity. Although many of our students are concerned with academic performance as measured by grades, they are also concerned about the meaning that the learning has for them personally. Internal incentives verbalized by students include "feeling good about myself for learning something new" or "feeling more professional" as a result of pursuing further education. Increased confidence and competence within the nursing profession are foremost considerations for the nursing student. Curiosity is also a strong motivator and readily evident in the student-selected clinical experiences. One student's rationale for choosing a nurse-midwife as a clinical mentor was that "I've always wanted to see what a nurse-midwife does and how different she is from the traditional nurse."

In conjunction with the five assumptions of learning, Knowles delineates the following six elements necessary to the andragogical model of education: (1) establishing a climate conducive to learning; (2) creating a mechanism for mutual planning; (3) mutually formulating learning objectives; (4) designing a pattern of learning plans involving learning contracts and student projects; (5) conducting the learning experience with suitable techniques and resources; and (6) evaluating the learning outcomes and rediagnosing the learning needs. Knowles emphasizes the need for mutual involvement of the educator and student throughout the learning process. Knowles (1980) views contract learning as the most successful method of learning because it commits the learner to a sense of ownership of the learning and the objectives he intends to pursue. In addition, contracts provide the learner with a visible structure for organizing the learning experiences.

The use of learning contracts for nursing students was initiated in 1982 in the "Theoretical Applications" course. Students were given the course syllabus, which contained general guidelines for lecture and clinical learning activities. The guidelines for writing a learning contract closely followed Knowles's elements of andragogical learning. Initially, students were furious because all the learning responsibilities were placed on them. After tempers cooled, however, the students became intrigued with the idea that they could select any clinical specialty area and any nursing theory they wished to pursue. They determined their learning objectives on the basis of their personal diagnosis of learning needs. They designed their own learning strategies to meet their objectives. Methods for evaluating the learning objectives were also identified and incorporated into the learning contract. (An example of a learning contract is found in Exhibit 1.) The student, his or her mentor, and the instructor extensively reviewed and discussed the learning contract. On completion of the course, students acknowledged that they had enjoyed their use of learning contracts because "I was able to select the learning that interested me, and it gave me the opportunity to try new things." Learning contracts are time consuming and can be initially confusing for the student and teacher; however, they create a spirit of collaboration and a sense of commitment that cannot always be found in the traditional classroom structure.

The learning climate in the School of Nursing is one of informality, promoting freedom of discussion, trust, and mutual respect. Faculty members regard students as nursing colleagues and encourage them to discuss concerns or issues. In all clinical nursing courses, planning of clinical learning activities is a mutual endeavor of the student and the teacher. Clinical mentors, selected by the students, are used in the upper-division clinical nursing courses. A contract with a clinical mentor involves extensive negotiation between the student, mentor, and faculty member. As mentioned, the final nursing course requires a more elaborate learning contract, which encompasses both theory and practice.

A variety of teaching strategies are employed in all the nursing courses. Student projects can be found in every lecture and clinical nursing course. In "Nursing Research," for example, the students write critiques of two nursing research articles they have chosen. A research proposal is the major learning activity, and the students choose their own research problem according to their interests. The results of their proposals are presented to the class, where sharing of knowledge actively occurs in a collegial manner.

"Nursing Management" also requires a paper that fosters student inquiry. Students are required to analyze the health care system in which their clinical experience occurred and to indicate its strengths and weaknesses. Potential for implementing change in the identified organization is also assessed and evaluated. Students are given the opportunity, through gaming and role playing, to practice management techniques such as handling group conflict, interviewing, and conducting performance appraisals.

"Public Health" provides students with a chance to select a project and present it to an appropriate audience. One student chose to tell nonnursing students—during a university-wide "Learnathon," which was attempting to raise money for community service agencies—why many nurses are pursuing their baccalaureate degrees.

Evaluation of learning in the clinical nursing courses results from a compilation of learner-collected evidence. The student performs a self-assessment, which is added to the teacher evaluation and the clinical mentor's evaluation (if appropriate), and discusses these evaluations in a final conference. All evidence is weighed equally and based on the learner's objectives and the course objectives. Rediagnosis of learning needs occurs at the final conference, and planning of future learning to meet

Exhibit 1. Franklin University School of Baccalaurate Nursing, Student Learning Contract.

Learner: _____   Course: ___Theoretical Applications___   Trimester: ___Summer 1982___

Learning Objectives	Learning Resources and Strategies	Evidence of Accomplishment	Target Completion Date	Methodology for Evaluation
At the completion of this trimester the student will be able to:				
(1) Perform a complete cardiac assessment on an infant.	Attend orientation class at Childrens Hospital on 6/1/82 on cardiac care of a neonate.	Demonstrate accurate cardiac assessment on an infant to clinical mentor.	7/22/82	Evaluation by mentor of my clinical performance.
	Spend two hours in Cardiac Clinic at Childrens Hospital.	Write brief outline containing key points in the performance of a cardiac assessment.		Evaluation of outline for performance of cardiac assessment by mentor and instructor.
	Perform a minimum of two cardiac assessments on infants in the ICU each clinical day under the supervision of clinical mentor.	Log entries of cardiac assessments done in clinical area.		Review of log entries by instructor.

(2) Improve interpersonal communication skills with staff, physicians, peers, and families.	Observe mentor's communication skills. Review transactional analysis, theory and literature on communication. After obtaining consent, tape-record two interviews with the families of infants in the ICU. Mentor, instructor, and peers to provide feedback regarding effectiveness of communication.	Log notations for type of communication styles utilized by mentor and faculty member. Develop a rating scale for effective communication to be filled out on me by my peers and instructors.	8/1/82	Written evaluation by mentor of my communication skills used in clinical setting. Evaluation by faculty member and peers at beginning and end of trimester (using rating scale).

these outstanding needs begins. The student assumes responsibility for communicating these needs or problem areas to his or her next nursing educator, which ensures continuity of the learning process.

Conclusion

An understanding of the characteristics unique to the adult learner is vital for faculty who are teaching in nontraditional baccalaureate degree programs and for students who are enrolled in these programs. Providing a motivating and stimulating climate for learning demands the use of varied and creative teaching techniques. Meeting the learning needs of students is at times difficult and can be achieved only through joint cooperation with students.

Adults initially will view any self-directed learning opportunities with shock and disorganization until trust between the student and teacher is established. Although we are dealing with students who are adults in the chronological sense of the word, they have been socialized through prior learning experiences to be dependent on the instructor for direction and guidance. Therefore, they cannot be expected to assume an adult learner role at the outset. Only after their individual needs are assessed and their learning objectives achieved through various teaching strategies and course assignments will they move gradually to a level of independent functioning, where principles of adult learning theory can become fully realized.

In summary, the adult learner is motivated to gain new knowledge, reexamine ideas, and challenge existing concepts of truth when learning experiences are individualized and flexible. It is our hope that, through the use of the andragogical model of teaching and learning, nursing educators will be able to foster a spirit of collegiality and mutual respect in the learning environment, thereby facilitating a valuable educational experience for the RN returning to school.

6

Teaching School Administration at Cleveland State University

Ernest M. Schuttenberg

This selection describes the implications of andragogical assumptions for course design and conduct in a graduate course in "Principles of School Administration." It shows how each of the assumptions was implemented in a five-week course, describes the evaluation procedures used, and makes recommendations for the improvement of graduate professional education in general in the light of this experience.

Ernest M. Schuttenberg was assistant professor of education at Cleveland State University at the time this article was written.

Special features:

- The responsibility of graduate schools to develop self-directed learners
- Implications of andragogical assumptions for the design and conduct of graduate courses
- Andragogical course objectives
- Climate-setting exercise
- Self-diagnostic exercise
- Peer helping
- Participative exercises
- Student feedback
- Evaluation of learning
- Evaluation of the course

Adapted, with permission, from "An Andragogical Learning Approach to Graduate Professional Education," in *Improving College and University Teaching Yearbook* (Corvallis: Oregon State University Press, 1975).

Graduate professional schools of education, medicine, law, engineering, and other fields are responsible to several publics for the caliber of their educational programs. Governmental or professional licensing boards, the client groups that are to be served by the graduates, and society at large are vitally concerned with the quality of learning of emerging professional practitioners. Especially at the present time, when graduates must confront issues of ever-increasing complexity, graduate professional schools must be continually on the alert for ideas which will improve not only their students' fund of knowledge but also their abilities to set goals, make decisions, solve problems, and evaluate their actions so that they will serve their clients and society responsibly.

In order for their graduates to serve the community more effectively, graduate professional schools and their faculties must examine the nature of the learning experiences provided for their students. Traditionally, students in college and graduate school have been taught with methods more appropriate for youth and children. Overconcern with mastery of predetermined facts and ideas, overreliance upon the recollection of details on examinations, and underutilization of student knowledge and learning resources may be appropriate for a group of learners who are passive, unimaginative, and unsophisticated. But most students in graduate professional schools are adults who hold jobs and have families and who are already active contributors to the welfare of society. If such students are preparing themselves to serve society at an even more complex level, should not their program of preparation for such service actively involve them in their own learning? As Werdell (1969, p. 14) argues, "The institution can develop self-directed learners only by innovating new teaching and learning models through which students can learn their own learning process, learn what they want to learn, and learn how to communicate this to other people."

This paper reviews the andragogical assumptions about the characteristics of adults as learners and examines some of the implications of these assumptions for the design and conduct of graduate professional courses in colleges and universities. In order to view an adult learning model in practice, a graduate professional course in educational administration is described. (The andragogical assumptions and their implications are listed in Table 1.)

The course entitled "Principles of School Administration" was designed and taught from an andragogical point of view. It is an introductory course required of all candidates for the master's degree in educational administration at Cleveland State University, an urban institution serving the greater Cleveland area. Students in other programs of study may also choose this course as an elective. The course objectives are andragogical in nature:

1. Gain a comprehensive overview of the field of educational administration.
2. Examine major national, state, and local issues affecting school administration in the light of personal educational philosophy and values.
3. Assess personal abilities in areas related to the role of educational administrator.
4. Formulate and accomplish personally significant measurable learning objectives in one or more of the following administrative areas: Curriculum, Staff Personnel, Pupil Personnel, School-Community Relations, School Business Management.
5. Review current literature and research in selected areas of educational administration.

Although the "Principles of School Administration" course is taught during every academic quarter, the course described in this paper was offered for five weeks during the summer session. Class meetings were held twice a week for three hours each session. In all, there were ten class meetings.

Twenty-eight graduate students participated in the course—twenty men and eight women. Most of the participants were public school teachers, although eight participants held other types of positions, such as administrative assistant, curriculum developer, guidance counselor, work-study coordinator, and university graduate assistant.

Table 1. Implications of Andragogical Assumptions for
Course Design and Conduct.

Assumptions	Implications
A. *Changes in Self-Concept Toward Increasing Self-Direction*	A1. Students participate in self-diagnosis of learning needs.
	A2. Students and teachers share in the planning process for learning.
	A3. Students and teachers share responsibility for personal and group learning.
	A4. Students and teachers share in the evaluation of learning.
	A5. Teacher solicits student contributions.
	A6. Teacher and students share spirit of mutuality as joint inquirers.
	A7. Teacher makes efforts to know students as individuals.
	A8. Teacher fosters psychological climate of acceptance and support.
	A9. Teacher fosters friendly and informal atmosphere.
B. *Role of Experience as a Learning Resource*	B1. Passive, information-transmittal teaching methods are minimized; active, experiential learning methods are emphasized.
	B2. Practical application is built into the learning experience.
	B3. Collaboration with other class members is fostered rather than competition.
C. *Readiness to Learn What Is Perceived as Essential*	C1. Students are encouraged to relate learnings to their career needs and plans.
	C2. Students are encouraged to work and share with others who have similar interests and and needs.
D. *Orientation to Learning as Problem Solving*	D1. Subject matter presentations are flexible enough to accommodate student concerns.
	D2. Student problem areas are identified and dealt with.

Twenty-four of the participants were candidates for the master's degree in educational administration or supervision or were seeking certification in administration, while four were majoring in other fields and were taking the course as an elective. The session of the course described in this paper was not particularly different in content or design from other sessions of the course taught previously. Nor were participant reactions different, in general, from those in past sessions.

At the first course session, several activities were introduced which were designed to foster a friendly and informal atmosphere (point A9 in Table 1). Name cards were used by the teacher and students, and the teacher greeted each participant by name (A7). Opportunity was provided for participants to meet in groups with others they did not previously know in order to learn about their experience and interests (B3). The teacher described his background and experience to the class and stated his role to be one of facilitator and resource provider in addition to that of information giver (A6). Student contributions and questions were encouraged (A8).

A statement of course requirements, based upon the course objectives, was distributed and discussed. There were four basic course requirements: (1) regular class attendance and participation in course activities, (2) reading of assigned portions of the textbook, (3) preparation and submission of two course reaction papers, (4) formulation and achievement of two personal learning objectives (a position paper and a review of literature).

The course reaction papers, due at the fifth and tenth class sessions, were to include personal comments in three areas: reactions to class sessions and outside readings; ideas, insights, or questions about school administration developed thus far; and thoughts or questions regarding personal motivations, abilities, or objectives for school administration. The purposes for assigning these reaction papers were to gain student feedback for use in course evaluation and modification (A5, D1) and to facilitate the relating of students' learning to their career needs and plans (C1). These reaction papers were not evaluated for purposes of grading.

During the first course session, participants were asked to

complete an "Administrative Knowledge Assessment Form" (AKAF) in duplicate. This form listed twenty-six areas of concern to principals and other school administrators. Each participant was asked to indicate on the form his present state of knowledge and experience in each area and to describe how the knowledge and experience were gained. This self-diagnosis was repeated at the end of the course and the two forms compared. There were several purposes for the use of the AKAF. From the student's point of view, it provided him with an indication of his learning needs (A1). Then, too, it pointed out areas for personal research (A2), as one of the learning objectives was to involve the preparation of a research paper on a selected topic in educational administration. The rediagnosis at the end of the course provided participants with an indication of some of the learning that had occurred during the period of the course (A4), and it pointed out areas of need for further study. From the instructor's point of view, the AKAFs provided a means for getting to know the students better (A7), and they made it possible to identify areas for added emphasis during the course (A2).

At the first class session, the instructor presented a theory session on management by objectives (MBO), a results-oriented system for administration that is increasingly being used in school systems. In order to provide practical experience with MBO (B2), this concept was used as an organizing system for the course. Each participant was asked to formulate in writing two learning objectives that he would endeavor to achieve during the course. One objective was to be the writing of a position paper on an educational problem area in which he was especially interested (D2). The other objective was to be the preparation of a review of the literature in an area of school administration that was of particular interest or concern to the participant. During the second and third class sessions, the instructor met with each student to discuss his learning objectives and to arrive at mutually acceptable goals (A3, A5, A7). Students were also encouraged to discuss their objectives with other class members to get ideas and suggestions (C2).

During the rest of the course, information giving (lectures, films, filmstrips), while being a part of almost every class session, was supplemented by numerous small-group discussions and simulation exercises (B1, B3). Participative exercises in the following areas were a major part of the course: an exercise in values and goals of education, analysis and future planning based on a case study of a high school, a role-playing exercise on educational leadership, problem-solving discussions using problems contributed by class members (C2), and simulation of a school board-teacher's organization negotiations sessions.

At the end of the course, a summary sheet was provided to each participant, listing the major theories, topics, and concepts that had been dealt with during the course. The students met in groups to review these items and to help each other in reviewing ways of applying them to problems in the field of educational administration (B3, C2).

Informal feedback from students was solicited at various times during the course (A5, A7). Formal feedback was received at the midpoint and the end of the course from the course reaction papers and through the use of various instruments. One instrument, the "Staff Development Feedback Sheet," was administered at the fifth class session and again at the end of the course. As the result of student interest determined by its first administration, an additional subject was added to the course (D1)—the topic of bringing about change in educational organizations.

In some areas of the course, andragogical principles were not applied to the extent that they might have been. These conditions were due partly to the short duration of the course (five weeks) and partly to lack of adequate planning. For one thing, while there was some sharing in the course planning by participants, much more responsibility in this area might have been given. Then, too, the amount of help and assistance in learning shared mutually by course participants might have been increased. Finally, the quality of the papers submitted in fulfillment of the learning objectives was determined unilaterally and graded by the teacher (although all papers were returned with extensive notations), and the course grades were assigned by the instructor without individual student consultations.

Accomplishment of Learning Objectives

In a course designed according to andragogical principles, how can the degree of learning, as stated in the course objectives, be measured? Table 2 lists the major theories, concepts,

Table 2. Major Theories, Concepts, and Topics Included in "Principles of School Administration" Course.

A. *The Administrative Process*
   1. Scientific management/human relations/behavioral science approaches
   2. Five major areas of school administration
   3. Relationship between educational values and administrative behavior
   4. Management by objectives
   5. Three dimensions of problem solving
   6. Functional staff participation
   7. The administrator as "man in the middle"
   8. Administrative accountability

B. *The Administrator as Leader*
   1. Administrative role/leadership role (Lipham)
   2. The Managerial Grid (Blake and Mouton)
   3. Consideration/initiating structure (Halpin)
   4. Continuum of leadership behavior (Tannenbaum and Schmidt)
   5. Transactional leadership (Moser)
   6. Theory X/Theory Y (McGregor)
   7. Hierarchy of needs (Maslow)
   8. Motivation-hygiene theory (Herzberg)

C. *The Administrator and Organizational Considerations*
   1. Centralized/decentralized organization
   2. Line/staff personnel
   3. Role conflict/role overload
   4. Ideographic/Nomothetic dimensions of organization (Getzels and Guba)
   5. Public schools as "Domesticated Organizations" (Carlson)
   6. Organizational Climate
   7. Organizational Change
   8. Professional negotiations

and topics dealt with during the "Principles of School Administration" course. The course was designed to provide an overview of school administration to which the student could relate the various theories, concepts, and topics discussed. Through readings, lectures, large- and small-group discussions, simulation exercises, and individual projects, the students explored these areas of content during the course sessions. At the end of the course, rather than require students to write an examination dealing with these areas, a process more in keeping with andragogical principles was employed. As indicated earlier, students were provided with a listing of the course topics, and they helped each other in reviewing the relationship of each to the practice of school administration. Topics that were not clear were brought before the entire class, and the teacher was able to provide clarification where necessary. The review sheets themselves were retained by the students for use in the future for review and further study.

The andragogical learning objectives required course participants to display behaviors appropriate to those required in a position of school administrator. In the "Principles" course, such behaviors included formulating two pertinent and meaningful learning objectives according to guidelines provided, accepting responsibility for preparing and submitting on time four papers in accordance with criteria specified, and, through regular attendance and active class participation, contributing to total class learning.

Unsuccessful course completion might result from failure to maintain regular class attendance, inability to plan or carry out learning goals, and inability to express oneself clearly in writing or inability to use research techniques effectively. In keeping with andragogical principles, however, the course was designed so that help in any of the above areas was available to each student if requested.

Participant Reactions

What are the reactions of graduate students to a course designed and administered according to andragogical principles? Since these principles reflect a concern with the learning needs of adults, it would be expected that adult student reactions would be generally positive. The feedback provided by the participants in the "Principles of School Administration" course supported this hypothesis. It was evident that the participants perceived that they had acquired useful learning from their experiences in the "Principles" course.

Conclusions and Recommendations

A study reviewing forty years of research on the learning outcomes produced by different techniques of teaching in higher education has revealed that "no particular method of college instruction is measurably to be preferred over another, when evaluated by student examination performances" (Dubin and Taveggia, 1969, p. 10). The same study recommends that "it is time for the researchers in the field to reconceptualize the problem as one of modeling the linkages between teaching and learning at the adult level" (p. 12).

This paper has suggested the hypothesis that the quality of learning in graduate professional courses is positively related not to a specific teaching methodology but to philosophical and psychological principles of adult learning. The data presented regarding the "Principles of School Administration" course indicate that the andragogical approach resulted in a satisfactory level of content learning, an opportunity for students to demonstrate a number of behaviors related to professional competency in their field of study, and the achievement by participants of a positive affective thrust toward continued exploration in the field of educational administration.

It is recommended that further study and experimentation regarding the application of andragogical principles to graduate professional courses be conducted in educational institutions. Some questions requiring investigation are the following: (1) In what kinds of courses are andragogical principles most and least applicable? (2) Are there distinguishable types of graduate students who respond most or least favorably to andragogical approaches? (3) Are there distinguishable types of instructors who employ andragogical approaches more effectively or less effectively? (4) What are the effects of andragogical course development on the overall accountability of a graduate school to its profession and to society?

An important educational objective for professional schools is to produce graduates who have a sound intellectual background for service, an ability to act responsibly in a professional manner, and a commitment to the solution of societal problems. The evidence reported in this paper suggests that andragogical approaches to learning are helpful in fostering these kinds of outcomes.

FIVE

✦✦ ✦✦ ✦✦ ✦✦ ✦✦ ✦✦ ✦✦ ✦✦ ✦✦ ✦✦ ✦✦ ✦✦ ✦✦ ✦✦ ✦✦ ✦✦ ✦✦ ✦

Applications
in Continuing Education
for the Health Professions

Although the threat of human obsolescence confronts all of humanity, given the accelerating pace of change in our society, it has a particularly strong impact on the professions—especially the health professions (see Dubin, 1972). The half-life of the knowledge, skills, attitudes, and values required by physicians, nurses, allied health professionals, and pharmacists is shrinking with increasing speed. Citizens worry about being treated by health practitioners who have not kept up to date and have reacted by passing laws mandating relicensing and continuing professional education. The health care professions and institutions have responded to the threat by mounting massive programs of continuing professional education; in fact, this is probably the fastest-growing aspect of all of education. And, since the clientele of continuing professional education consists exclusively of adults, these programs have tended increasingly to be based on principles of adult learning.

This chapter opens with a description of a pilot project for physicians at the University of Southern California, in which the central theme is self-directed learning. The selection presents the need for and assumptions and goals of the project and the major program components, including needs assessment, individualized learning plans, information brokering, and the use of peer resource groups. Then follow three selections focused on the continuing education of nurses. Selection 2, by the American Nurses' Association, sets forth a policy statement and guidelines for self-directed continuing education in nursing. Its provisions could easily be adapted to other professions. The application of the andragogical model to highly technical training in cardiovascular nursing at Doctors Hospital in Little Rock is presented in selection 3, and selection 4 describes an innovative in-service education program in which primary responsibility is placed on the clinical nursing units at St. Mary's Hospital in Waterbury, Connecticut.

1

Self-Directed Learning
for Physicians at the
University of Southern California

University of Southern California

"Sitting in a classroom listening to a lecturer talk about many things one may not have a need to apply is not an ideal learning experience for physicians," according to Phil R. Manning, M.D., associate vice president for health affairs continuing education, University of Southern California Health Sciences Campus, and organizer of the USC Development and Demonstration Center in Continuing Education for Health Professionals. So, in October 1980, the center launched a three-year pilot project to test an innovative program of continuing education for physicians, based on the andragogical model. Over one hundred physicians have participated in the pilot program and have given it highly positive evaluations.

Special features:

- The meaning of self-directed learning for physicians
- Objectives of a self-directed learning program for physicians
- Information brokering
- Peer resource groups
- Role expectations
- Needs assessment

Adapted, with permission, from *Manual for Participants*, published by the Self-Directed Learning Project for Physicians, Health Science Campus, University of Southern California. This publication was supported in part by NIH Grant LM 03427 from the National Library of Medicine.

• Individualized learning plans (contracts)
  Objectives
  Learning resources and strategies
  Evidence of accomplishment
  Validation of evidence

The Self-Directed Learning Project for Physicians is a three-year study designed to explore nontraditional avenues for continuing medical education. It is sponsored by the USC Development and Demonstration Center in Continuing Education for Health Professionals and is funded by grants from the National Library of Medicine and the W. K. Kellogg Foundation.

Background, Assumptions, and Project Goals

Self-directed continuing education has been a major goal of medical and adult educators. There is evidence that adults learn more deeply and permanently on their own initiative than with traditional teacher-oriented classroom approaches. Indeed, a prime characteristic of the adult learner is the need and capacity for self-direction. Adult learners who are professionals interested in continuing education have another noteworthy characteristic: they are most interested and motivated to learn for action, to perform, to solve problems, to make decisions, or otherwise to have impact in their life work.

All physicians have some concept of their own needs for continuing education. This concept is implicit in the choices they make, such as to read one journal article and not another and to attend one session at a professional meeting and not another. The physician who depends on participation in formal continuing medical education programs deals with perceived need for learning by participating on an intuitive basis in programs that seem relevant. The program may or may not present information in a style or medium acceptable to all participants, and the actual learning outcomes of such programs are usually indeterminate.

The self-directed physician learner can undertake a different approach to continuing education. In its broadest meaning, "self-directed learning" describes a process in which individuals take the initiative, with or without the help of others, in diagnosing their learning needs, formulating learning goals, identifying human and material resources for learning, choosing and implementing appropriate learning strategies, and evaluating learning outcomes. Other labels found in the literature to describe this process are "self-planned learning," "inquiry method," "independent learning," "self-education," "self-instruction," "self-study," and "autonomous learning." The trouble with most of these labels is that they seem to imply learning in isolation, whereas self-directed learning usually takes place in association with various kinds of helpers, such as instructors, tutors, mentors, resource people, and peers. There is a lot of mutuality among a group of self-directed learners.

The characteristics of teacher-directed and self-directed learning should be viewed as on a continuum, rather than dichotomous. No doubt there are learning situations in which we are indeed dependent (as when approaching an entirely new and strange area of inquiry), in which our experience is in fact of little worth (as when we have had no previous experience within the area of inquiry), in which our readiness to learn is really determined by our level of maturation regarding the area of inquiry, in which we are rightly focusing on accumulating subject matter, and in which we are actually motivated by external pressures. What makes the difference between pedagogical and andragogical education is not so much the difference in the assumptions underlying their theory and practice as it is the attitude of the learners. If self-directed learners recognize that there are occasions on which they will need to be taught, they will enter into those taught-learning situations in a searching, probing frame of mind and will exploit them as resources for learning without losing their self-directedness.

The practicing physician is well suited to a self-directed learning approach. For the most part, physicians have effective communication skills, a well-developed inquiry and problem-solving orientation, and the ability to learn from unfamiliar material and from problems encountered in their practices. There are other personal and professional characteristics that make a self-directed approach to continuing medical education both feasible and promising. Unfortunately, there are also barriers to a self-directed approach. For example, most physicians have accumulated more than twenty years of teacher-directed educational experiences and have developed those learning skills and strategies required to excel in teacher-directed learning environments. Self-directed learning requires a different set of skills and strategies, and these must be discovered and applied by the effective self-directed learner. Another difficulty is that there is an inadequate basis for selecting from overwhelming professional literature, often leading to apathy or anxiety. There is often insulation from feedback and norms provided by peers.

The Self-Directed Learning Project is based on the assumption that physicians can best determine and satisfy their own educational needs. The goal is to provide a system that facilitates and supports the needs of the self-directed physician learner.

Six project objectives have been stated:

1.   To establish a mechanism to help medical libraries become more responsive to the needs of the practicing physician community.
2.   To identify and circulate educational resources concerned with physicians' self-determined educational needs.
3.   To establish methods for validating self-directed study in a manner acceptable to quality assurance boards and medical societies for membership and relicensure.
4.   To facilitate the development of self-directed learning skills among physician participants.
5.   To improve the quality of medical practice and patient care through self-directed continuing medical education.
6.   To provide a program model for application of self-directed learning strategies in the continuing education of health professionals.

Major Program Components

Three educational strategies are integrated in this unique continuing medical education program: learning plans, educational brokering, and peer resource groups or networks.

Individualized Learning Plans. Participating physicians develop a brief, but formal, learning plan. The plan clarifies the physician's objectives and outlines a workable course of action. An educational specialist assists physicians in documenting educational needs and constructing manageable learning plans.

Information Brokering. The medical library-based information broker serves participating physicians by linking them to appropriate teaching/learning resources. The broker identifies available community resources to assist physicians in reaching their educational goals. In addition to printed and audiovisual materials, the broker identifies specialized resources—such as consultants, clinics, courses, and equipment—that may be necessary for successful completion of the learning plan.

Peer Resource Groups. Groups of three to five physicians provide support to the individual members. Although the participants are involved in their own learning projects, they assist one another by information sharing, problem solving, providing technical assistance, and informal personal interaction. The group also serves as a motivating force to complete the self-determined learning plan. Individual physicians maintain direction of their own programs. The peer resource groups meet on a monthly basis over a four-month period.

Participating physicians have the opportunity to self-direct their learning activities in order to maximize the impact of the effort and time devoted to continuing medical education. At no cost to the physician, a range of support services is provided by a medical education resource team. Physicians may receive Category I continuing education credit for their participation. An agreement to participate includes a commitment to act as resources to colleagues and a willingness to provide project staff with information necessary to evaluate and improve the program.

Role Expectations

Physician Participants. Participants agree to undertake at least one self-directed learning project during a four-month period. A brief description of intended objectives, planned activities, method of evaluation, and time estimate must be written in a learning plan format to document each self-directed learning project. In addition, participants agree to act as resources to fellow participants engaged in self-directed study, primarily in peer resource groups. On occasion, physicians may be asked to complete questionnaires or provide other program-related information to research staff.

Peer Resource Group. Participants join two to four other physicians in a group meeting held once a month. Group meeting agendas are devised by the group and are devoted to facilitating members' self-directed study. Members provide formal and informal assistance to one another by critique, problem solving, and information sharing and by serving as an evaluation source for completed learning plans.

Educational Specialist. The educational specialist provides support services to individual participants and to peer resource groups. Technical assistance in needs assessment procedures and documentation of the learning plan are primary services provided to participants on an individual basis, including examples, models, protocols, and literature pertinent to educational planning for the self-directed physician learner. The educational specialist attends peer resource group meetings, records the group agenda, acts as a resource, and generally facilitates the process through coordination of logistics, scheduling, and dissemination of materials.

Information Broker. The information broker is a medical library-based resource person who serves participating physicians by securing and arranging access to appropriate education resources. In addition to providing printed and audiovisual materials searches, the broker identifies courses, seminars, consultants, clinics, equipment, or other specialized resources that may be necessary for successful completion of the learning plan. The broker is available for individual assistance and attends group meetings as a resource to participants.

Research Assistant. The research assistant assists physician participants and project staff in arrangements, scheduling, and data collection necessary for project operation and group meetings.

Needs Assessment

One of the first and most important steps self-directed physicians take in pursuing a learning goal is the needs assessment. During this phase physicians may simply reflect on topics in their practice they are interested in learning more about, or they may conduct a systematic process to identify discrepancies between their skills and accepted medical practice. For each of these techniques, numerous ways can be devised to identify the learning goal to study. The following methods are provided as examples and should not be considered exhaustive of the techniques self-directed physicians can use during the needs assessment phase.

Intrinsic Interests. This method of needs assessment requires physicians to reflect on their practice and/or recent topics being discussed by experts in their specialties or medical societies. After sufficient reflection physicians list topics of interest. Topic lists may also be generated from recent (last year) journal indexes, seminar topics from formal Continuing Medical Education (CME) programs, skill tests generated by topic experts, and audiovisual resource lists available from state and national groups who were likely to have conducted a needs assessment before development of recent resources.

A prioritization of the topic list must then be performed to identify high-interest and high-impact topics. The prioritization is usually accomplished by considering such things as available resources and realistic time available to the physicians to pursue certain topics.

Examinations. This method of needs assessment may require physicians to review test content descriptions provided by their licensure and/or specialty boards. The physicians would conduct a self-analysis by rating the content areas according to their perceived weaknesses and strengths. At this point physicians may wish to take self-assessment examinations, if available or devisable, to compare to their self-analysis and/or use the prioritization criteria to make their final topic selection.

Audit of Practice. This method of needs assessment re-

quires physicians to perform an analysis of their practice to discover topics for consideration that will directly relate to patient
care. One method frequently suggested requires physicians to
audit their patient records. This process is used to discover the
disorders they treat most often, the problems that give them the
most difficulty solving, the conditions that cause the most se-
vere complications or cost their patients the greatest expense
and disability. At this point physicians would prioritize the list
as suggested above and select the patient problem to study. Recent articles and other educational resources concerning the
topic would then be collected to enable physicians to quickly
identify areas to pursue in the learning plan. Physicians may
also call on consultants, specialists, and medical school faculty
to provide a criterion of performance for managing patients
with the particular problem or condition selected to study.
Physicians can then compare their own management of patients
with these problems and determine to what extent it matches
the ideal or criterion performance devised by the consultants.

  Another method of generating the list of potential areas
of practice to study can be obtained by use of a patient survey.
With this method physicians would ask their patients to express
their satisfaction with the care they received for various health
problems. This information can be used with other prioritization criteria and the discrepancy approach described above to
establish a standard of practice.

The Learning Plan

  A learning plan, sometimes called a "learning contract,"
can be used to describe four basic components of an intended
educational experience in any subject matter:

1. The *objectives,* or a description of what the learner expects
    to be able to do as an outcome of the experience.
2. The learning *strategies,* or a description of the activities and
    resources necessary to prepare the learner to accomplish
    the stated objectives.
3. The *evidence of accomplishment,* or a description of the in-

formation to be collected to measure the extent to which the objective has been met.

4. The *criteria and means of validation,* or a description of the persons, standards, and procedures that will be used to judge the evidence.

In the Self-Directed Learning Project, a physician's learning plan will serve as primary documentation of the self-directed educational experience. It is designed by the physician at the outset of the experience and may be modified in part or in whole as the experience progresses. At the completion of the activities specified in the plan, including the evaluations of the evidence of accomplishment, the learning plan and associated documents provide a basis of support for the soundness of the educational experience. Those kinds of learning that are engaged in for purely personal development can perhaps be planned and carried out completely by individuals on their own terms and with only a loose structure. But those kinds of learning that have as their purpose improving one's competence to perform in a job or in a profession must take into account the needs and expectations of organizations, professions, and society. Learning contracts provide a means for negotiating a reconciliation between these external needs and expectations and the learner's internal needs and interests.

Each component of a learning plan is described briefly below.

Objectives. Objectives are clear statements of the intended outcomes of an educational experience. Educational outcomes may be in the form of knowledge, psychomotor skills, or attitudes. Objectives are stated in performance terms; that is, they describe what the learner will be able to do, using specific action verbs. Further, an educational objective that is stated well is specific and unambiguous about the outcome to be measured, rather than global and general:

Too general: To learn more about treating respiratory distress in the newborn.

Too process oriented: To read four articles about in-
                                 tensive respiratory management
                                 of the newborn.

Specific measurable objective: To select "early criteria" for de-
                                 termining the need for mechani-
                                 cal ventilation in premature
                                 neonates.

  Sometimes it is more communicative to describe the educational aims or outcomes of a project by writing a general goal
and a set of more specific supporting objectives. The specific
objectives usually relate to the general goal in one of two ways:
(1) the objectives list smaller parts or steps necessary to achieve
the overall goal, or (2) the objectives list a representative sample of outcomes expected of a learner who can meet the overall
goal.

  It is a good idea to write down a general goal or a first
draft of intended objectives in a chosen topic area, then spend
some time reviewing relevant resources before deciding on a final list of objectives to guide your study. Finally, it is important
to keep in mind that the objective and the evaluation components of the learning plan are closely related, if not matched.
Since the objective defines the intended outcome of the learning experience, it is likely that the evidence to be collected in
evaluating accomplishment of the objective will be described in
the objective itself. For example, if a learner's objective is to devise a protocol for managing flail chest patients, then the evidence of accomplishment will probably be a written copy of the
protocol. For this reason it is important that objectives be specific and feasible to measure. In this project physicians are provided the services of a medical education specialist in documenting educational objectives and other aspects of the self-selected
learning plan.

  Learning Resources and Strategies. A self-directed learner
is free to choose from an array of resources, including print and
audiovisual media, lectures, rounds, conferences, formal programs, tutors, consultants, and clinics. Further, the resources
and strategies can be selected to correspond to the learner's

styles and preferences for learning. Self-scored learning-style profiles and inventories are available to help identify a participant's predominant information-processing modes and learning-style preference.

In this project physicians are provided the services of an educational broker to search, collect, acquire, refer, and otherwise arrange access to appropriate resources. Physicians may select, from a collection of potential resources, those methods and materials best suited to their educational objective and personal preferences.

Frequently a combination of resources and methods will be used to reach a single objective or set of related objectives. This is necessary because most resources will not be as comprehensive as might be needed and because of the complex nature of some objectives, especially those learning objectives that require outcomes beyond simple acquisition of knowledge.

Evidence of Accomplishment. For each objective some evidence must be collected to help measure the degree to which the objective has been accomplished. Most often the evidence to be collected is implied if not stated explicitly in the objective. Different types of evidence are required for assessing the accomplishment of different types of objectives.

Accomplishment of an educational objective aimed at acquiring knowledge or new information can be demonstrated by a report of knowledge acquired, as in essays, oral presentation, or exams. Objectives aimed at higher levels of understanding (comprehension, application, synthesis, evaluation) may be demonstrated by examples of using learned information, such as might occur in action projects, products, simulations, problem solving, and research efforts.

Criteria and Means for Validating Evidence. For each objective specified in the learning plan, criteria must be identified for use in judging the learner's evidence of accomplishment. The criteria will vary according to the type of objective and nature of the evidence associated with its accomplishment. For example, appropriate criteria for knowledge objectives might include comprehensiveness, depth, precision, clarity, accuracy, usefulness, scholarliness. For skill objectives more appropriate criteria may be speed, flexibility, precision, outcome. Often criteria may be based on norms, external standards, and/or useful comparisons of performance to peers and designated specialists.

In addition to specifying criteria for judging evidence of accomplishment, the learning plan should indicate the means by which the criteria are to be applied. For example, if the evidence of accomplishment is a report, then who will read it and what are their qualifications? By what means will the chosen evaluators express their judgments—rating scales, descriptive reports, or other means or measures?

Target Dates. Each objective should be viewed as an independent effort for the purpose of estimating the time required for completion. Time constraints of a busy practice considered, a single objective should be specific enough to manage completion in four to eight weeks. A collection of related objectives may take much longer, but each individual objective should carry a separate time estimate. Participants are expected to complete one or more objectives during a four-month interval.

2

American Nurses' Association's Guide for Self-Directed Continuing Education

American Nurses' Association

This guide for self-directed continuing professional education, by the American Nurses' Association, is so congruent with the andragogical model that I thought it should be included in the collection. Its provisions could easily be adapted to any profession.

Special features:

- The meaning of continuing education in nursing
- The American Nurses' Association philosophy of continuing education
- Documentation of self-directed learning activities
- Variables in self-directed learning
- Examples of self-directed learning activities
- The self-design process
- Criteria for approval of a self-directed learning project

The American Nurses' Association believes it has the responsibility to develop standards for nursing education and to devise methods for gaining their acceptance and implementation through appropriate channels. Nursing education includes basic education, graduate education, and continuing education.

Reprinted, with permission, from *Self-Directed Continuing Education in Nursing*, a publication of the American Nurses' Association, 1978.

Continuing education in nursing consists of planned, organized learning experiences designed to augment the knowledge, skills, and attitudes of registered nurses for the enhancement of nursing practice, education, administration, and research, to the end of improving health care to the public. Defined broadly, continuing education is a lifelong learning process that builds on and modifies previously acquired knowledge, skills, and attitudes. The structure and content of continuing education must be flexible in order to meet the nursing practice needs and career goals of nursing personnel.

ANA believes that:

- Continuing education is essential for maintaining competence in nursing practice.
- Faculties in schools of nursing have a responsibility to assist students in conceptualizing nursing as a health career that requires lifelong learning.
- Continuing education is necessary for the personal growth and professional maturity of the individual.
- Continuing education should communicate concepts and theories of nursing science and should facilitate their incorporation into nursing practice.
- Providers of continuing education should continually assess and periodically evaluate the effectiveness of educational offerings.
- Providers of continuing education should assist in the field testing of nursing knowledge and competence that may later be included in preservice or graduate programs.
- Continuing education should utilize the theories of adult learning.

ANA further believes that it has the responsibility to assist the state nurses' associations to plan and initiate continuing education approval and recognition programs (CEARP) through

- Developing guidelines for approval of continuing education activities.

- Designing a system to evaluate the effects of continuing education offerings on nursing practice.
- Providing consultation services.

Certain continuing education needs of practicing nurses are national in scope, however, and can be met best by the American Nurses' Association because of its capability of assessing common continuing education needs. Such needs include knowledge of national legislation affecting nurses and trends in nursing that are common to individuals and groups of nurses. As a provider of continuing education, ANA can also disseminate standards for nursing practice and work toward their implementation.

The ultimate responsibility and accountability for continuing education to enhance professional practice rest with the individual nurse. Many nurses practice in areas that are professionally or geographically isolated, however, making access to continuing education activities difficult. Further, individuals learn in different ways (learning styles) and at their own pace, and they learn those things that are of interest and relevance to them (learning needs). Individuals vary in motivation and readiness to learn. Thus, traditional methods of delivering continuing education, such as conferences and workshops, may not be available and may not meet special learning needs or learning styles.

A self-directed learning activity is one for which the learner takes the initiative and responsibility for the learning process. Self-directed learning is either designed by the learner or designed by others. Most persons engage in some type of self-directed learning, which may or may not be planned or structured. For some persons self-directed study is the most effective way to learn. Its greatest advantage is that it provides options to individuals for meeting specialized learning needs.

Nurses who participate in mandatory or voluntary systems of continuing education are required to document their learning activities. Learning by traditional methods has been relatively easy to document because historically it is based on accepted measures of success—for example, demonstrated change in knowledge, skills, or attitude. In contrast, nontraditional learning ordinarily has not been documented; its merit has been in the value perceived by the individual. Since approval bodies are beginning to recognize self-directed learning activities, careful documentation is essential.

As more states develop plans for recognizing self-directed learning, use of this document will help achieve a uniform approach to facilitating interstate transferability of continuing education records.

For individual learners, these guidelines should be viewed as suggestions and not as the only method of approach to this form of learning. Many nurses engage in a wide variety of self-designed learning projects without the formal structure suggested here. But for those who wish to seek approval, structure is needed and these guidelines suggest one approach.

Individuals seeking recognition for self-directed learning are advised to request specific requirements from their state nurses' association or licensing body before beginning a project, since some states have well-defined guidelines for approval of self-directed learning activities. Approval bodies are encouraged to support diversity in content and process as long as the learning outcome or professional development demonstrates relevance to the individual's practice. Each approval body must deal individually with philosophical issues, such as the depth and scope of learning projects or the amount of self-directed learning that is acceptable.

Purpose of the Document

This document has four purposes:

1. To introduce the concept of self-directed learning that encompasses two dimensions—self-designed and other-designed.
2. To provide guidelines in the self-design process.
3. To provide criteria for approval of self-designed, self-directed learning for use by approval bodies, such as a state

licensing body or a continuing education approval and recognition program of a state nurses' association.

4. To provide a substantive contribution to the acceptance of self-directed learning as a legitimate form of continuing education learning.

Definitions

Self-directed learning may encompass a wide range of learning activities. A self-directed learning activity (self-designed or other-designed) is one for which the learner takes the initiative and responsibility for the learning process. Self-designed and other-designed activities are differentiated by the extent to which the learner controls the learning variables. In self-designed activities, the learner controls the majority of the learning variables; in other-designed activities, someone other than the learner controls the majority of the learning variables.

The learning variables are as follows:

1. Identification of learning needs
2. Topic and purpose of the learning activity
3. Objectives or expected outcomes
4. Appropriate learning experiences
5. Learning resources
6. Environment
7. Time
8. Pace
9. Methods of evaluation
10. Methods of documentation

Examples of Self-Directed Learning Activities

Self-designed (the learner controls the majority of learning variables):

Informal investigation of a specific nursing problem

Individual scientific research

Self-guided focused reading

Independent learning projects

Other-designed (the learner controls a limited number of learning variables):

Correspondence course

Self-contained learning packages

Directed reading

Computer-assisted instruction

Programmed instruction

Either self-designed or other-designed:

Study tour

Clinical application

Work project with shared control of variables

The Self-Design Process

The self-design process includes planning, implementation, evaluation, and documentation. The steps that follow are suggested to assist the individual learner with self-directed learning. They also provide a format that may be used in submitting a self-designed project to an approval committee.

A. Planning (NOTE: Any step in the planning process may be modified during the implementation phase of the project.)
1. Identification of learning needs
Learning needs may be felt needs of the individual or needs ascribed by others (such as a supervisor). The individual determines which needs may be met through self-designed study and establishes some learning goals and priorities.

2. Selection of specific focus for the project
    The focus of the project should relate to professional competence and needed practice. A statement of purpose should be developed. It may be helpful to describe the relationship between this learning activity and previous or future ones undertaken by the individual.

3. Determination of expected outcome objectives
    The expected outcomes are expressed as objectives for the learner. The objectives should be measurable, attainable, and more specific than the statement of purpose.

4. Assessment and selection of resources and learning experiences
    The objectives will influence the type of resources and learning experiences selected. If a variety of learning resources is available, the learner will need to determine which are most appropriate for this project. Following are examples of resources that may be used alone or in combination:

    a. Materials
        Audiotapes and records
        Client records
        Computer-assisted instruction
        Correspondence courses
        Learning modules
        Media packages (slide-tapes, filmstrips)
        Nursing books and periodicals
        Nonnursing literature
        Pamphlets and brochures
        Pictures, charts, diagrams
        Programmed instruction
        Radio
        Telephone
        Television

    b. Human resources
        Allied health professionals
        Clients (patients)

Clinical nursing experts
Colleagues, peers, co-workers
Educators (nursing and other disciplines)
Families
Librarians

5. Determination of evaluation methods
    Some form of evaluation is essential so the learner can
    measure the extent to which objectives have been
    achieved. Selection of specific evaluation tools or tech-
    niques depends upon such factors as the nature and
    scope of objectives, available resources, and learner
    preference.

6. Development of documentation procedures
    Documentation provides tangible evidence that objec-
    tives have been achieved. Following are examples of
    documentation:
    a. A written research or other professional paper,
        with or without reviewer's comments
    b. A letter of acceptance for publication from a pro-
        fessional journal
    c. Written verification of successful mastery of a
        clinical skill (Verification by an expert in the field
        may be needed if the approval body requests it.)
    d. An annotated bibliography
    e. Successful completion of a written exam prepared
        by an expert in the field
    f. Written case study, with or without reviewer's
        comments (If previously accepted as a part of
        ANA's certification process, a copy of the notifi-
        cation of certification is acceptable.)

7. Projection of project time schedule
    An estimate of the total amount of time (hours, days,
    weeks, months) required to complete the project will
    assist the learner in planning effective use of time. This
    plan may include target dates for the completion of
    various segments. The learner will also determine a
    pace and environment suitable to her own learning
    style and conducive to meeting the objectives. Addi-

tionally, when seeking approval of the project, the learner will need to include the number of contact hours she requests for the project.

B. Implementation

As the learner carries out the project, the proposed plan may be modified. Expected outcomes or objectives may change during this phase with new developments or expanded knowledge. The learner's needs or interest may change, making the original plan inappropriate. Additional learning resources may be located, or different learning experiences may be sought. Such changes (with rationale) should be incorporated into the final report, but they do not require renegotiations with the approval body.

C. Evaluation

Formative evaluation by the learner occurs throughout the process. It assists the learner in progressing toward the attainment of the objectives and allows for ongoing improvements of the original idea. In summative evaluation, occurring at the end, the learner determines the extent to which the stated objectives have been met.

D. Documentation

Upon completion of the project, a final report is submitted to the approval body. The approval body may have a form or an outline for the final report. If not, the report may be in any appropriate form (see A-5) that gives evidence of learning. Additional information may be necessary to describe how the objectives were met and the time required to complete them.

E. Submission for approval

Individuals who live in states that do not have an application for self-directed learning activities should submit a narrative description of their independent learning project, utilizing the preceding steps as a guide. The date, name, address, and license number should also be included.

Criteria for Approval of Self-Designed Project

The following criteria are suggested for approval of a self-designed, self-directed learning project by a continuing education approval and recognition program of a state nurses' association or by a state licensure board.

A. For prior approval of a proposed plan
   1. Learning needs
       a. Evidence is provided that the learning project is based on the individual's identification of her own learning needs.
       b. The description of the project indicates that self-designed study is a realistic method of meeting the identified learning needs.
   2. Focus of the project
       a. The title indicates a specific area of focus.
       b. The purpose describes the relationship of the content of the project to the learner's professional practice and competence or to the bodies of knowledge that contribute to nursing practice.
       c. An overview of the project is provided in the description.
       d. If applicable, the relationship between this learning activity and previous or proposed ones done by the learner is described; for example, it shows a relationship to the learner's long-range goal.
   3. Objectives
       a. The objectives are clearly stated.
       b. The objectives appear to be attainable in the proposed time.
       c. The objectives are measurable.
       d. The objectives indicate learner outcomes.
   4. Resources and learning experiences
       a. Adequate resources are identified.
       b. Appropriate learning experiences are identified or described.
       c. Learning experiences relate to the achievement of objectives.
   5. Evaluation
       a. The plan for evaluating the expected outcomes is based on the objectives.
       b. An evaluating method is proposed.

6. Documentation (A procedure for documentation is de-scribed.)
7. Estimated time schedule
   a. An estimate of the total amount of time (hours, days, weeks, months) for the project is given.
   b. The estimated time appears realistic for the proj-ect.
   c. The (estimated) number of contact hours the in-dividual requests is realistic for the project.

B. For postcompletion approval
   In addition to the first three steps outlined above, the fol-lowing criteria are considered in the approval of a com-pleted project:
   1. Resources and learning experiences
      a. Appropriate learning resources were used.
      b. Learning experiences were appropriate to the ob-jectives.
   2. Content
      a. The content of the completed project is accurate and current.
      b. The content is presented in a logical manner.
      c. The content is consistent with the objectives.
   3. Evaluation
      a. Evidence is provided for the attainment of objec-tives.
      b. The evaluation methods used indicate that the ob-jectives were attained.
   4. Documentation
      a. Documentation includes the time involved for completing the learning project.
      b. The number of contact hours requested by the in-dividual is realistic for the learning activity.

3

Teaching Nurses
Advanced Skills
at a Metropolitan Hospital

Carol B. Dare

This selection addresses another dimension of the question whether the andragogical model can be used with highly technical subject matter. It is difficult to think of any content more technical and demanding of proficiency than cardiovascular nursing. This is the actual course syllabus that is given to the learners to orient them to the philosophy and rationale for the self-directed learning program, its objectives (in behavioral terms), precourse instructions, the designing of learning contracts, the use of learning modules and other resources, and evaluation procedures.

Carol B. Dare is a critical care nursing educator in Little Rock, Arkansas.

Special features:

- Statement of philosophy
- Course objectives in terms of behavioral outcomes
- Precourse instructions
- Orientation to self-directed learning
- Introduction to learning modules
- Devising learning contracts
- Evaluation of learning

Adapted, with permission, from a syllabus for the Cardiovascular Nursing Program at Doctors Hospital, Little Rock, Arkansas, designed by Carol B. Dare.

This course provides a comprehensive and integrated approach to the management of the adult cardiac patient, with the goal of restoring the patient to and facilitating the maintenance of a maximal level of health.

It is recognized that nursing can make a significant impact on decreasing cardiovascular morbidity and mortality and improving the quality of life—both inside and outside the formal coronary care setting—in persons with cardiovascular disease.

It is further recognized that cardiovascular nursing requires skills and knowledge beyond that which can be acquired in basic nursing education and in general career experience. It demands of the nurse an expanded professional role in the areas of diagnosis and management. Cardiovascular nursing challenges the nurse to accept more professional responsibility and develop expertise in assessment and technical skills.

It is further recognized that not all cardiovascular nurses have the need for identical educational preparation in order to function as competent practitioners in their own areas of clinical practice. Therefore, this Cardiovascular Nursing Program focuses on cardiovascular nursing in a variety of clinical settings, with built-in flexibility to meet the individual professional needs of nursing practitioners in their own specific areas of clinical responsibility.

Therefore, in order to meet the individual needs of nurses from all specialty areas and all levels of clinical expertise who desire increased knowledge of cardiovascular nursing and increased competencies in cardiovascular nursing practice, a self-paced, self-directed program is offered based upon the concepts of adult learning. This program provides the flexibility necessary to meet the individual needs of the nurse, the unit, the institution, and, above all, the patient.

Course Description

This course focuses on a holistic approach to nursing of the adult patient with cardiovascular disease, designed for the professional nurse, and based upon the concepts of self-directed learning. Background is presented on cardiovascular anatomy and physiology, with emphasis on practical application. Coronary artery disease is presented as a clinical entity, with angina, myocardial infarction, and sudden death being viewed as manifestations of this disease. A step-by-step approach is utilized in the presentation of prevention, etiology, recognition, diagnosis, treatment, and rehabilitation of patients with coronary artery disease.

The course provides self-directed learning experiences designed to meet the individual needs of each participant. Based upon an individual needs assessment, each participant formulates a learning contract with guidance from her supervisor and the course coordinator. Several self-learning modules—consisting of pertinent reading, audiovisual material, and/or clinical experience—are each followed by check points which assess acquisition of knowledge of critical data. Lectures and qualified resource people are available to supplement the independent learning activities as the participant desires. Each learning module is designed with one or more specific competencies in mind, and testing is based on assessment of these acquired competencies. In addition, material is presented as described in the core curriculum for "Advanced Cardiac Life Support" as prescribed by the American Heart Association. It is anticipated that a minimum of 240 hours will be spent in course activities.

Upon completion of the course, the nurse will hold certification in cardiovascular nursing practice that is rich in the generalities of caring for the adult cardiovascular patient as well as the specifics relevant to her own area of professional nursing practice. These individual competencies are mutually arrived at by the participant, her nursing supervisor, and the course coordinator. The competencies met during the course are clearly outlined in an addendum to the course certificate. Advanced Cardiac Life Support (ACLS) certification will be granted to those participants who successfully meet the criteria established by the American Heart Association.

Additional learning goals will be established and documented in a Professional Development Plan upon course completion. This ongoing learning contract will be formulated by the participant to meet continuing educational needs, designed to enhance continuing levels of clinical expertise.

Course Objectives

Upon completion of the course, the nurse will be able to:

1. Identify her own role in relation to the cardiac patient and the Coronary Care Unit (CCU) team, also identifying the role of coronary care in the reduction of cardiovascular morbidity and mortality.
2. Explain and apply the anatomy and physiology of the cardiovascular system and identify how it relates to the body as an integrated whole in promoting homeostasis.
3. Describe the pathogenesis, pathophysiology, and manifestations of coronary artery disease, with emphasis on prevention, early recognition, and nursing management of angina. She will also recognize coronary artery disease as being a continuum, with angina and myocardial infarction (MI) as progressive manifestations of this entity, identifying sudden death as a sequela of this disease. She will do a differential diagnosis of chest pain aimed at recognition of angina (stable and unstable) and MI.
4. Discuss procedures and tests indicated for diagnosis and evaluation of ischemic heart disease and MI.
5. Perform basic arrhythmia interpretation, utilizing a systematic approach to pattern recognition. Differentiate normal from abnormal 12 lead ECGs and interpret rate, rhythm, axis, ischemia, infarction, and selected miscellaneous changes.
6. Perform a comprehensive cardiovascular history and physical examination on a patient with an uncomplicated MI, planning appropriate nursing care based on the information gained and demonstrating knowledge of pathophysiology and pertinent psychoemotional factors. Nursing care should be planned according to patient needs, relating medical and nursing management to the patient's condition.
7. Discuss drug therapy appropriate for cardiovascular pa-

tients, including indications, contraindications, desired effects, side effects, precautions, route of administration, and dosage for each of the relevant drugs.

8. Discuss principles of appropriate oxygen therapy in the cardiovascular patient, demonstrating ability to perform this function. Demonstrate basic understanding of acid-base balance by ability to analyze arterial blood gasses, and suggest appropriate measures to correct abnormal values.

9. Function with a high degree of competency in a cardiac arrest situation. ACLS certification will be granted to participants who successfully meet the objectives outlined in the ACLS provider core curriculum.

10. Recognize major complications of acute MI, demonstrating specific knowledge of pathogenesis, pathophysiology, prevention, treatment, and prognosis. Perform appropriate emergency measures for the major complications of acute MI, specifically demonstrating early recognition and appropriate treatment of the warning and lethal arrhythmias.

11. Demonstrate knowledge of principles of hemodynamic monitoring designed to identify and serve as a guide in the management of these complications.

12. Describe factors involved in post-MI rehabilitation, including patient education, risk factor modification, physical activity, sexual activity, and drug therapy; and develop an individualized rehabilitation program for a post-MI patient.

13. Demonstrate knowledge of related pathology, such as conditions requiring permanent pacing, cardioversion, and other situations.

General Precourse Instructions

You are about to embark upon an adult learning experience in cardiovascular nursing practice. The course is structured with the flexibility to allow for individualization of learning experiences based upon the needs of the individual learner. Each student, because of past experience and present and future professional expectations, comes to the course with learning needs that probably differ from those of her fellow students. The course coordinator, in cooperation with you and your head nurse/supervisor, will assist you in structuring a series of learning experiences that will meet your needs at this time, within the constraints dictated by the core curriculum. In order to accurately assess your present level of competencies and determine your perceived and actual needs, a Competency Rating Scale is included in this packet, which will give you and the coordinator a good feeling of where you are in your cardiovascular nursing development, where you and your head nurse feel that you need to be upon completion of this course, and where you plan to go in fulfilling your responsibility for ongoing professional development. Additional tools are provided to help identify what kind of a learner you are, as well as how you learn best.

This course is a self-directed adult learning experience. In order for you to more fully understand the reasons for this specific course design, included in this packet are some contrasting assumptions about childlike, traditional learning (pedagogy) and adult learning (andragogy). The basic difference is that, in an adult learning experience, the adult learner is provided with the opportunity to be self-directing and therefore learn what interests her, when it interests her, and in the way that it interests her, thereby increasing the likelihood that learning will actually take place.

For additional information on the concepts of self-directed learning, you are referred to the handbook *Self-Directed Learning* (Knowles, 1975). This book is easy, fast reading; and its concise, commonsense approach to adult learning principles will help you understand the whys and hows of self-directed learning that this course employs. This orientation would undoubtedly enhance the quality of the learning experience before you. Copies are available for loan through the course coordinator.

Introduction to Learning Modules

This course, as stated earlier, is a self-directed learning experience, based upon the principles of adult learning. Because of what we know about adults as learners, lectures will not be the primary learning modality used in this course. Instead, a variety of learning modalities will be employed, including pertinent reading materials (textbooks, journal reprints, and handouts), audiovisuals, clinical experiences, talking to a qualified expert, and any other resources you identify as being potentially meaningful to you, including lectures upon request.

In order to provide organization, structure, and direction to you in determining which activities you plan to utilize in meeting your objectives, learning modules have been developed to coincide with groups of specific objectives in each category. There are forty modules available for the core objectives for the course.

The modules are merely self-contained learning packages that address specific topics and are each designed to meet one or more objectives. All of the modules have at least three common components:

1. *Objectives.* These clearly and behaviorally state what you may expect to be able to do upon completion of the module. These objectives coincide with the objectives listed on the competency rating scale. As you work through the module, scrutinize the objectives individually, to make sure that they are relevant to your nursing practice. Any objectives that you consider irrelevant should be discussed with the course coordinator for possible omission from your individual lesson plan. These objectives should be kept closely in mind and referred to often during completion of the module.

2. *Suggested Activities.* This is a list of relevant and available resources (including reading, audiovisual, clinical, and other resources), which can be utilized in meeting the objectives. You should utilize those activities that you feel will be relevant to you. During the first day of class, you will be given extensive opportunity to pursue the available resources until you become quite familiar with them. Of course, as the course progresses, you will get a better feeling of what tools you can best utilize to facilitate your learning. You are by no means limited to the resources listed on this page, but these may serve as a guide.

3. *Evidence of Learning.* This documentation will be maintained in a portfolio and discussed with the course coordinator on a weekly basis. Potential options could include:

a. *A posttest.* This tool is based directly upon the objectives for each module, and it can be utilized for self-assessment and documentation that learning has taken place. Here, it is important to comment on the "nice-to-know" versus the "need-to-know." You will encounter a great deal of information in your studies which, although very useful, is not critical to your safe care of the patient (that is, you will probably not cause increased morbidity or mortality to your patients by virtue of not knowing this information). This "nice-to-know" information is therefore not included on the test, although it might be useful to know. Because only the critical "need-to-know" information is included on the test, you must make 100 percent on each test. As stated earlier, in addition to documentation of exposure to the critical elements for purposes of credible certification, the test is a self-assessment tool for your use in verifying that you know the critical information. Therefore, the test is self-administered when you feel that you are ready, and self-graded. Because the test is designed to evaluate what you know (instead of how well you can second-guess and take tests), you may take the test as many times as is necessary for you to make 100. Remember, the bottom line is what you know, rather than how you learned it, so although returning to the books is recommended for questions you miss (especially if you don't know why you missed them), it is not required that you do so (this is adult learning). If you prefer not to return to the literature to research vague information, the course coordinator is available to you for clarification of those questions you do not know the answer to. For purposes of documentation and credibility, it is strongly recommended that you take all of the tests. If you have a problem with this, please discuss it with the course coordinator.

b. *Clinical practicum sheets.* These are to be completed by you and your preceptor, indicating the content and quality of your clinical experience.

c. *Application tools* (for example, 12 lead ECGs). These may be completed in order to document learning.

d. *Follow-through patient.* A patient will be followed from admission through discharge, demonstrating your ability to integrate the entire course of his illness. This will be discussed further in the appropriate module.

Other options can be explored on an individual basis. For example, you may opt to give a presentation to the class on a topic you are particularly familiar with or interested in. Other options might include preparing a learning module or posttest on a particular subject.

Although you might be asked to take a posttest for the purpose of self-assessment of retention and ongoing course evaluation, there will be no comprehensive examination for the purposes of documentation of learning. It is therefore very important that, whatever method you choose to document, the information you present is valid and credible.

Instructions for Devising Your Learning Contract

As outlined on the Competency Rating Scale, the objectives for the course are divided into thirteen major categories. Each of these categories is further broken down into more specific objectives/competencies, which coincide closely with the learning modules. Having identified the objectives that you plan to meet, your next task is to devise a learning strategy to meet them. This is what you will do today (the first day of class). The components of this task are as follows:

1. Determine the order in which you plan to pursue the objectives. (This can be individualized, although a general order should be followed for the sake of logical flow and adequate background before tackling the more advanced topics.) A list of modules and suggested prerequisites is provided to assist you.

2. Identify the relevant modules for each objective, and determine what activities you plan to employ to meet each objective. The module numbers which correspond with each competency are noted on the Competency Rating Scale.

3. Write down on the attached calendar the dates you plan to work on/complete each activity/objective.

Facilitating tasks would include:

1. Familiarize yourself with the available resources.
   a. Look through the text references in order to acquaint yourself with what is available to you.
   b. Some of the audiovisuals are annotated, and this information is available on the teaching cart, though the length of each of the AVs is stated on the activity sheet in the related module.
   c. Look over the list of human resources and optional lectures.
   d. Think creatively about other options not mentioned above.
2. Go to each module and look at the objectives. Determine which of those you feel you have already met (you have done this on the Competency Rating Scale), thereby isolating those you need to work on.
3. Cross-referencing from the objectives to the activities, determine (tentatively) which activities you plan to employ in meeting the objectives. (This can be renegotiated at any time.)
4. On the attached schedule, plot your individual lesson plan in the form of a tentative timetable for completion of each module or objective (whichever helps you think more clearly and feel more in control). In making these decisions, you should consider your interest in the subject, the depth you feel you require in the subject, how much you already know about it, and the amount of time you feel you will need to complete each activity you have tentatively selected. Keep in mind that these dates may be renegotiated because you may find that the activities you have presumptively selected may be too few or too many to actually meet the objectives. (*Please Note:* Plotting a lesson plan will be a formidable task, but it is important in order to assure that you pace yourself appropriately to complete the course in the prescribed six weeks, so take your time in doing it. The whole day is allotted for this task, and I will help you to whatever extent you require. YOU CAN DO IT!)

Evaluation

Now comes the time for evaluation. It has two components:

1. As I stated in our first meeting, this course has been a shared learning experience for us. You have concentrated on becoming a self-directed learner in acquiring skills in cardiovascular nursing practice. I have endeavored to find better ways to facilitate learning and coordinate this course. The course evaluation, as well as the notes you have made along the way on your activity sheets, will assist me in meeting my personal objective.

2. In terms of self-assessing the extent to which you have met your objectives, there should be no surprises (you have been in close touch with this for the duration of the course). However, if you want to do a final self-assessment, you may pursue at least one of the three following options:

   a. The first option is a posttest, which is identical to your pretest; if you choose to take it, it will document to you and the world that learning has taken place.

   b. The second test in this section is a final exam that I used in the old days before I became "enlightened." If you are still somewhat uncomfortable about knowing what you have learned, you may take this test.

   c. A third option available to you would be to retake some (or all) of the posttests that you took upon completion of the modules. If you take these, it might be interesting as an inferred evaluation of your cognitive retention. You could also review your own tests, being sure to review some of the questions you got right the first time, as well as those you missed.

However, regardless of which, if any, method you employ to evaluate yourself, be assured that learning has definitely taken place. No doubt, you have met your original objective of wanting to learn more about cardiovascular nursing practice. Because of the active involvement you took in this learning, you now own the knowledge (rather than having borrowed it for six weeks). It is yours to do with as you wish. Your success as a competent cardiovascular nurse depends on you, which brings me to my second point.

Probably the most exciting thing that you have gained in this course is that you have gotten to know something new about yourself—that you are an adult learner who is responsible for your own learning—that you are capable of being self-directed . . . that you can take advantage of a variety of resources to meet objectives that you yourself have set . . . that you can be creative in designing an educational program just for you . . . and that you are valued—by yourself, by your peers, and by me. Thank you so much for what you have taught me and what you have given me—a piece of yourself.

4

In-Service Nursing Education Through Clinical Units

Jessie Albanetti, Donna Carroll

This selection describes how principles of adult learning were applied to the design and operation of an innovative program of in-service nursing education in which primary responsibility is placed on the clinical nursing units.

Jessie Albanetti is assistant director of staff education, and Donna Carroll is director of staff education for the Department of Nursing at St. Mary's Hospital, Waterbury, Connecticut.

Special features:

- Basic beliefs underlying this model
- Involvement of head nurses
- Involvement of unit coordinators
- Assessment of learning needs
- Taping of learner presentations as resources for future learning
- Orientation to resources
- An "Educational Activities Calendar"
- Evaluation of results

The "un-model" is an innovative approach to unit-level education that allows participants a high degree of flexibility in designing a plan of education relevant to their specific needs in terms of content and available time. The approach utilizes hu-

Reprinted, with permission, from "The UN-Model: A Humanistic Approach to Unit-Level Education," *Nurse Educator*, 1977, 2 (3), 23-24.

manistic principles of adult education with an emphasis on active participation in striving toward personal and professional growth and, ultimately, improved patient care.

The "un-model" evolved as a result of several factors:

1. Limited education manpower.
2. Our belief in our role as facilitators of learning.
3. Our belief in concepts of adult education.
4. Our belief in the value of participatory learning.

Two members of the Staff Education Department were faced with the major responsibility for unit-level education on seventeen clinical units. The task seemed insurmountable. In addition, as we explored our roles and our philosophies regarding education, we concluded that it would be both impractical and highly undesirable to try to determine the learning needs for so many persons and then to plan schedules and present educational offerings accordingly. We feel strongly that valuable education—true learning—is that which is desired and sought after by the individual; is relevant to his needs; and is further assimilated through sharing with others. We believe that adults want to learn and will learn what is important to them. Thus, we needed a plan that would offer participants freedom to identify their learning needs and choose methods of sharing information. As facilitators, we felt our job was to build a framework for the identification of needs and then assist the staff with the implementation of their own plan, by providing information regarding resources and supporting all efforts.

Head Nurse Participation

We began by meeting with head nurses to identify our philosophy of "unit-level education" and explaining to them that their help would be required only in the setting of expectations. Since we knew expectations to be highly motivating, the support of head nurses regarding them was essential. We believed that if the head nurses communicated the expectation that the staff should plan and carry out educational activities, then the staff would meet that expectation—and we were right!

The next step was to recruit "unit education coordinators." This role was filled by a nurse from each clinical unit who either volunteered (preferably) or was selected by the head nurse. The length of this appointment was determined by each unit. Most units had many eager volunteers among nurses who felt the need to exercise their leadership abilities. The coordinator from each unit met with the staff from her unit to design their educational plan. A questionnaire listing broad categories of possible areas of learning (for example, treatments, procedures, medications) was designed to assist the nurses in identifying their educational needs. The coordinators distributed the questionnaire to the staff members, and each listed her own learning desires under each category. Any uncategorized "miscellaneous" needs were also identified by the nurses. The coordinators utilized these suggestions to plan the calendar of presentations with the staff.

It was suggested that those identifying a particular need should research and present that topic as a means of increasing learning; however, this was not required. The number of presentations to be made each month was determined by the staff, based on their own needs and situation. It was suggested that topics be narrow and presentations short (fifteen to twenty minutes), to avoid postponement due to lack of time during busy periods. Each unit was encouraged to determine how to enable staff from all shifts to participate. We made some suggestions to fuel the fire of ideas, but many units came up with their own unique and excellent approaches.

Taping of presentations is encouraged to give absentees access to the information. The cassettes are available on the unit for one week after recording takes place, and are then catalogued in the library for use by any interested personnel. Although we prefer a more personal means of communication, we feel it is important to have the information recorded for reference purposes and for those who cannot possibly be present.

At each presentation a summary and attendance list is

made by a "secretary," and copies are filed on the unit and in the Staff Education Department. Some units appoint a secretary for each month, some have a more or less permanent secretary, and others just ask a member of the group to act as secretary at each presentation.

Use of Available Resources Encouraged

As facilitators, we initially made ourselves available to guide coordinators and staff members, to provide information regarding resources, and to offer help in any area. Recognizing the wealth of information available in the hospital library, we planned a "Know Your Library" program with the librarian. This program, which was open to all nursing personnel, included a tour of the library, focusing on locations of various resources; instruction in the use of the *Cumulative Index to Nursing Literature*; and a list of the names of the audiovisual films and cassettes, the AV hardware, and the journals available in the library. The thirty-minute program was conducted three times daily for five days and then twice each month. It will be continued twice monthly indefinitely. Library statistics show a significant increase in use of facilities by nursing personnel since the institution of unit-level education and the "Know Your Library" program.

As an additional attempt to communicate educational activities and facilitate intraunit as well as interunit sharing, we have devised a monthly "Educational Activities Calendar," which is distributed to all clinical units. This calendar indicates the full schedule of presentations on all units for the month. Coordinators are required to send their projected calendar for the coming month to the Staff Education Department by the 25th of each month. We then prepare a mimeographed calendar on yellow paper, which is clearly distinguishable from the many other papers posted on unit bulletin boards. Centralized educational activities are also included on this calendar, and some of the coordinators have taken the initiative of keeping their head nurses and co-workers apprised of coming events. A current list of recorded presentations catalogued in the library is also attached to the calendar each month.

This approach relies heavily on the support of the head nurses through their setting of expectations and on our belief that as learning becomes more routine and less painful it becomes self-motivating. Although in the beginning we offered suggestions to help the coordinators and their co-workers develop their plan, the entire approach allows for a great deal of freedom and encourages each person's unique contribution. The few "requirements" are primarily the responsibility of the coordinator, who submits calendars, summaries, and attendance lists. This approach encourages the acquisition of new information and allows for the personal discovery of its meaning by the individual.

Several Positive Results

The roles of coordinator and participant allow personnel to recognize and utilize their own imaginative contributions.

Our approach has resulted in a number of beneficial accomplishments aside from the successful planning and sharing of education among nursing personnel and the resultant improvement in patient care that the nurses have reported. It has provided the opportunity to serve as unit education coordinators for those who wish to demonstrate their leadership abilities. It has promoted a sense of comradeship and fostered enthusiasm and teamwork in all unit functions. This benefit is perhaps the most valuable of all and has been mentioned countless times by many nursing personnel as being a direct result of the "working together" required in the planning and implementation of unit-level education.

The plan was begun on five medical units. After two months head nurses were asked to evaluate it and their staff's response. The results were all favorable and very encouraging. Comments indicated the plan was well accepted, personnel were participating eagerly, and staff felt the programs were improving the care they gave to patients. After four months we asked all personnel in these areas to evaluate unit-level education. Again responses were positive. Staff members felt the plan helped meet their individual educational needs and provided for better patient care. They reported consistently that they enjoyed participating in their own education.

At this point the remaining units became involved in unit-level education. We followed the same approach used in the initial areas, and the response was enthusiastic. The plan has remained self-sustaining, with Staff Education acting as the resource liaison. Coordinators' meetings are held approximately every six weeks for the sharing of ideas, problems, and relevant information. Our philosophy has thus far been supported and of course our satisfaction is great. We would be remiss not to mention our belief that the total cooperation of all nursing personnel at St. Mary's Hospital as well as complete administrative support contributed decisively to the success of unit-level education. However, we feel that true commitment to a sound philosophy by the educational facilitators and the setting of expectations by the head nurse can lead to significant success even where a degree of indifference among personnel may exist.

SIX

◆◆◆◆◆◆◆◆◆◆◆◆◆◆◆◆◆◆◆◆◆◆◆◆◆◆◆◆◆◆◆◆◆◆◆◆◆◆◆

Applications
in Religious Education

Religious institutions of most denominations have been shifting their focus from a primary concern with the instruction of children and youth to at least an equal concern for the education of adults. Many denominations and an increasing number of local churches have added adult education specialists to their staffs, with the result that their programs have become more congruent with principles of adult learning.

This chapter presents two case descriptions of programs that were based self-consciously on the andragogical model. The philosophy and strategies of the ecumenical Biblical Andragogy Clinic, headquartered in Mississauga, Ontario, are explained in selection 1. It suggests that a solution to a major contemporary religious education problem for churches and synagogues lies in the development of small communities of adult learners. Selection 2 is a seventeen-year longitudinal case study that documents the steps for successfully converting a social system —in this case the Catholic Archdiocese of Detroit—into a learning community. It demonstrates that major organizational change can be achieved through educational means.

1

The Biblical Andragogy Clinic

Eugene Trester

This selection describes the rationale and procedures of one of
the most innovative applications of the andragogical model to
religious education that I have seen. The program described is
conducted by the Biblical Andragogy Clinic, headquartered in
Mississauga, Ontario. The clinic is a charitable, nonprofit, ecumenical organization founded for the promotion of adult biblical learning.

Eugene Trester is director of the clinic.

Special features:

- The challenge to religious educators of adult learners
- Focus on learning, not teaching
- Formation of learning communities
- Leadership training through Facilitators' Clinics

Contemporary biblical scholarship alerts us to the fact that the
Bible was formed in a community context. Adult learning the-
orists stress that adults learn best in a community atmosphere
fostering cooperation, caring, and mutual respect.

This article suggests that a solution to a major contemporary religious education problem for churches and synagogues lies in the development of small communities of adult
learners. This challenge and proposed solution for religious educators will be dealt with under the themes of (1) the gap between

Adapted, with permission, from "Adult Biblical Learning in Community," a paper presented at the international convention of the Religious Education Association, Toronto, 1979.

adult religious understanding and modern biblical scholarship, (2) the future church and adult biblical learning, and (3) biblical critical learning in local communities.

The Gap: Adult Religious Understanding and Modern Biblical Scholarship

Biblical research has made amazing advances in recent decades. Yet it becomes increasingly obvious that the wealth of knowledge currently available in the realm of biblical scholarship has somehow tragically failed to flow out into the lives and minds of adults (Smart, 1970).

Modern biblical scholarship, enlivened by the findings of archeology, linguistic studies, and the historical sciences, has life-giving potential when it satiates the spiritual-intellectual appetites of modern adults. The insights of biblical scholarship need to grace the table of contemporary adults. The fruit of specialized biblical studies should be used to nurture and empower people in their day-to-day living.

The integration of scientific advancements in religious knowledge into contemporary adult life is a prerequisite for a vital adult faith and for balanced mental health. Adults need to live their religious lives in the present age.

Brown (1975, p. 5) phrases our current educational challenge in these words: "The fairest way of judging Christian theological endeavors of the past is on the basis of whether or not they used the knowledge at their disposal. And we Christians of today are liable to be judged harshly by the future if we do not use the knowledge at our disposal in reflecting upon God." The real challenge for the religious educator resides in the fact that, in spite of the increasing technicality and complexity of biblical studies, their purpose always is to open to adults the springs of living water contained in the Scriptures. The fruits of modern biblical criticism need to be placed at the disposal of adult believers. The task of the religious educator is to make this lavish golden harvest of religious understanding accessible to believing adults for their spiritual nurture.

Boys (1979) has suggested that biblical scholars have an

educational problem; that the erudition of the biblical scholar is proving to be an obstacle to education; that nonspecialists, even those fairly well educated in theology, can hardly follow the increasingly esoteric discussions. She urges that biblical scholarship needs to be solicitous for the integration of its findings into the life of churches and synagogues.

Current Educational Efforts

The past fifteen years, in particular, have witnessed a concerted and sustained effort on the part of gifted biblical specialists to communicate the wealth of scholarly biblical research to ordinary believing adults. This communication has taken the form of sound yet readable books, booklets, and pamphlets; high-quality journals of popularization; and insightful columns and articles. Many of these same generous scholars have faced the rigors of addressing hundreds of audiences with presentations and workshops. Cassettes, recordings, radio, and television have brought their message to further thousands.

Many talented biblical specialists have made important contributions toward a solution to this massive contemporary adult religious education problem. However, it would seem that our efforts to date have been confined to the limitations of a single educational paradigm. Alternate paradigms need to be investigated. Perhaps more appropriate educational technologies need to be brought to bear upon this religious education challenge.

I suggest that if a major change in the landscape of adults' abilities to grasp and assimilate modern biblical scholarship in respectable depth is going to happen, it will happen only when we shift the focus from the activity of the teacher, however qualified and gifted, and begin to refocus attention on the learners, and what goes on when real learning happens in adults.

Knowles (1970, 1972) notes that our generation has moved into a more sophisticated era of thinking about learning, in which we have to talk more about the basic and fundamental things if we want to improve education. The real improvements in education are not going to come in the form of new tech-

niques for making it more interesting, more relevant, or even
more participative. Knowles suggests that we have finally begun to absorb into our culture the ancient insight that the heart
of education is learning, not teaching, and so our focus has
started to shift from what the teacher does to what happens to
the learners.

This observation from a leader in the field of adult education has significant implications for religious education of
adults and specialized biblical scholarship. The prevailing assumption has been that the vocabulary and the very complexity of biblical scholarship are too difficult for ordinary adults. I
am suggesting that the germ of the problem lies rather in the
fact that religious educators of adults have not understood and
been at ease with the basic processes in the facilitation of adult
learning. Challenged and motivated adults are able to assimilate
and articulate biblical knowledge at far greater depth than we
previously had reason to imagine.

The Future Church and Adult Biblical Learning

Without a doubt, one of the most significant dynamics
emerging in contemporary church life, that has strong implications for Christianity's future, is the growing reassertion by laity
in recent decades of their rightful place in the ministry of the
church (Cooke, 1979). This is to state that an important recent
development concerning Christianity's relationship to society
has been the increasingly significant role of adults in the various
social undertakings of the churches. Informed adult Christians
are indispensable to the challenge of translating Christian values
and attitudes into social, political, and economic institutions
(Cooke, 1976). Religious educators recognize that the emergence of informed adult Christians hardly happens by chance or
by the recital of magical incantations.

Simmons (1976, 1978) observes that, in this important
venture of religious growth, individual adults need the assistance
of a sponsoring community. It is extremely difficult for the
ordinary Christian to achieve adult faith without a high level of
community sponsorship. And if the community expects the

individual adult to reach adult faith, it must be prepared to provide a model, a religious vocabulary, a challenge to growth, and
a forum for working through to a new understanding of faith.

A key to Christianity's future is community; but essential
to modern-day communities are competent, well-trained adults,
people who can reflect in the context of faith and experience.
But to begin to reflect theologically, adult Christians need the
biblical and theological insight that enables them to relate their
understanding of Christ and Christianity to their own experience. The formation of such community is a basic function of
contemporary Christianity.

Christopher Mwoleka, a bishop in Tanzania, emphasizes
that, for each community to be a community with a human
face, it has to be small enough to enable a network of interpersonal relationships to develop and grow among all its members.
A sense of belonging must be fostered through services prompted
by mutual concern. A prominent contemporary theologian,
Karl Rahner (1974), observes that the experience of the church
is the experience of community. The church of the future will
be one built from below by basic communities.

Thus, religious educators and theologians on several con-
tinents are reflecting on lived experience and recognizing that
human, supportive, and sponsoring communities are a vital and
indispensable context that enables the emergence of adult faith.

Biblical Critical Learning in Local Communities

From the perspective of the professional religious educator of adults, what is needed to bridge the gap between ordinary
adults' present biblical background and the advances of modern
biblical critical scholarship is a learning dynamic that incorporates the findings of modern biblical critical scholarship, that
utilizes the assumptions and premises of modern adult education, and that fosters interdependent learning in a community
context.

In my estimation, the net result of adult religious education needs to be more than personal enrichment. It needs to be
the development of leadership in a community of trust. Chris-

tianity is in critical need of leaders. Authority will grow where well-founded knowledge and learning are evident. The context of this development is in the formation of communities of learning.

Biblical Andragogy is an adult biblical interdependent learning program. As a solid adult learning program, it makes available to adult learners the best insights of modern biblical scholarly research in a community learning context of positive affirmation. The learning methodology that guides this adult education program is based on the andragogical theory of adult learning.

Biblical Andragogy is designed to be an on-the-spot leadership training program that familiarizes adults with their Judeo-Christian roots. As a prerequisite for adult Christian ministry, Biblical Andragogy inaugurates for adults the thrill and excitement of interdependent scholarly biblical learning in a supportive community context.

The sequenced academic content of the Biblical Andragogy program is a developmental overview of the Hebrew and Christian (Old and New) Testaments inspired by the insights of modern biblical scholarship. The educational methodology of this leadership training program is hewn from the theory and practice of modern adult education—andragogy.

Biblical Andragogy and its antecedents have been undergoing experimentation, modification, and testing at the grassroots level for a period of seven years. The scholarly content of this biblical overview learning program is assured by the active supervisory role played by William H. Irwin and J. Terence Forestell, prominent biblical specialists at the University of Toronto. Ongoing expertise in adult learning theory is offered by Malcolm S. Knowles and adult learning specialists at the Ontario Institute for Studies in Education, Virginia R. Griffin and Ron Hine.

A central focus of activity of the Biblical Andragogy Clinic of Mississauga is the operation of two-week Facilitators Clinics, in which adults who are representatives of potential learning communities come together to assimilate a solid overview of the Hebrew and Christian Scriptures, as interpreted by modern critical biblical studies, in a community context of interdependent adult learning.

Adult participants in the two-week Facilitators Clinics assimilate the biblical content and absorb the andragogical learning methodology and subsequently carry the Biblical Andragogy program to their home communities. The graduates of the Facilitators Clinics recruit twelve adults to make a sizable commitment to adult biblical interdependent learning, with a view to developing their own leadership skills. This is to enable competence and confidence on the part of the adults in the facilitation of the biblical learning of other adults in the future.

Participants of Biblical Andragogy comment: "We have participated in the development of a caring and respectful community. We were, more than we realized, a group of persons constantly nourishing each other as faith people. When we sang and prayed and reflected upon our studies, a sense of really being a community in the Lord was established. This was a time when we all really relaxed and unwound and were refreshed. Quite something when you also consider that our studies were serious business."

Biblical Andragogy is premised on the assumption that groups of adult learners are the richest potential source of creativity if they interact supportively, noncompetitively, and collaboratively.

To gauge the academic depth and the adult learners' abilities, Biblical Andragogy has been offered through the University of Toronto (Toronto School of Theology) as an introduction to the Old and New Testaments over a four-year period as an off-campus program at the Master of Divinity level. When they were examined by the biblical specialists at the conclusion of each phase, the adults' comprehension of the academic material attested positively and strongly to the competence of the learners and the power of the interdependent learning process.

2

Adult Education
in the Archdiocese of Detroit

Jane Wolford Hughes

This selection is a dramatic description of the evolution of a comprehensive program of adult education, based on principles of adult learning, in the Archdiocese of Detroit. It exemplifies a phenomenon I have witnessed often: A program is initiated by a leader who intuitively applies principles of adult learning and then discovers that there is a theory supporting that intuition—andragogy. With the support of a theory, the leader is able to take the program to heights previously unimagined. This is in essence a seventeen-year longitudinal case study that documents the steps for successfully converting a social system—in this case a Catholic archdiocese—into a learning community. It demonstrates that major organizational change can be achieved through educational means.

Jane Wolford Hughes is director of the Institute for Continuing Education of the Archdiocese of Detroit and a member of the United States Catholic Conference's Committee on Education and National Advisory Committee on Adult Education.

Special features:

- Formation of an Institute for Continuing Education
- Establishment of adult education centers
- Making lectures more effective
- Taking advantage of teachable moments
- Addressing a broad range of human needs
- Dealing with critical social issues
- Using television for learning
- Training parish facilitators: the "Expansion Program"

351

- Creating a religious climate
- Influencing the clergy
- Providing consultation services
- Integrating adult education into the total system

In 1966 the term "andragogy" was hardly known in the Church, and adult education methods were little used. Adults were still being taught principally like children. And yet, there were stirrings.

In Detroit, excited by the potential of Vatican Council II, Cardinal John F. Dearden brought together 120 articulate, questioning people from all sectors of the archdiocese to dialogue with him about what had happened at the council. The six weekly sessions pointed to one direction: people wanted, needed, and demanded more knowledge about their faith. By late spring the cardinal had appointed me director of adult education. He also made the Institute for Continuing Education (ICE) autonomous and equal to other educational offices, thus giving it status and stretching room.

ICE stated its purpose as "the development of the mature Christian" and plunged into seventeen years of pioneering, research, and experimentation. Many of our innovative programs and processes have been studied and copied across the United States and around the world, and we have been awarded many creativity awards from the Adult Education Association of Michigan.

Of course, we had some problems. In the beginning our newness was both a blessing and a danger, and challenges had to be met with considerable finesse. There was the need to provide educational opportunities through which the potential of the adults could unfold in openness and freedom; but, at the same time, we had to convince those who were distrustful of the adult education process. So, in the beginning, without using new labels or language, we tried to be faithful to the precepts of adult education in seventeen newly formed adult education centers, which opened in the fall of 1966:

Various forms of needs assessment were used.

Teacher-facilitators were given the basic principles of how adults learn.

A learning climate for adults was provided.

Participants were encouraged to build community through interaction and acceptance of one another.

Chairpersons were assigned to establish a friendly, caring atmosphere.

Half of the class time was given over to discussion, and participants were encouraged to share insights and experiences on the topic. Then they were urged to apply the conclusions to their daily lives.

After evaluation, ICE centers were expanded to twenty-five and courses offered twice a year on such topics as Scripture; ecumenism; contemporary morality; marriage; psychology; government; liturgy; ethics; human relations; basic Christianity; communication; Vatican II documents; and appreciation of film, drama, literature, painting, and music. Not all were purely religious topics, but we felt any experience that helped adults discover God or cope with the demands of their lives was right for us to offer.

The SIGNS Series

In the fall of 1966, as we were opening the centers, we also started the SIGNS Series. In addition to its educational value, the lecture series served three other purposes: (1) It gave high visibility to adult education as a ministry of the Church. (2) It dispelled the fears most adults have that they are no longer capable of learning and whetted their appetite for more learning. (3) It presented opportunities for contact with some of the world's great thinkers.

The SIGNS Series was well publicized, and we had excellent response. The facilities were chosen in anticipation of the number wishing to participate, and we usually filled the rooms, even those holding 1,000–3,000; but the average was between

400 and 600. Because programs were presented in evening, one-day, or two-day sessions, we were able to draw those who were reluctant to commit themselves to the six- and eight-week courses.

In ten years, over forty SIGNS speakers challenged and—as the audiences became more sophisticated—were challenged by Detroit Archdiocesan audiences. We were fortunate in having outstanding people in their fields. In 1977 the SIGNS Series was discontinued for another phase of adult education, which we will describe later.

In the 1960s and 1970s, when adult education was struggling with the interchangeable roles of teacher and learner, the lecture method was frequently scorned. I feel a need to defend that method—when it is used effectively. The preparation and quality of the speaker and the participants' motivation to learn are two essential factors in the lecture's effectiveness. In addition, ICE has long made it a practice not to seat the audience lecture style, but to place the participants at round tables and provide time immediately following the lecture for interaction. This dynamic is then followed by questions to the speaker, which were formulated by the *group*. At every lecture the participants are provided a learning kit, which includes reprints and articles pertinent to the topic, a bibliography, listings of agencies and opportunities for action, and an evaluation form. Present in the lecture hall are displays of books and audiovisuals for immediate sale and browsing. We also audiotaped and videotaped every SIGNS lecture, as well as all present lectures. The tapes are available for purchase for a nominal sum by the parishes.

Taking Advantage of Teachable Moments

Much study has been devoted to "motivating" adults to learn. One means frequently noted is the "teachable moment." In each parish and diocese, there are "teachable moments," which the adult educator should be alert to and wise in using. Obvious ones are times of sacramental preparation or the Rite of Christian Initiation of the Adult, but we are not confined to these.

In 1967 the archdiocese was preparing for its synod, and

the cardinal wished to involve as many participants as possible in designing the future. This called for an *informed* people. ICE began a massive adult education program called "Seeking Progress Together." It drew 80,000 adults and 100,000 students and young adults, who organized, studied, and discussed each of the nine study topics for ten weeks. From these "Speak Up" discussion sessions came the recommendations for change that have helped shape the present operation and structure of the Detroit Archdiocese.

The synod process has been studied by many bishops in the United States, Europe, and Australia. It became the prototype of the 1975-76 "Liberty and Justice for All" consultation process for the National Conference of Catholic Bishops' Catholic Bicentennial program. The involvement of the people in the synod (which was promulgated formally in May 1969) put clear focus on the adult education principle of "realizing the potential of everyday experience."

Another "teachable moment" in Detroit came after the archdiocesan *Insight Survey* defined areas of confusion and levels of faith development. In 1972-1974 ICE responded to the survey with the Church, World, Kingdom (CWK) Program, which used the study-discussion technique. Parish facilitators used various forms of learning experience and visuals, as well as the diocesan-prepared basic texts. An average of 30,000 adults actively participated in each of the four phases, which covered the topics of Church, Jesus, Christian morality, and spirituality.

It is difficult to judge the depth of the penetration of the CWK topics, since the program attempted a saturation educational method, whereby religious education at all levels, homilies, prayers of the faithful, visuals at liturgies, educational articles in parish bulletins, flyers, and closed-circuit television reached untold numbers of people.

The fifth topic chosen by the CWK participants was social justice, which was merged with the national program, "Liberty and Justice for All," in the fall of 1975. ICE was asked to pilot the national program, prior to its general participation, and consequently redesigned the materials and prepared filmstrips to enrich the printed texts.

Reference was made earlier to programming that helps

people cope with the world in which they live. At times this calls for programs not ordinarily sponsored by the Church. For five years, beginning in 1971, we offered adult basic education in parish locations. Through this cooperative program with the public school system, we were able to help some one thousand educationally disadvantaged persons each year. Most of the adult students were not members of the parishes. Somehow they saw the Church centers as less threatening than the schools where they experienced childhood defeat. They accepted our invitation and continual reassurance that they "could make it." We had to drop the program because of staff cutbacks but have enabled some parishes to provide it through direct cooperation with their public school district.

The nurturing of the Church needs to be evident at other times and in other situations: in providing English as a second language, in preparation for a change in life-style, in retirement, and in providing skills to gain greater economic stability. In the economic crisis with the automobile industry, ICE brought the parishes into contact with specialists in programs on writing job résumés, coping with stress, budgeting, and similar problems faced by laid-off workers.

Television for Learning

From 1967 through 1976, ICE worked with the University of Detroit television studios on programming that was transmitted to the archdiocesan schools. The adults gathered to view the television, were provided with printed back-up materials, and entered into lively discussions. One program in particular was especially popular: "What's It All About?" which used the New York Times *Student Weekly* as a text. The key items in each issue of the paper were discussed by a panel of experts chosen to give a balanced view on the subjects.

In 1968, after the race riots in Detroit, ICE joined with a community group in preparing a program intended to heal some of the hurts and to help city officials understand the attitudes of both blacks and whites. This program was aired on educational television. Discussion booklets were mailed to those re-

questing them. Both call-in and written expressions of attitude
and attitude change were sent in: there had been a change since
the dreadful summer of 1967! Also in 1968, we were part of a
series on the History of the Black People—again, an effort to
merge the gap between races.

In 1969 ICE was involved in an ecumenical six-talk series
for educational TV, "Can Christians Be One?"

Other popular television programs centered on Scripture,
understanding of the pastoral letter of the American Hierarchy,
"Human Life in Our Day," and three different Lenten Series.

Adult Education Leadership

Until 1976 ICE's focus had been through a broad lens.
Learning opportunities were offered in different ways, in different places, for different persons. Opportunities were planned
for the person in the pew as well as for those in leadership positions. Adult education had been accepted—not universally certainly, but by a good segment of the archdiocese. At this point
we sharpened our focus to concentrate our total efforts on
training and enriching the adult education leadership in the parishes. In shifting our emphasis, we multiplied the effectiveness
of adult education. Who could know better the needs of their
people than those involved in the same daily struggle?

A large committee of those working in the parishes and
the ICE staff planned the overall vision of what we called "Expansion." We brought Malcolm Knowles in for three sequential
workshops in January, March, and May of 1977. Persons were
required to register for all three. Certificates were granted for
those who attended *and* developed their self-directed learning
projects. The three days examined "The Emerging Role and
Technology of Adult Education," "Helping Adults Learn," and
"Organizing and Administering Programs of Adult Education."
We had 200 participants (more than we wanted, but enthusiasm
cannot be turned away). The *Expansion Handbook,* bulging
with practical articles and charts, was one of our most popular
items for sale.

"Expansion" caught on like the fiery red of its brochure,

and we continued in skills development on various facets of adult education for the next four years and still offer an occasional workshop as requested. The most popular is a two-day workshop on public relations, which actually involves the participants in designing their own flyers and brochures and setting up a public relations schedule. A good percentage of parishes produce their own attractive brochures and are pleased with the response they bring.

From our experience as well as our logic, we determined that the adult religious educator must have qualities not usually demanded of a person in a public institution. First and foremost, he or she must be a person of faith, whose fundamental direction, values, and attitudes spring from living the life of Jesus Christ. These must be integrated with the skills, sensitivity, and understanding of the adult educator.

We found in situation after situation that even when the adult learning is in a nonreligious subject the climate should be one of religious atmosphere. In other words, no matter what the person is learning, the life of Christ within that person must be affirmed and this affirmation consciously felt by the learner. Simply stated, adult education in general provides opportunities for the person to become more fully himself or herself. Equally simple would be the goal of adult religious education to aid the person to become "fuller in Christ." In other words, adult religious education aims at conversion. It is fairly obvious, then, that adult religious educators, if they are to be facilitators of such radical change, must have come to grips with conversion and be able to share it.

The subtle reason behind the prerequisite comes from the lived experience of those in adult religious education, whose faith supported and sustained them in difficult and unsympathetic conditions. Faith as well as fire can change the rough iron of "simply a job" to the steel of what is a call to ministry.

As part of our responsibility in the development of leadership in adult education, we saw the need to play the advocacy role with both Catholic institutions of higher learning and seminaries. The former were urged to provide adult education development courses on undergraduate and graduate levels. The direction of the seminaries is not so much to produce adult educators as to provide comprehensive understanding for all priests about andragogy, and the various methodologies to utilize. In most national surveys—as recently as the winter of 1983—one of the most frequently named impediments to parish adult education across the United States has been the lack of knowledge of, indifference to, or the outright blockage of adult learning programs by the clergy.

To me the fault lies with the system. While the Roman Catholic Church, through the American Hierarchy, has placed adult education "at the center of the teaching mission of the Church," the priest leadership in the parishes has not been prepared for the change in methods as well as thinking that must undergird adult education. In most instances where adult education is resisted, the pastor has not made the transition from the educational style in which he was taught and/or is uncomfortable in the andragogical role of *enabling* the adult to make mature faith decisions, and wishes to remain the authority figure who *tells* the person what to believe and how to act.

However, in a needs assessment taken in the late 1970s by a professional firm in the Archdiocese of Detroit, 77 percent of the priests interviewed admitted that they did not understand adult learning and would be willing to receive some training. We responded to their willingness with courses at the provincial seminary and workshops that would appeal to them. A successful series on Scripture, with fifteen full-day workshops over a period of four years, was presented by a noted Scripture scholar. A high proportion of the participants in these lecture/dialogue/questioning days have been clergy, and the same persons—clergy and lay—keep coming back. Consequently, there is a great richness of Scripture study in the parishes. Priests also enter into the adult education process because they have experienced it and the benefits from it. We have not limited attendance to these or any other workshops to "clergy only" because we strongly feel that the interaction between laity and clergy provides healthier, more real, and more enjoyable learning experiences.

The Office of Priestly Life and Ministry and ICE have en-

tered into collaborative efforts so that the continual exposure
of the priests to adult education will continue to acclimate
them. The subject of collaboration is to be a significant factor
in the future of ICE and will be described at greater length later
in this article.

When we talk about the enrichment of adult education
leadership—both clergy and lay—we naturally gravitate toward
experiences and insights into personal spirituality. Enrichment
also encompasses the areas of self-understanding through the
study of life cycles, faith growth, burnout, coping with stress,
time management, and human relations. All of these have been
part of the ongoing leadership development.

Another factor in our service of developing leadership is
individual consultation—usually at the parish with the adult
education leaders and committee. Through this arrangement,
parishes can have their needs and problems addressed. An ICE
staff person meets with five parishes weekly for a few hours or
longer. We avoid designing programs for them but help them
master the skills and insights to manage their own.

Adult Educators Association

Our close relationship with the adult educators gave birth
to the Adult Educators Association in 1979. It was the first,
and perhaps only, such diocese association in the country. We
meet bimonthly. The meetings are very well attended. There is a
real support community melding through shared experiences,
updating on the state of the art, fresh professional development,
prayer, and some gourmet-catered light lunches (for which we
charge). The structured part of the meeting is in the morning,
then wine and cheese, lunch, and the freedom to chat with anyone you wish, or stay as long as you can, in a one-to-one exchange about the ministry of adult education. We have tried to
utilize the principles of adult education in these meetings: the
learning freedom, sharing, and self-direction are evident. In between, we have an informative newsletter.

Collaboration—A New Era

Through the years the growth and acceptance of adult education have been obvious. Success has also made it pervasive, affecting other offices and services in the archdiocese. All of us have been changed in the process. We have become acutely aware that all staff offices are, in effect, working directly with adults, even though for some the end objective is to serve children and youth.

The movement to this conclusion came gradually. ICE began taking lead responsibility for large diocesan projects and programs in which other offices were involved. The exposure to adult education principles of those in the project altered their sense of how successful learning experiences could be designed. ICE became more and more a part of the planning operations of other offices. We acted as consultants. We cosponsored. We taught. We facilitated. Today the listing of our yearly objectives clearly states the fact: We are involved in three times as many collaborative programs as those offered primarily and solely by ICE.

It will, therefore, not be difficult for ICE to be absorbed into the Department of Education. As a result of a restructuring plan, dedicated to the concept of lifelong learning, there will no longer be any separate offices (for schools, religious education, adult education, and so on) within the department. Under the leadership of our new archbishop, Edmund C. Szoka, the archdiocese is committed to an integrated educational thrust to serve *all* age groups, with adult education as the primary force. A benchmark in diocesan educational design, the plan is still inert—but exciting—on paper, and it will be the task of all the department leaders to bring it to vibrant reality. It holds great promise.

SEVEN

◆◆◆ ◆◆ ◆◆ ◆◆ ◆◆ ◆◆ ◆◆ ◆◆ ◆◆ ◆◆ ◆◆ ◆◆ ◆◆ ◆◆ ◆◆◆

Applications
in Elementary
and Secondary Education

In one of the most important educational documents of this century—the report of the UNESCO International Commission on the Development of Education, *Learning to Be* (Faure, 1972)—the proposal is made that, in order to prepare human beings for a world of accelerating change, all of education should be organized around the concept of lifelong learning. A primary mission of elementary and secondary schools would then be to develop the skills of self-directed learning. As it is, adult educators attempting to apply the andragogical model face obstacles because adults have not learned the skills of self-directed learning in their earlier schooling. How different our task as adult educators would be if the schools were indeed turning out lifelong learners.

But the question is invariably asked, "Will the andragogical model really work with children?" This chapter presents three case descriptions of programs in which aspects or adaptations of the andragogical model have been applied in the education of children and youth. Selection 1 presents the "Challenge Education Program" pioneered at Simon Fraser University in British Columbia. It demonstrates that students in elementary and secondary schools will respond to the challenge of self-

363

directed learning and that communities will respond to the challenge of joining with the schools in sharing responsibility for the enterprise. Another approach to community-based education— at the Jefferson Elementary School in Rochester, Minnesota—is described in selection 2. It provides an especially useful set of guidelines for specifying learner outcomes, possible means and methods of achieving particular outcomes, and performance measures. Selection 3 describes a totally new way of organizing a high school—Bishop Carroll High School in Calgary, Alberta— around the concepts of learner-centered instruction, resource centers rather than classrooms, team teaching, modularized curriculum, independent study, and flexible scheduling.

1

Challenging Students to Excel

Maurice Gibbons, Gary Phillips

In the face of the crescendo of criticism of our public schools, there is strong pressure for our educational system to "go back to the basics." This direction of movement might have been appropriate in the nineteenth century, and even the first half of the twentieth century. But is it appropriate for a world of accelerating change? Would it prepare children and youth for the twenty-first century? A group of educators in western Canada believe not, and they have been demonstrating that students in elementary and secondary schools will respond to the challenge of self-directed learning—the prerequisite of lifelong learning. This selection describes an approach that involves the whole community in providing resources for self-directed learners.

Maurice Gibbons is professor of education at Simon Fraser University in Vancouver, British Columbia. Gary Phillips is director of Learning Unlimited at North Central High School in Indianapolis. Gibbons and Phillips worked together in 1978–79 to inaugurate a center for the study of self-education at Simon Fraser University.

Special features:

- Assumptions on which "challenge education" is based
- Five basic challenges
- Structural elements in challenge education

Adapted, with permission, from "Walkabout: Searching for the Right Passage from Childhood and School," *Phi Delta Kappan*, 1974, *55* (9), 596–602; and from "Walkabout: Exploring New Paths to Adulthood—Self-Directed Learning Challenges Students to Excel," *Phi Delta Kappan*, 1978, *3* (5), 1–8.

- Preparing students for self-directed learning
- Developing process skills (instead of teaching content)
- A support system for challenge education
- Using student advisory committees
- Educational brokering
- Using community resources in partnership
- Networking
- Contract learning
- Involvement of parents
- A new role for teachers
- Helping students through the transition
- Monitoring students
- Celebrating students' accomplishments

> With a single, bold stroke, secondary administrators and their teachers can educate students in the basics, eliminate many discipline problems in schools, improve the individual effectiveness of their students as emerging adults, and help to reverse the social trend toward apathy and fatalism— all without increasing the cost of education.

As visionary as the introductory sentence may appear to some, these goals can be achieved now, without any major breakthroughs in knowledge about learning or the processes of human development. These goals are within our reach when we are willing to bring together, as a shared responsibility, the three greatest influences on student accomplishment—namely, the school, the home, and the natural inclination of students to motivate and direct themselves. When these three forces become congruent and are directed toward goals that are both clear and valuable to students, the potential for learning is almost unlimited.

The major premise around which our proposal for "challenge education" is built will break no new ground here. Simply stated, it goes something like this: Students learn most effectively when they are responding to challenges that they know will directly and significantly affect their lives.

A minor premise is equally uncomplicated: Challenge

education is essentially a process of self-education, a continuing process in which students learn to direct the course of their actions toward desirable ends.

While the two theoretical premises are not new, the methods through which challenge education can be implemented in contemporary secondary schools is new.

We are convinced that now is a propitious time for challenge education. Never have we been in a better position to describe an experience- and performance-based program that promises so much and has been so thoroughly tested. Several years of development have led us to a new understanding about how experience-based programs should be designed and implemented. In the pages that follow, we have attempted to summarize that hard-earned knowledge.

What Is Challenge Education?

- Challenge education is a form of schooling in which all students learn to voluntarily and independently pursue excellence.
- In challenge education students challenge themselves to learn and accomplish as much as they think they can master in academic, practical, creative, social, and physical pursuits.
- In challenge education each student negotiates his or her challenges with a committee comprised of a teacher and a parent.
- In challenge education responsibility is shared by the teacher, the student, and the parent. Each has a specific role to play.
- In challenge education the resources of the school are coordinated with the resources of the home and the community to create a potent, congruent influence on the student.
- In challenge education students learn to plan and implement a personal curriculum so that by graduation they are already functioning in independent but mature ways.
- In these ways challenge education leads to a smooth transition to adulthood and to a life of learning.

In summary, challenge education is a new method of developing skills for self-education.

Why Challenge Education?

We think many school practices cultivate apathy and crush initiative. Further, many schools seem to be applying those practices with greater and greater force, causing themselves more problems. In such schools teachers are often required to behave in entirely routine ways and are monitored to ensure their conformity.

Students have almost every minute of their time designed and directed for them. They are told what to do, when to do it, how to do it, and for how long. As a result, they make few contributions of their own initiative; they learn nothing of disciplining their own behavior; they take no responsibility for their education; and they graduate still completely unprepared for the real tasks of adulthood.

How can schools more successfully educate students in the basics, solve their discipline problems, significantly increase the personal effectiveness of their students, and proudly declare a major contribution to reversing the social trend toward apathy and fatalism—all without increasing the cost of education? That can be done with a single, bold stroke by administrators and their teachers willing to establish a program of challenge education based on learning contracts that are negotiated by committees each made up of a teacher, a student, and a parent—or a parent substitute from the community—who share the responsibility for educational achievement.

By bringing these committees together to review the students' learning plans, the school assembles the three greatest influences on student accomplishment—the school, the home, and the almost untapped power of students to motivate and direct themselves. When these three forces become congruent and directed toward clear and valued goals, the potential for learning is unlimited.

Teaching for self-education not only leads to excellence but is entirely consistent with the demands of growth and the ideal conditions of learning. Moreover, it prepares students for the personal decision making and self-directed learning demanded of them immediately after graduation.

Elements of a Challenge Program

The most useful structure for self-education is a challenge program. Through individualized challenges students develop their own activities in the five basic challenges:

1. *Adventure.* A challenge to the student's daring, endurance, and skill in an unfamiliar environment (rock climbing, sailing, wilderness hiking, and some forms of self-exploratory, meditative, or spiritual adventures).
2. *Creativity.* A challenge to explore, cultivate, and express one's own imagination in some aesthetically pleasing form (sculpture and painting, handicrafts, poems, plays, gourmet foods, computer art, films, music).
3. *Service.* A challenge to identify a human need for assistance and provide it; to express caring without expectation of a reward (volunteer work with the old, ill, infirm, and retarded; construction of playgrounds, hiking trails, parks; cleanups of eyesore lots).
4. *Practical skill.* A challenge to explore a utilitarian activity, to learn the knowledge and skills necessary to work in that field, and to produce something of use (finely honed secretarial skills, stock market analyses and estimates, computer programming, a travel guidebook for high school students, a repair service for home appliances, and a collection of movie reviews written for the local newspaper).
5. *Logical inquiry.* A challenge to explore one's curiosity, to formulate a question or problem of personal importance, and to pursue an answer or solution systematically and, whenever possible, by investigation. (How does a starfish bring about the regeneration of a lost arm? How does one navigate in space? What are the ten most important questions man asks but can't answer?)

Once students successfully complete a preliminary activity in each category, they are challenged to extend their accomplishments as far as possible. Teachers can then direct all their efforts to assisting students in setting and meeting their challenges. In addition to challenge areas (which constitute the "subjects" in this form of self-education), the following structural elements will also help the teacher to create a framework for student decision-making and action:

1. *Contracts.* The students negotiate with parents and teachers what they will learn in each challenge area, how, and in what length of time. They also negotiate how their work will be evaluated. The learning contract is then written up and signed by all parties.
2. *Semester timetable.* An incremental pattern is established for each term or semester, including such steps as diagnosis, exploratory activities, preliminary tasks, prerequisite mastery learning, intensive challenge tasks, demonstration of accomplishments, and evaluation.
3. *Diagnostic-prescriptive system.* Each student's ability in access and mastery skills is systematically diagnosed. Appropriate training is then prescribed.
4. *Monitoring schedule.* Dates are arranged with students for regular review of contracts and progress toward goals.
5. *Presentations.* Students arrange to demonstrate their accomplishments to others at the end of the contract period. The final presentations are public and are considered to be major events in the program. Other students, parents, and members of the community are included in the audience.

   The first step is convincing students that self-education is important to them, that they can do it, and that it will benefit them now and as long as they live. In the beginning self-education will be strange compared to familiar teacher-directed learning. Some students will feel "This isn't school at all." But the reality of self-education can be established by such activities as the following:

1. Model self-education yourself and promote it enthusiastically.
2. Reward students for each independent act, each sign of self-reliance. Include parents in this scheme.

3. Use admired local, national, and international heroes as models of self-education.
4. Build pride in the students for being able to act successfully on their own, to exercise freedom responsibly.
5. Create self-fulfilling prophecies of their early success and then be sure they do not plan excessively ambitious projects they are ill equipped to complete. Once they have the right attitude, they are ready to learn the basic skills of self-education.

From the teacher's point of view, the basic content of a self-education program is process. In the familiar teacher-centered classroom, students are usually taught content and skills associated with subjects. In teaching for self-education, however, students are taught how to conduct the processes involved in designing, implementing, and managing their own learning in the challenge areas. In all cases the process skills selected for teaching are essential prerequisites of the students' learning. They are selected because they increase the students' power to function independently and because they will be used by students regularly for the rest of their lives. The skills involved in the process can be discussed in terms of the following categories:

1. *Access skills*—skills such as reading, speaking, and writing, which are essential for gaining further access to knowledge.
2. *Mastery skills*—studying, problem solving, and organizing skills essential for mastering a body of knowledge.
3. *Planning skills*—decision-making skills. (How to decide about one's learning program? What goals? What experiences? What means of evaluation?)
4. *Management skills*—skills necessary for managing one's time, effort, and resources in order to learn.
5. *Interpersonal skills*—learning to relate to people of all ages, both older and younger, and to assume different roles successfully.

One of the most important functions of the teacher in

self-education is to organize the resources—particularly the human resources—necessary for the program to function. A support system for a challenge program must have the following elements, at least:

1. *Student advisory committees.* A typical committee would be composed of the student, a teacher, and at least one parent or substitute adult who would help to guide the student through his contracted project. Typical activities would include advising the student on what experiences to seek, negotiating learning contracts, checking on progress, and establishing contact with people in the community.
2. *A people-and-places brokerage.* This would include a listing of experts who are willing to work with young people and teach them their specialty. It would also include sites where students can conduct such activities as on-the-job training, research, adventure, and volunteer service. The teacher, with student and parent help, would organize this market and then act as broker between the student and the volunteer or site sponsor.
3. *School and community agencies interface.* The teacher selects from the hundreds of agencies and services available in the community those that can be useful in the program, and organizes them so that agents will come to the school and students can go to them. Examples include training in mental health agencies for working with the severely retarded; social workers running workshops on interaction skills; and police and others taking students along for "a day in the life" experiences.
4. *Self-education network.* When teachers are running a small program in a large traditional school, it is particularly important that they establish a network which includes school officials, people in the community committed to self-education, and teachers in other schools involved or interested in self-education. Officials should be kept informed about the program and should be given every possible good reason for feeling supportive toward it. Supporters in the community can be very helpful to the program, both politically

and educationally. It is axiomatic that innovations only occur and survive where the innovator has associations with others—at least one other—who are also committed to the idea.

As students begin meeting with their advisory committees to negotiate learning contracts in each of the challenge areas, teachers can begin their one-to-one and small-group meetings with students to diagnose their levels of performance, teach them the self-education process, and assist them in dealing with the difficulties they will face.

Once they realize they are responsible for their actions, students have difficulty deciding what to learn. Most will be unable to organize their time and keep to their own schedule. When difficulties arise, many will want to give up. In dealing with these issues, teachers are addressing the fundamental problems of learning. They are helping students to take charge of their own education and to give shape to their own lives. They are acting as professional educators.

Tasks of Planning Committees

The main instrument for organizing a challenge program is the negotiated learning contract. The key to the contract is the negotiation among the participants to determine the challenges, the learning strategies, acceptable demonstrations of achievement, and the role of each participant in the program. The planning committee should meet at least five times. During these meetings an important set of tasks must be accomplished.

Securing the Commitment. In the first meeting with the parents and student, the teacher's main task is to secure their commitment to become involved in the challenge program.

Involvement means different things for different participants. For parents it means accepting a specific responsibility to cooperate with the school and their child in his or her learning efforts. This means becoming informed, contributing to the learning contract negotiations, and participating in their child's learning activities.

For the teacher it means a new role in which he or she will assist students not by delivering the curriculum to them but by helping them to master the process of selecting and shaping their own.

For the student it means not being dependent on the teacher or the school for direction in learning but, rather, to take an increasingly responsible role in his or her own pursuit of excellence in education.

During the first meeting, the responsibilities for each participant should be outlined. Students should come away with a clear idea of the kind of challenges they are willing to set for themselves, challenges which will also meet school requirements and the expectations of their parents. The parents must decide if they are willing to contribute, and suggest ways in which they can best help their children to meet their obligations. It is the teacher's responsibility to clarify the expectations of the school.

Negotiating the Contract. The second meeting should begin with reports by all the participants, in which they affirm their commitment to the program and state their expectations as clearly as possible. Candor is essential.

Assuming that all participants are willing to take part, the negotiating process begins. The contract will include specific activities in several challenge areas. If it is the student's first challenge experience, the teacher would be advised to prepare a list of suggestions. Once the student has created a vision of himself performing successfully in a particular field of activity, the activity can be broken down into the specific contractual outcomes he will pursue.

Two dangers must be avoided. First, the challenge must not be so ambitious that the student has no hope of ever achieving the goal. Second, the challenge must not be so modest that the student can fulfill it without effort. Both can be extremely destructive. The three major participants negotiate a set of objectives and enabling activities until all participants reach agreement and all are clear about both what the student will achieve and what each participant will do to contribute to that achievement.

The commitments of all three participants are then clearly

stated in the contract. Besides stating what the student will do, and by when, the contract specifies what the committee will accept as proof that the student has achieved his goals. That is, everyone must be able to tell when the student has finally done what he set out to do. When this contract is written up and signed by all participants, the active stage of the learning program can begin.

With adequate preparation these meetings may be conducted in an hour or less. When a program is starting out, it may be necessary to conduct these planning sessions on professional days, but after the program is operating, they can be conducted while students are working on their challenge activities.

Helping Students Through the Transition. If students have spent many years in a classroom where learning has been directed by the teacher, they will experience a profound trauma as they attempt to take over the responsibilities for directing their own learning.

We can anticipate that they will begin in high excitement and set ambitious goals, but they will soon find it extremely difficult to get tasks done, to overcome obstacles, and to fulfill the many requirements of preparation for such things as field activities. Some will be immobilized by the complexity of the tasks that confront them.

The changeover from teacher-directed to self-directed learning is a monumental task. All participants must recognize the supreme challenge that taking responsibility for oneself involves, and they must be resolved to tolerate this transitional experience. Many programs, unfortunately, are terminated when students descend into the dark night of the soul that occurs when they discover how difficult self-education is. Parents want to withdraw their children from the program, and students want to escape to more comfortable dependency in a teacher-directed classroom. But it cannot be emphasized too strongly that this is the moment of truth in challenge education, the moment at which students are ready to take the most important step forward. Once the personal dissonance is recognized as an inevitable but necessary step to independent learning, it can become the focal point for strategic teaching.

The teacher can help the student to confront his failure and to reaffirm his potential for successful self-direction. During the meeting conducted at this stage, the contract may be renegotiated, a more detailed and realistic plan of action may be drawn up, and extraordinary assistance may be provided to ensure the student an early success.

Parents and those working with the students in the community must also play new roles, making sure to communicate that they value independence and initiative and to reaffirm the students' vision of themselves acting skillfully and responsibly on their own. The students must leave the meeting with renewed hope that they can be successful where they were unsuccessful before, but none of their well-meaning supporters must rescue them and thereby rob them of the independent victory they need.

Monitoring Students. If at all possible, students must be able to report a success during the first of the monitoring meetings. They have had difficulty fulfilling the terms of their initial contract; they have renegotiated that contract; and they have tried once again. Everything should be done to help them become successful for this meeting. If by chance a student is still unsuccessful, then a program must be set up immediately which almost guarantees immediate success.

Schools generally make the mistake of meeting with parents only when there is a crisis, but regular meetings serve a number of purposes, even when there is no serious issue to be resolved. First, they provide a goal for the students. Students are more likely to maintain their programs rigorously, knowing that these programs will be examined and discussed. Second, the meetings provide an opportunity for the team to identify potential problems and head them off before they become explosive issues. Third, the meetings provide an opportunity for the team to continuously raise the level of challenge for the students, where appropriate. Finally, these meetings enable all the participants to continue their interactions, to reward and support student progress, and to continue to create opportunities for students to keep pursuing excellence in their fields.

Celebrating the Students' Accomplishments. From the

moment the students first contemplate entering the challenge program, they realize that whatever they accomplish will be demonstrated before an audience of teachers, relatives, friends, members of the community who have been part of their program, and students of other ages anticipating their own challenge programs.

During this demonstration they will describe the challenges they set for themselves and the achievements that resulted. This may involve modeling clothes they designed and tailored, showing slides of a summer cabin they designed and built, showing videotapes of their early dancing performance and a performance after a semester of practice, displaying paintings or poems, or demonstrating their ability to speak a foreign language or to type rapidly and accurately or to tear an engine down and reassemble it. This final session is completed by a ceremony in which teachers, relatives, and other members of the community celebrate the students' achievements and welcome them into the world of adulthood.

If we can imagine a school career terminating with a year in which the students are fully responsible for planning and executing their own educational activities, then we can begin to conceive of a school system in which the first eleven years are designed to prepare the students to meet that challenge.

2

Involving the Community
as a Resource for Learning

Robert Sande

Contemporary educational thinking strongly endorses the notion that all the resources of a community should be involved
in the educational process. Such terms as "community school,"
"community education," "the educative community," and
"community lifelong learning resource system" are current in
our literature. This selection describes what it calls a "school-
based management system," which is designed to use creatively the abundance of existing community resources to develop
self-directed learners. It portrays a Jefferson Community School
Council as the instrument for establishing linkages among all
elements of the community. The table at the end of the selection, which specifies student learner outcomes, possible means/
methods, and anticipated performance measures, provides a
comprehensive set of guidelines for designing educational programs that are adaptable to a variety of situations.

Robert Sande is the principal of Jefferson Elementary
School, Rochester, Minnesota.

Special features:

- Involving the community through a school council
- Philosophy of Jefferson School
- Characteristics of a self-directed learner
- Desired learning outcomes
- Means for achieving them
- Performance measures

Excerpted, with permission, from a proposal by the Jefferson Elementary School to the Northwest Area Foundation for a grant that was
funded in April 1983.

School-based management is a valuable and viable way to bring all elements of the school community to bear on the process of developing productive self-directed learners. This child-centered outcome requires sensitive, responsive, flexible management of the educational environment in order to focus a rich array of school community resources to respond to the range of individual differences among students. From this perspective, school-based management is a functional and highly practical approach to the efficient use of resources for individual children.

The Jefferson Community School Council is a way to establish a working rapport among all elements of the school community. This approach to school-based management focuses on developing the unique talents of each child affected by the system through (1) increasing the level of interest in the educational system among parents, nonparent residents in the community, staff members, and students; (2) broadening the decision-making base to include active involvement of all of these segments of the school community; (3) strengthening communication among school, home, community, central office, and school board, thereby enhancing support through a sense of "ownership" resulting from a genuine process of shared governance.

Philosophy of Jefferson School

We of the Jefferson School community believe, as Thomas Jefferson did years ago, that education—especially the education of our children—is a prime ingredient in the successful functioning of our democratic society as well as the well-being of our citizens. Due to the complex age in which we live, we recognize the advantages that children gain today by developing the skills that lead to becoming self-directed learners. This requires a new commitment toward helping each individual reach his or her potential physically, intellectually, socially, and emotionally. It means recognizing that children have various learning styles and that tailoring education to the needs of those to be educated is essential.

We are committed at Jefferson School to promoting an environment in which children want to learn and are successful learners. We stress basic academic skills, critical thinking, and problem solving, as well as skills that will broaden personal interests and increase knowledge in expanding new information areas of our era. We are aware that becoming independent and self-directed learners means understanding that there is a direct relationship between privileges and responsibilities. It also means continuously developing positive self-concepts, so that interrelating with others can become a learning and growing experience for all involved. This positive self-concept starts in the home and continues at school as parents become partners with the school in the education of their children.

Thomas Jefferson envisioned a democratic society, enlightened through education, becoming a model for the world. Jefferson School embraces this concept and looks forward to becoming a learning resource for the entire community, just as it uses the community as a resource for itself in order to enhance the idea that learning is enjoyable, important, and in our lives a never-ending process.

School-Based Management and the Self-Directed Learner

Learning is an internal process of human development which begins at birth and continues throughout life. It is an inherent feature of being human. Children bring to school natural curiosity and a built-in desire to learn about their world. Motivation for meaningful learning is a personal thing—an internal dimension of an individual.

The Jefferson School-Based Management and Self-Directed Learner Project is based on the premise that self-motivation and self-direction can be nurtured in the learner and maintained throughout the learner's lifetime. The skills and attributes of the self-directed learner do not grow in isolation but are woven into the academic content and can, therefore, be channeled by professionals and parents using the skills, concepts, and knowledge of formal learning. This formal learning is seen as a mutually responsible and cooperative enterprise involving students, educators, administrators, and families.

School-based management is a process by which children, teachers, parents, administrators, and school communities share authority in making decisions about their school. The Jefferson Community School Council is responsible for implementing the school-based management concept and for enhancing the present academic program and evaluation system by encouraging development toward self-direction in the learner. Criteria for all action taken by the council will be whether or not development of the self-directed learner is promoted in areas of social, emotional, physical, and intellectual growth. Development of the following characteristics in the learner is the reason for, and function of, school-based management:

1. *Insight.* Has sufficient self-knowledge to evaluate own strengths and needs.
2. *Social maturity.* Is comfortable in social climate; works well in groups or with another; sensitive to needs of others.
3. *Creative thinker.* Is able to use creative-thinking strategies —such as fluency, flexibility, originality, elaboration, evaluation, planning, decision making, problem solving, and forecasting—to process the information learned.
4. *Apply strategies.* Is able to apply the appropriate strategies to a given situation or lesson to create new, unusual ways of dealing with challenges and/or problems.
5. *Responsible, efficient work style.* Is able to choose and pursue individual tasks and follow through to completion.
6. *Positive self-concept.* Shows predominately positive attitude—has self-confidence.
7. *Adaptation to change.* Is tolerant of change; able to evaluate new situations and make judgments according to needs.
8. *Motivation.* Has intrinsic motivation; has enthusiasm for learning; seeks new knowledge.
9. *Risk taking.* Is able to take risks; to make and accept mistakes in self and others; to learn from mistakes.
10. *Personal learning style.* Is able to use learning methods best suited to individual needs.
11. *Individualized process.* Enters and progresses through school system at a rate determined by maturation/developmental level.

12. *Participation in decisions.* Is a participant in decisions that concern personal and classroom activities.
13. *Mature decision maker.* Chooses options which may not be the same as group, but are not harmful to self or others.
14. *Communication skills.* Is able to express self orally and in writing effectively; has good listening skills.

Each dimension of the management system, as well as all future strategies considered by the Jefferson Community School Council, must be related in some way to promoting growth of these key characteristics.

In Table 1 school community activities are ordered in accordance with the basic project focus—the self-directed learner. The work of the Jefferson Community School Council will be directed toward imaginatively and flexibly achieving these outcomes.

As the council becomes experienced in making decisions consistently centered on these basic components of self-directed learning, it is anticipated that "means/methods" and "performance measures" will be defined with greater precision. The "student learner outcomes" may also be revised and refined. It is in the identification of "means/methods" that the curricular, personnel, and budget decisions involved in school-based management are embedded.

An awareness of the developmental process is essential in making these decisions. The child's understanding of the world at different stages of development has an integrity and coherence of its own, based on a complex interaction between a person's physiological development, self-awareness, and environment. Experiences at different ages of the same event are fundamentally different. The event may be experienced, interpreted, and integrated differently, depending on individual developmental levels.

Table 1. Guidelines for Designing a Self-Directed Learning Program.

Student Learner Outcome (Objectives)	Possible Means/Methods	Anticipated Performance Measures
Increase positive attitude and motivation toward learning.	Provide a stimulating environment.	Child self-evaluation instruments.
	Evaluation of student work emphasizing reinforcement theory.	Parent and/or child surveys and attitude scales.
	Provide individualized challenges.	Tally parent comments to teachers.
	Expand students' choices and enrichment.	Tally parent comments to principal.
	Teacher awareness of a developmental process.	
	Guidance program.	
Increase active participation and involvement in learning activities.	Systematically develop a hierarchy of skills for self-direction.	Participation in goal-setting conferences involving student, parents, and the teacher.
	Provide a rich variety of discovery and "hands-on" activities.	Child self-evaluation processes.
	Classroom government involving responsible student decision making in response to real issue, including routine classroom duties and solutions to emerging problems of group living/interaction.	Surveys of perceived effectiveness of various active learning strategies.
	Student council.	
	Provide individual, small-group and whole-group activities.	
	Participation in school-based management.	

Maintain and/or improve academic achievement.	Teacher structuring of time management to allow for greater individual attention. Guidance program. Provide a variety of individual challenges that are meaningful and realistic for a full range of abilities. Expand enrichment possibilities. Use of computers. Field trips and resource persons that make learning relevant. Teacher awareness of a developmental process.	California Achievement Test. End-of-level reading tests. Chapter tests in mathematics. Spelling test scores.
Increase self-awareness and self-evaluation and the ability to accept own mistakes and learn from them.	Flexible use of "circle groups" to enhance self-awareness. Materials which focus on processes of self-awareness. Autobiographical topics for written expression. Guidance program.	Self-concept measures. Participation in goal setting and progress report conferences. Child self-evaluation processes and/or parent surveys.
Improve quality of self-direction in study situations and ability to follow task through to completion.	Carefully structured development and practice of a hierarchy of skills for self-direction. Use of computers. Provide a range of opportunities for planning and organizing independent projects suitable at different levels of development and for students of varying levels of ability. Guidance program.	Teacher observation checklists. Child self-evaluations and/or parent surveys.

(continued on next page)

Table 1. Guidelines for Designing a Self-Directed Learning Program, Cont'd.

Student Learner Outcome (Objectives)	Possible Means/Methods	Anticipated Performance Measures
More able to take risks, as well as to handle other stress situations appropriately.	Evaluation of student work, emphasizing correct responses.	Teacher observation checklists.
	Circle groups.	Child self-evaluations and/or parent surveys.
	Guidance program.	
Improve creative-thinking, decision-making, and problem-solving skills and the appropriate application of them.	Small-group brainstorming activities that promote productive thinking strategies across all content areas.	Tabulate incidence of successful problem solving observed on playground in child-to-child disagreements.
	Provide opportunities for learning and practicing decision-making processes and dealing with resulting consequences of chosen alternatives.	Students given current problem in school and/or community and are able to use the decision-making process to come to a workable solution.
	Teacher awareness of a developmental process.	Creativity measures.
	Provide for student-designed plan for efficient use of supplies and energy.	
	Provide simulation activities that include a variety of strategies to be used in order to complete the given task.	
	Computer: provide activities which encourage divergent thinking and the creation of other materials beyond what is given.	
	Participation in school-based management.	

Improve communication skill.	Provide instruction and guidance in productive group dynamics. Circle groups. Nonteaching personnel participation in relevant classroom discussions. Family participation in workshops and training sessions. Participation in governing units. Cooperative learning experiences. Peer tutoring/cross-age tutoring. Guidance program.	Random sampling of progress reports. Evaluation of talk sessions, group sessions, and workshops by participants. Teacher observations/interviews with students involved in tutoring.
Enhance self-esteem and self-confidence.	Consistent use of positive reinforcement. Provide successful learning experiences. Identify student special interests, talents, and skills and relate class and group activities to those individual differences. Circle groups. Teacher awareness of a developmental process. Teacher models expected behavior. Peer tutoring/cross-age tutoring. Guidance program.	Self-concept measures.

(continued on next page)

Table 1. Guidelines for Designing a Self-Directed Learning Program, Cont'd.

Student Learner Outcome (Objectives)	Possible Means/Methods	Anticipated Performance Measures
Improve interpersonal concern for others and acceptance of strengths and weaknesses of others.	Provide student opportunities for helping and sharing in learning and social situations.	Random sampling of progress reports.
	Circle groups.	Use of questionnaires to assess group climate and individual awareness of group responsibilities.
	Plan interaction which fosters appreciation of human differences.	
	Teacher awareness of a developmental process.	
	Develop foster grandparent relationship.	
	Guidance program.	
	Develop big brother/big sister/buddy partnerships.	
	Develop positive relationships with adults in the school setting.	
Improve personal responsibilities, constructive participation in groups.	Provide instructions and guidance in productive small-group situations.	Random sampling of progress reports.
	Provide appropriate small-group activities.	Participant self-evaluation of group and workshop activities.
	Circle groups.	
	Family participation in workshops and training sessions.	
	Cooperative learning experiences.	
	Peer tutor/cross-age tutoring.	
	Guidance program.	

Goal	Strategies/Activities	Indicators
Decrease disciplinary problems and at the same time increase appropriate behavior.	System for developing skills and attitudes for accepting responsibility for behavior within classroom and extending throughout building. Teacher awareness of a developmental process. Emphasize positive consequences in guiding behavior. Guidance program. Students made aware of cost of vandalism and school security system.	Number of disciplinary reports. Amount of vandalism at Jefferson School.
Maintain and/or improve attendance.	Guidance program. Teacher awareness of a developmental process.	Attendance records.
Improve feeling of belonging and identification with the school.	Sharing of school responsibilities through student council. Parent/family participation in workshops and training sessions. Family participation in school events. Participation in school-based management. Awareness of aspects of budget through student participation in the school community council. Teacher awareness of developmental process.	Number of positive communications to teachers, principal, and/or council. Level of participation by students in school activities.

3

Individualized Education at a Catholic High School

Bishop Carroll High School

For over ten years, Bishop Carroll High School has successfully used a continuous-progress approach to individualized education with emphasis on independent study. At first glance it may seem to be another of the "alternative schools" that flourished and then faded in the 1960s. But it is different: Instead of deemphasizing the transmission of subject-matter content, it provides a rigorous system for helping students structure the means for their acquiring the content. It provides a tested answer to the question I often put to my colleagues in secondary education, "Why aren't our high schools doing more to prepare students to be self-directed learners?"

Special features:

- A school building with resource centers for nine curriculum areas and without traditional classrooms and student desks
- A teacher-adviser program tied directly to individualized independent study
- Teachers working in teams and aided by a large support staff
- A modularized curriculum divided into nine areas of knowledge, with graduation requirements in each
- Flexible student scheduling, including opportunities for learning experiences in the community for credit

Adapted, with permission, from *Bishop Carroll High School: A Profile,* published by the Bishop Carroll High School, Calgary, Alberta, Canada.

In 1971 Bishop Carroll High School in Calgary, Alberta, Canada, opened its doors. Its program is based on a continuous-progress, individualized approach to education for all students in grades 10-12.

Continuous-Progress Approach

The Bishop Carroll program developed through the five-year Model Schools Project sponsored by the National Association of Secondary School Principals and directed by J. Lloyd Trump. Thirty-two schools were selected as project participants, thirty in the United States, one in Germany, and Bishop Carroll in Canada. The project was based on a commitment to student-centered education and included changes in curriculum, staffing methods, and instructional patterns. Currently the school is a member of the Learning Environments Consortium, under the direction of William Georgiades, which is a self-help group of schools committed to personalized learning.

The Bishop Carroll program is based on the concepts of continuous-progress instruction and individualized education. The curriculum is modularized, and students move through courses at their own pace, evaluate their own progress, and choose times for testing according to their own rates of achievement. Students work toward predetermined learning goals in courses that may be of particular interest to them while fulfilling specified requirements for graduation. Student groupings vary according to achievement levels and student interest, and scheduling is flexible.

Students are evaluated according to individual progress rather than through comparison with other students. Working through individual study plans, students do not wait for other students to catch up, nor are they frustrated by work that is too difficult for them. The relationship between time spent in school and credit earned has been abolished; instead, there is a direct relationship between achievement and credit.

There is flexibility to match students' learning styles with teaching strategies. The role of the teacher is defined as separate from the roles of support staff, and the program provides conditions for teaching that recognize differences between teachers and capitalizes on the special talents and interests of each staff member. Teachers provide instruction through large-group presentations, small-group discussions, and individual meetings with students. Learning takes place in a number of spaces, and neither students nor teachers are programmed to study or teach in particular places at particular times every school day.

Flexibility a Key

Two of the elements which facilitate the individualized approach to education at Bishop Carroll are a school building flexible enough to accommodate the innovative program and a reorganization of staffing which changes the role of teachers.

The school building, while not an essential element for the success of the program, was new in 1971 and does not include traditional classrooms but provides major areas used as resource centers for each of the nine subject areas into which the curriculum has been divided. Each center contains study carrels, tables and chairs, equipment, printed materials, and audiovisual resources appropriate to the subject area. The school building also includes seminar rooms, labs, shops, a media center, gymnasium, cafeteria, reference library, theater, art gallery, diagnostic fitness center, career resource area, and individual offices for teachers. The building provides areas for students to follow individualized learning plans that include three kinds of instruction: independent study at learning centers, large-group presentations, and small-group discussions or seminars.

Staffing at Bishop Carroll reflects the curriculum emphasis on individualized instruction. In a staffing program that includes a system of support service provided by three types of aides, teachers serve in professional roles as both learning facilitators in a particular subject area and as teacher-advisers to an assigned group of students.

Subject area instruction includes several elements. Working in teams, teachers are responsible for motivational presentations in a particular subject area to large groups of students. In

these sessions teachers may provide information, circulate sup-
plemental written materials, or make oral assignments to students. Individual teachers may schedule themselves to meet
with smaller groups of students for seminars in particular subject courses. Scheduling is flexible, and the majority of teacher
time is spent as a subject area resource person.

A portion of each teacher's time is set aside each week
for curriculum planning. In regularly scheduled biweekly sessions, teachers work together to develop curriculum materials
for use in subject area resource centers. Teachers also have time
to work individually to map personalized schedules for individual students assigned to them in the school's teacher-adviser
program.

As subject area specialists, teachers are also responsible
for maintenance and staffing of subject area resource centers.
They prepare curriculum materials, monitor student progress,
and are always on site during certain hours to provide assistance
to individual students or informal groups of students working in
that center. There is some specialization, but, for the most part,
teachers are responsible for providing assistance and direction to
students in all course material within the subject area.

Teacher-Adviser Program

The remainder of teacher time is spent providing assistance to students in the teacher-adviser program. Each teacher
serves as teacher-adviser (T-A) for twenty to thirty-five Bishop
Carroll students. Students are assigned to a T-A when they enter
the school and remain with the same T-A throughout their high
school careers. New students are assigned to each T-A each year,
and T-A groups include students from all grade levels.

The teacher-adviser is personally responsible for providing
assistance to student assignees in all areas of their educational
progress at Bishop Carroll. They work in cooperation with professional counselors, subject area teachers, and the administration in monitoring advisees.

There is continual contact between the teacher-adviser
and each advisee. At the beginning of the year, teacher-advisers

meet individually with assignees to plan personalized student schedules for the year. Individual meetings continue at least once a month during the year for review of student academic progress, diagnosis of problems, and prescription of solutions. All members of a single T-A group meet with their teacher-adviser twice each day, as well, for check-in where attendance is recorded and for check-out at the end of the day. In addition, teacher-advisers are available during regular school hours for special consultations with individual advisees.

A close relationship develops between the teacher-adviser and the advisee. Teacher-advisers are responsible for keeping student progress records, meeting with parents of advisees at least twice each year, and reporting home on student progress. They serve as mentors to their advisees, referring students to subject area teachers for special instruction, becoming aware of personal needs of individual students, and providing support to students as they work through their personal study plans.

Use of Paraprofessionals

Support staff relieve teachers of many noninstructional duties. Three types of aides provide support services for teachers, performing tasks which would take up as much as one third or more of a traditional teaching day:

1. Instructional assistants who have two years of postsecondary training in a particular subject area supervise independent study areas, aid in materials preparation, and assist in evaluation of students.
2. Clerical aides are responsible for typing, duplicating, record keeping, and other clerical tasks normally performed by teachers. There is one clerical aide for each subject area team of teachers, approximately one for every four teachers.
3. General aides supervise study and nonstudy areas, arrange for audiovisual equipment, file, and perform other tasks.

This paid support staff frees teachers to concentrate on instruction, curriculum development, and direct monitoring of individual student progress in the teacher-adviser program. This support staff is not in addition to professional staff but in place of some certified teachers.

Modularized Curriculum

A modularized curriculum provides flexible time that can be scheduled to include a variety of learning experiences for all Bishop Carroll students, regardless of age or talent. With the guidance of teacher-advisers, students can arrange for supervised, self-directed, and school-directed individualized study and work at school, at home, or in the community.

All students must meet specified requirements in the school's "Nine Areas of Knowledge" while acquiring the 100 credits necessary for graduation:

1.	English Language Arts	Minimum of three five-credit courses, one at each grade level
2.	Fine Arts	Minimum of one three-credit course
3.	Health Fitness and Recreation	Minimum of one three-credit course
4.	Mathematics	Minimum of one five-credit course
5.	Modern Languages	Minimum of one three-credit course
6.	Philosophy and Religious Studies	Minimum of one three-credit course
7.	Practical Arts	Minimum of one three-credit course
8.	Science	Minimum of one three-credit course
9.	Social Sciences	Minimum of ten credits, five of which must be grade 10 Social Studies

In the nine subject areas, each course is assigned a number of credits toward graduation. Students must earn a minimum of 100 credits to graduate, although most students earn more. There is no time limit for fulfilling requirements, nor are students required at all times to be at grade level in all courses.

Each student follows a personal performance schedule of independent study, planned with and approved by the teacher-adviser to include time for independent study and scheduled group sessions. The student is responsible for working according to his or her personal schedule, which can be changed whenever necessary.

Group sessions and independent study time are scheduled for all students and teachers in a two-week cycle of instruction. In a typical two-week schedule, students may attend large-group sessions and small-group sessions in each of the major subject areas. These sessions, which are the responsibility of the subject area teams, are approximately thirty minutes in length and complement the students' independent study.

Students proceed at their own pace through courses, using learning guides prepared for each unit. Working through the guides, students spend time in subject area resource centers in study and in projects guided by subject area teachers. Learning guides are supplemented by small-group discussions, seminars, audiovisual materials, videotapes, and some large-group presentations. Within the course students advance in units, which may or may not be sequenced, after achieving 60 percent proficiency on unit tests. Most tests are administered in the school testing center.

Reporting Progress

Student academic progress is monitored by teacher-advisers. A *Student Progress Report* booklet is assigned by the T-A to each student at the beginning of the year. The booklets serve both as planning guides for students and as formal reports of student progress. Following meetings with teacher-advisers, student goals for the year are listed in the booklets. As course work is completed, entries are made in a "Course Completion Record" kept up to date so that student, parent, and teacher-adviser are aware of student progress toward year-long goals. At each formal report period, a report to parents is made via forms in the booklets which note work completed to date, work planned for the next report period, and work to be completed by the end of the year. At all times, students, teachers, and parents are aware of the student's progress toward meeting yearly goals and toward fulfilling graduation requirements.

As units are completed, students receive written confirmation which includes test performance and comments from teachers. Percentage grades—an Alberta Education requirement—are given at the completion of each course. Grading, forced attendance, and peer comparisons are deemphasized to reduce tensions among students, and there are few discipline problems in the school. Letter grades are not given, and there is no honor roll.

Community Learning

In addition to in-school instruction, students have opportunities to gain credits by participating in work experience and by doing special projects both inside and outside of the formal school setting. Students can, with teacher-adviser approval, arrange to spend time in the community in offices, industries, museums, institutes, or other locations to supplement instruction in particular subject areas. In this way much of the community becomes a classroom, as students work outside the school building in individual learning situations arranged by the school.

EIGHT

◆◆◆◆◆◆◆◆◆◆◆◆◆◆◆◆◆◆◆◆◆◆◆◆◆◆◆◆◆◆◆◆◆

Applications
in Remedial Education

People who failed, dropped out, or did not keep up with their classmates in school present special problems when they return to school as adults to catch up. They are in a double bind: they are adults in age, size, life roles, experience, and self-concept, but they are learning what they perceive to be childish content —reading, writing, and arithmetic. It is therefore especially important that they be treated as adults—that their dignity and self-esteem be respected, that their learning materials and tasks be geared to application in the adult world, and that their adult experience be taken into account and made use of as a resource.

The two case descriptions in this chapter exemplify the application of adult learning concepts to this special group of learners. Selection 1 describes the Predischarge Education Program (PREP) of the Department of Defense Schools, Pacific. Addressed to the military personnel the program is designed to serve, it sets a climate of adultness and orients the prospective student to a new kind of relationship with teachers who see their role as facilitating self-directed learners. An andragogical approach to a different set of learners—immigrants who want to learn English as a second language—is presented in selection 2.

1
Developing Basic Competencies at Department of Defense Schools

Department of Defense Schools, Pacific

An example of an attempt to apply principles of adult learning to education in the military services is the Predischarge Education Program (PREP) of the Department of Defense (DOD) Schools, Pacific. This selection describes how the program is presented to the military personnel it is designed to serve. It is one of the clearest and most enthusiastic portrayals of the role of learning facilitator that I have seen.
   Special features:

- Special characteristics of reentry learners
- Role of teachers as facilitators
- Learning as an enjoyable activity
- Role of self-directed learners
- Evaluation without grades
- Individualized learning
- Team teaching
- Building positive self-concepts

The Department of Defense Schools, Pacific, functions on a cross-service basis by operating on Air Force, Army, Navy, and Marine installations throughout the Pacific and Southeast Asia areas. Responsibility for providing educational programs which are equal to (or exceed) stateside accreditation standards spans

Excerpted, with permission, from a brochure published by the Adult Education Division of the Department of Defense Schools, Pacific, 1976.

elementary, secondary, and adult needs of United States service-men and their dependents.

District III of the DOD Schools, Pacific, encompasses a geographical area which includes United States military bases in the Philippines, Thailand, and Taiwan. The Adult Education Division of District III Schools conducts "PREP," a program that offers refresher, remedial, deficiency, high school completion, and other secondary-level courses for eligible military personnel.

The program is designed for military personnel with 180 days of active duty who have no high school diploma and for those who are lacking in academic requirements necessary for entrance into college or other postsecondary and vocational programs. The active-duty VA benefits provided for PREP are in addition to postservice benefits extended under the original GI Bill.

Although PREP is primarily for active-duty military personnel, United States government civilian employees and adult dependents may enroll on a space-available, tuition-paying basis.

PREP is offered throughout the continental United States by county school systems and community colleges, and in overseas commands by DOD Schools and private colleges wherever United States servicemen are stationed. Although other educational institutions conduct PREP in the Pacific and in Southeast Asia, DOD Schools have by far the largest program, with an active enrollment approaching 3,500 students taking almost 5,000 separate courses.

District III PREP began at Subic Naval Base, Olongapo, Philippines, in the spring of 1971, and by 1972 the program had expanded northward to Clark Air Base, Philippines. In March 1973 the DOD Schools were directed to implement PREP Centers at all United States military installations in Thailand. This was followed by the inception of three more centers on Taiwan, Republic of China. Currently there are fourteen adult learning centers within District III.

The conduct of PREP by the Adult Education Division of District III Schools affords both career military and those planning to leave active service educational benefits never before offered. The improvement and certification of basic skills, or attainment of a fully accredited high school diploma, hold tremendous potential for upgrading military performance, enhancing overall career development potential, and giving those who wish to leave the military better opportunities for occupational pursuits or college and vocational programs.

Many students who enroll in PREP see the necessity for improving reading, language arts, and math skills while moving toward high school diploma completion. Others need encouragement that they can succeed. PREP students are unique individuals, but they have certain similarities. Many are burdened with unpleasant memories of past high school experiences. They "dropped out" because the traditional school system was not relevant to their lives. Many still feel hostility toward authority, and some harbor a feeling of helplessness about how to broaden career opportunities within the service or what to do once their tour of duty is ended. Often there is a lack of basic skills for which the student has had to overcompensate for many years. Many people lack a positive self-image and have a fear of failure. They have little confidence, especially where "school" is concerned, and this lack of certainty may carry over into their assessment of their own worth.

We care about these real fears, feelings, and concerns. Our goal is to help the individual students discover how they can overcome some of the problems they face and how they can be involved in decision-making processes that affect their lives.

This is one way our program is unique—teachers spend much time with individual students. Very often in their past, adult learners have known little personal involvement with teachers. Often it is this teacher/student relationship—that personal touch—that helps break down the learning barriers of the initially reluctant students, enabling them to develop a more positive attitude about themselves and to feel motivated beyond anything they have previously known. This warm, caring atmosphere seems to go far in alleviating possible apprehensions and preconceived ideas that PREP is "just another school."

Another unique feature in PREP's student/teacher interchange is that every teacher is a learner. Each teacher does not really "teach" in the usual sense: he or she is seen in the role of

facilitator, of helping the student learn how to learn. In doing
this, teachers are asked many questions about subjects relevant
to the student. Often they do not know the answers, and the
learning procedure becomes a search together for solutions.
Through this attitude of searching, seeking, and finding together, adult learners begin to see and live learning as the day-to-
day, ongoing process it really is.

The individualized, open learning approach used in PREP
differs from traditional teaching on one hand and the "free,"
"progressive" schools on the other. The free schools, which are
often confused with Open Learning Centers, connote an absence of structure and teacher impact. The open learning concept does not diminish the role of the teacher. The role of this
"learning leader" perhaps is more important than in a traditional classroom—important because the teacher is influencing
internal and personal motivation of the students by promoting
self-confidence and arousing a desire for learning. However, the
teacher in a Learning Center is not an authority figure but, rather, attempts to relate to the learners on an equal, human basis
by acting as a leader, tutor, counselor, and friend. The teacher
helps the student learn and accept ideas about what should be
learned as differentiated from traditional concepts which imply
the teacher has knowledge to be forced into the learner, who is
an empty vessel to be filled under pressure. There is a structure
in a Learning Center though it is less apparent and more informal than a classroom. The individual programs for each learner
and a sharing of the management of learning activities among
teachers require a sense of direction and goals on the part of
each staff member, combined with an awareness of the progress
of each student.

The teacher in an Open Learning Center is a facilitator
of learning rather than a source of knowledge. Our goal is to
teach people how to discover, to make learning fun, and to initiate a lifelong process. Therefore, the emphasis is on the art of
seeking information rather than the science of teaching facts.
If learning becomes a continuous, enjoyable, natural process,
then our students are learning to cope with change, a necessity
in a rapidly changing world. Our teachers help and influence,

but don't direct. Improvement of the student's self-concept is the foremost goal of open learning. Many people are prevented from learning because they don't think they can; when they gain confidence, they learn. Traditional methods drove them out of school, but PREP strives to make learning attractive and a practical lifelong process. Inherent is the respect for individual differences: interests, backgrounds, and abilities (*respect, not tolerance*).

The establishment of a warm human relationship between teacher and student without connotation of superior/inferior is important as it extends the learning process into open communication. To maintain such a rapport, trust—which is developed from honesty, acceptance, and open cooperation—is essential. Even though the interaction between instructors and students appears to be informal, the informality is a guarded one on the part of the teachers. A great deal of responsibility is involved when one is influencing a person's internal goals and motivations. A hastily tossed-out remark, a "cute" reply, or a look of impatience will be interpreted with a lot more importance than was intended.

Evaluation in an Open Learning Center is continuous and essential, but grades are not. Documented grades of "F," or any evidence which connotes a failing performance, are shunned. An adult learner either receives credit or he does not; hence, there is no immortal record of failure on the part of each student. If a student begins at a given level of knowledge and progresses upward, it is more important to emphasize advancement and not simply the rate of movement. Tests are given and grades sometimes computed, but their purpose is to indicate mastery of material. The teacher suggests alternative materials for reinforcement and indicates whether learning has been sufficient for credit (keeping in mind individual differences), but there are no directives and no failures. Additionally, emphasis is always on the positive rather than the negative. It is much more important to emphasize a learning effort which is 75 percent successful rather than dwell upon the remaining 25 percent in which the learner was not as proficient. Encouragement and praise make criticism easier to accept. A nonthreatening atmosphere where thoughts and opinions can be freely expressed without fear of criticism or ridicule is essential to the Open Learning Center.

Rather than carrying out a set curriculum, someone else's, teachers in an Open Learning Center are constantly creating, revising, implementing new ideas and scrapping old ones. Curriculum is in a constant state of flux; when one is dealing with individual students and developing core courses, a premium is placed on creativity and innovation. A lot of communication and the discovery of student needs, weaknesses, and desires are critical in determining individualized programs. The curriculum or course content becomes important only in relation to the needs and goals of the learner. The goals of open learning promote and encourage exploration and diverse and critical thinking. Expression of ideas is encouraged; rote memory and regurgitation of facts are discouraged. The inquiry method is the most thought-provoking and least threatening way to promote greater depth of thinking or finding alternative ideas. Challenges to accepted ideas, ideas expressed in books and course content, are accepted and discussed. Keeping in mind the adult status and experience of the PREP student, instructors avoid imposing their values on the learners; in fact, they generally avoid expressing their values unless there is a definite reason for doing so. Flexibility is essential as each learner requires a different approach, a different program, and a different attitude on the part of the teacher. While plans and expectations are essential, the teacher must be prepared to deviate from these, must have alternatives, and must be continuously questioning, changing, and innovating.

This individualized approach to learning seeks to motivate students by helping them find and work on their own needs and interests, and by giving them individual assignments and individual tasks based on this uniqueness. Students see more relevance in coming to the Learning Center when they know they are going to be involved in work which is recognized as personally rewarding rather than attending a "school" where they will face a predetermined curriculum.

Teachers in a Learning Center are required to be "generalists," to cross subject lines, to work in subject areas for which they are not primarily trained. "Specialists" in each area are available if necessary (every teacher, because of aptitudes and interests, will tend to master at least one area in depth), but teachers in general are familiar with the entire environment of the center and can use the majority of materials with ease. This takes time; usually teachers will start out in one area where they are comfortable and expand from there. Instruction in the Learning Center is not really "teaching" in the classical sense: the teacher not only helps the student learn but also learns along with the student, as opposed to being the "expert" in a given subject discipline. A lack of knowledge about specific subject areas can be a very positive attribute for a teacher to possess: the phrase "I don't know either, let's see if we can find out together" has produced a positive response from many students. Will Rogers once said, "Everyone is ignorant, only on different subjects." In essence, the syndrome in teaching of "this is my area" (or sacred cow) is not followed in the Open Learning Center.

Why? Adult learners tend to be person oriented rather than subject oriented. Adult students are hurt if their teacher refers them to someone else for a simple question. It is also a useless procedure to keep someone waiting while "the teacher" is busy with someone else, or is not there on a given day. According to our concept, the teacher is a helper for learning, and it is unnecessary for an instructor to have an extensive background in a subject to teach it. More important is the ability to ask the right stimulating question and to be willing to learn with the students.

In each Learning Center, a person known as the lead teacher works on the staff but also is the designated contact person for the area principal and the District Schools Office, and is essentially the individual in the Learning Center who deals with the local military community. The lead teacher concept as developed in British schools is highly successful and is totally different from the American idea of a principal. This concept of team teaching, which can be described as a sharing of the management of learning activities, promotes mutual understanding of problems in the Learning Center by sharing accountability for its success. Teachers work in counseling and administration, and the lead teacher participates in the education. Team teaching requires the ability to get along with others. This means acceptance of individual differences (the same as with our students!), sharing the load, helping each other, not assuming rigid roles, keeping an open mind, and being flexible. Rigid, authoritarian types who are set in their ways are not effective in a team-teaching situation.

In essence, what we are trying to accomplish in an Open Learning Center is the recognition that there is no standard student and that each person is an individual who is going to learn in his own way and in his own time. The Open Learning Center in many cases allows the first successful feeling the student has experienced about himself and his ability to learn, to think, and to create. We believe the most valuable thing we can do is create an inspiration in that student, a spark, an excitement about learning. And this, we feel, in the relatively short time we work with an adult learner, is the flavor that will perhaps carry him past what a traditional school situation would accomplish. We believe that learning is an emotional and an exciting process, and if we can tap this excitement, which comes out in so many different ways, then we have provided a very worthwhile service to the community and to society.

2

Teaching English
as a Second Language
to Immigrant
Community College Students

Zilda Souza DePaula

Important as it is to show respect for the experience of learners when the learners are well-educated adults, it is doubly important with less educated and immigrant learners. Their self-respect is about all they have going for them. This selection describes an andragogical approach to teaching English as a second language by one of the more dynamic and imaginative teachers I have met.

Zilda Souza DePaula is program director, International Culture, Central Piedmont Community College, Charlotte, North Carolina.

Special features:

- A person-to-person needs assessment process
- Creative use of the media for promotion
- Getting administrative support
- Creating a learning climate
- Common characteristics of foreigners
- Identifying learning levels
- Planning extracurricular activities

Adapted, with permission, from a document published by the Central Piedmont Community College, Charlotte, North Carolina, to "provide information for anyone offering a program in teaching English as a second language to adults, using the andragogical approach."

Looking at our multilingual brochure and at the college catalogue, I cannot deny that my dream came true. Patience, determination, and an open market did allow me to change public
opinion about the need for an English as a Second Language
program for adults in Charlotte, North Carolina. Since the
summer of 1971, when the first class (with eight students) was
organized, I could see some of the instructors changing their reaction to our new program. They changed from prejudice and
indifference at first, to curiosity and support later on. I remember when one of the top administrators, believing that we didn't
have enough foreign students to justify a full-time teaching position, asked me: "What is your definition of English as a Second
Language, anyway?" To others from surrounding institutions,
who wrote to us candidly, and trying to find a catalogue definition, we answered: "English as a Second Language (ESL) is a
special program designed to meet the needs of foreign-born students, for whom English is a second language."

As the program started to grow and received community
support, we received hundreds of letters and visitors from near-
by institutions. One English teacher asked if I could help her to
define their course objectives. Then, in 1973, we printed our
original brochure in three languages: Greek, Spanish, and
English. We stated our objectives this way: "In consonance with
the Central Piedmont College's philosophy of giving the student
what he or she needs as an individual, our English as a Second
Language program is taught with two basic objectives: (1) to
overcome the communication problem in order to promote a
quicker adjustment within the life of the community (foreign
nationals, legal residents, and intracompany transferees are not
required to have a high school diploma to enter this program);
(2) to make an easy transition from a person who has little or
no proficiency in English to one who is a proficient, happy, ad-
justed, and useful citizen." These students are seeking English
for professional and social purposes. An important factor that
helped our efforts was the fact that CPCC is conveniently located in the heart of the world's largest textile manufacturing,
distribution, and technician's training center.

Assessment of Needs and Initial Responses

Visiting several churches during the spring of 1971, I discovered many foreign-born people attending those churches but unable to understand the language. Going to shopping centers and supermarkets, I saw many foreign faces and heard foreign languages and dialects. Many of the people I saw were orientals from Korea, Taiwan, Hong Kong, and Japan. I saw Spanish speakers from South and Central America and the Caribbean Islands, and very soon I discovered that many of the restaurants in Charlotte were owned, managed, and operated by Greek immigrants.

I was sure that the need did exist and that the market was open to an ESL program for adults, even though the principal of one of the adult centers made clear to me that the effort was worthless, because his center had tried it in previous years without success. "They are not motivated," he concluded. Nobody else seemed to be interested either.

One reason for failure in previous years I discovered later. None of the previous instructors had the experience of teaching ESL to adults. Unfortunately for the foreign adults, the teachers tended to ignore the students' background. I discovered that the previous adopted book was "The New Streamlined English Series," originated in 1930 for teaching adults how to read and write. The fundamental assumption that they were illiterates certainly caused a massive dropout and a resentful cultural shock.

To assess the needs for the program, we wrote letters to nearly 500 foreign names listed in the local telephone directory. We wrote letters in Spanish, Greek, Italian, and in English, informing the foreign population about the new ESL program to be offered. Because many were not able to respond in English, they came in person to confirm that they would come to class. They came because our letter explained that "they only could get ahead on their jobs by being able to speak the language well, in order to make use of their full potential, and by continuing their education in this country." The letter also reminded them that as taxpayers they were helping the local community college to operate, although they were left out because they were not motivated to come to school. The ones who were United States citizens or second-generation immigrants wrote encouraging us "to go ahead and make easier the transition for newcomers."

The first class, in the summer of 1971, was offered off campus at the CPCC Adult Education Center at Garinger High School. In the summer of 1972, when the college decided to offer the program on campus, the course already had ninety-three students representing twenty-two foreign countries.

Getting Administrators and the Community Involved

Using the resources and talents of the students, I took my class to the WSOC television station to participate in the program "The Hour of Opportunity." The television program was a tremendous success, and our story was already becoming well known to the faculty and administrators. They started moving from the initial indifference to curiosity. A very positive community response from the news media took place on August 17, 1972, when the *Charlotte News* published a front-page article entitled "Problems Routine to Her." Among other information the newswriter said: "Mrs. DePaula teaches English to foreigners at Central Piedmont Community College. She does it with considerable success. When she began teaching the course last summer, there were eight students in one class. This summer there are 93 students, representing 22 foreign countries, in three classes." By fall 1979 the number had increased to 800 students from 82 countries. Another newswriter asked me: "What is the secret of the success?" and I replied: "I guess that it is the international environment of the classes and a new sense of belonging, which generate the motivation. In addition to that, a happy student always brings a friend."

Responsibilities and Standards in Handling Foreign Students

Today's ESL for adults is just one of the segments in the lifelong learning experience. It is a part in the world's perspective of international education. The lifelong experience might start in one continent and might continue abroad. That could be the case for one of our textile engineers from Japan, or from Germany, who signs up for the Intensive English class while engaged himself in a training program, sharing or learning additional skills. It could also be the example of an immigrant (legal resident) seeking English for getting ahead on the job, or a full-time foreign student (holding a student visa status) trying to upgrade her command of the English language. No matter what nationality, a foreigner outside his or her native environment is generally subject to the same kinds of sociocultural pressures, which generate social stratification and cultural shocks. Consequently, before we are able to teach ESL, a certain degree of reading on international cultures becomes a prerequisite.

Creating the Environment. Creating a good learning environment is a psychological move expected from any reputable adult educator. So, in order to create such an environment, the ESL instructor must not ignore the impact of the foreign culture, which can become traumatic for those who leave their native countries to live abroad: the mores and the roles are different; socialization techniques vary and provide for different behaviors. Part of the cultural shock is due to loss of identity that occurs when the immigrant is faced with new values. Part of it derives from the intense feeling of isolation from others because of language barriers. Faced with acculturation demands, the student confronts alternatives that might result in either assimilation or refusal to adapt, followed by cultural and social withdrawal. It is a good feeling when a student comes to us, confiding that "today's lesson, or intellectual nourishment, was like medicine."

How to create the learning environment? The first step toward overcoming the cultural shock is to help the students relax about the common goal of learning the language "collectively." The classroom is the living lab. All are there with the same purpose of overcoming the language barrier, and the instructor is there to help them define their goals and to certify that they are moving at the expected rate.

The anxiety due to long absence from school can be minimized by an easy, informal, and friendly environment. Since the outside responsibilities (family, social, and at work) of adult learners do interfere with class performance, it is imperative to relate the lesson content to real-life experiences. Therefore, before you decide to order your textbook, make sure that the content is aimed at adults. When strongly motivated, they come to class voluntarily and with good sense of responsibility. We advise you to make the classes challenging and alive. They want to be involved. Give them opportunity to evaluate and make suggestions. The instructor should never ignore their experience and background, especially when they are willing to share it with classmates. In fact, group discussions focusing on problem solving, case studies, and open-ended stories dealing with controversial values are strongly encouraged. Interaction is essential. For most of the newcomers, the classroom time might become the main event of the week, since the social life is yet to be structured. We recommend the organization of an international club, or at least a quarterly party for welcoming and farewell, in order to provide opportunity and time to socialize and to help students to get acquainted with each other.

Identifying the Learning Levels. Any English teacher can design an elementary placement test. The first and easy step is to find out if your ESL student is illiterate. Give the student a list of ten words, preferably action verbs, such as *sit, stand, stop, go, drink, dance.* Those verbs provide you with a body language type of response. While the student is looking up the words, using a dictionary, you will have a chance to measure the student's dictionary skills. Next, you can use the Science Research Associates' *Reading for Understanding—Junior RFU.* This box, with 400 cards, offers you the convenience of multiple choice, and the first 80 cards are easy for dictionary usage. It also provides for checking vocabulary knowledge and pronunciation skills. The three levels of proficiency are divided into three sublevels of increasing difficulty:

> *Beginner:* Learning how to imitate by listening and repeating easy patterns; using vocabulary to satisfy daily needs; learning questions and answers with

more listening and repeating patterns; replying, reacting, participating, and interacting in order to assimilate the language and culture; learning the alphabet and phonetics; situational dialogues; learning objective sentences with more listening and repeating patterns; starting interest in verbs needed for effective expression and everyday dialogues; spelling for functional purposes.

Intermediate: Using situational dialogues and working with meaningful vocabulary to improve oral communication; building up vocabulary; communicating for survival; facing emotional and cultural shocks; becoming familiar with verbs; learning principal parts of sentences and negative and interrogative forms of verbs; situational simple dialogues; reading and understanding; questions and answers; dialogues oriented for building up a functional vocabulary; using synonyms and opposites; writing short messages; learning prepositions and two-word verbs; using the dictionary.

Advanced: Interacting to help overcome oral communication problems through short speeches and slide presentations about the students' countries; speech correction and coordination of ideas for effective dialogue; reading and understanding; increasing fluency to the point where student may begin academic work; obtaining basic knowledge of idioms and usages; fluency in conversational English; discussion of contemporary issues (subjects chosen by students); reaction to film presentation, faculty or guest speaker, excursions, and so on; English composition and writing skills.

Planning Extracurricular Activities. Extracurricular activities are entirely welcomed, mainly because they represent additional opportunity for interaction. The students enjoy field trips, trips to sightseeing places, mountains and beaches, historical landmarks, and the like. By not ignoring the background of your students, you might be able to have a talent show using their artistic and cultural talents for international festivals and other international events. At CPCC the "Christmas with International Students" certainly became the international event of our college during the month of December. Today the faculty and administrators look forward to attending the international buffet and the talent show. Usually the event is covered by the local news media. Another way of planning is to activate the international club and to list the extracurricular activities that members want to be implemented.

A Closing Remark

The assumptions of andragogy are totally valid, and many of its methods and techniques are applicable during all phases of teaching ESL to adults.

Never in the history of education has so much emphasis been placed on the value of audiovisual approaches, self-paced packages, individualized instruction, and alternative delivery systems. Since all learning skills for immigrants are taught in English, how can they cope with the lack of English in the life-long learning society? Without an ESL for adults, the foreign population will have no chance.

NINE

Conclusion:
Effectiveness
of Andragogy
in Various Settings

Usefulness with Different Types of Learners and Programs.
Clearly, as the case descriptions in this book demonstrate, practitioners have found that the andragogical model can be applied, in whole or in part, to a wide variety of educational activities and programs in a wide variety of institutional settings. It appears not to be culture bound; it has been successfully applied in North America, Europe, Africa, Brazil, and Australia with individuals from every socioeconomic level. It appears not to be highly content limited; it has been applied in situations dealing with scientific and technical content as well as the "soft" content of the humanities and social sciences. It appears not to be age restricted; selections in this book span the life cycle.

Certain elements in the andragogical model have been more widely applied than others. Climate setting is probably the most widely adopted element, but self-directed learning, contract learning, individualized instruction, experiential learning, process designs, peer helping, self-diagnosis, and self-evaluation are prominent practices. And evaluative comments about their effectiveness have been strongly positive.

What We Have Learned from Practice. In the almost two decades of experimenting with the andragogical model, many problems have been identified and as many solutions have been devised regarding its application. Some of these problems and solutions are discussed explicitly in Chapter Three, selections 7 and 8, and in Chapter Four, selection 3. Others are implicit in the other case descriptions. Many others have been reported to me by practitioners. Here are some of the things I think we have learned:

1. The andragogical model is a system of elements that can be adopted or adapted in whole or in part. It is not an ideology that must be applied totally and without modification. In fact, an essential feature of andragogy is flexibility.

2. The appropriate starting point and strategies for applying the andragogical model depend on the situation. In some situations—for instance, in new institutions or programs starting from scratch—it may be appropriate to apply the model totally and at once (see Chapter Two, selections 1, 2, and 3; Chapter Three, selections 1 and 4; Chapter Four, selection 1; Chapter Six, selection 1; Chapter Seven, selection 3; Chapter Eight, selection 2). In most instances, however, it would probably be more appropriate to experiment by applying the model to one unit of the program, such as a unit of a course or one course or one department in an institution or a workshop or a special project (see Chapter Two, selections 3 and 4; Chapter Three, selections 2, 5, 6, and 8; Chapter Four, selections 2, 3, 4, 5, and 6; Chapter Five, selections 1, 3, and 4; Chapter Six, selection 2; Chapter Seven, selection 2). People tell me that if such an innovation is labeled "a pilot experiment," it is likely to meet less resistance than if it is labeled "a program change." Probably the most common starting point, because it is the easiest and least conspicuous, is the climate-setting element. Once the innovator and learners have had a small success and have gained some security in experimenting, then other elements of the model can be piloted and the model can be spread to other activities.

3. Learners will be able to participate more responsibly and enthusiastically in an andragogical learning experience if they have some preparatory orientation to it. All that most

learners know about education is derived from their prior experience as a student in didactic teacher-directed schooling. If they are suddenly expected to take responsibility for planning and carrying out their own learning, they will tend to be confused, resistant, and resentful. Accordingly, programs based on the andragogical model provide for some front-end exposure to the assumptions about learners in the andragogical model and to the skills of self-directed learning (see Chapter Two, selections 6 and 7; Chapter Three, selections 3, 7, 8, and 9; Chapter Four, selections 2, 3, 4, 5, and 6; Chapter Five, selection 3; Chapter Seven, selection 1).

4. Learners—especially adults who are reentering an academic program after years of absence from academic study—experience some anxiety with this new approach to education until they have had experience with it and come to understand how it works. This anxiety can be reduced if learners are provided with support groups consisting of fellow learners, more experienced learners, and supportive faculty members (see Chapter Two, selection 8; Chapter Three, selections 1, 2, 5, and 6; Chapter Four, selections 1 and 3; Chapter Six, selection 2; Chapter Seven, selection 1).

5. Most teachers, trainers, and resource people know only the pedagogical model; they have no idea about how adults learn. Therefore, faculty training (or, if you prefer, reorientation or development) is crucial to the successful implementation of the andragogical model. Faculty development programs range from single-shot one-day workshops to long-term continuing education strategies (see Chapter Two, selections 4 and 6; Chapter Three, selections 2, 4, and 5; Chapter Four, selection 3; Chapter Six, selections 1 and 2; Chapter Seven, selections 1 and 3).

6. Many institutions have policies, rules and regulations, and traditions that are not congruent with the andragogical model. Norm-referenced grading, compulsory attendance, rigid time schedules, and required content-oriented syllabi are often treated as sacred cows. Many practitioners, however, have found imaginative ways to adapt to traditional systems without sacrificing the essence of the andragogical model. A number of

them have mentioned to me that they were surprised at how much they could "get away with" as long as they did their innovating within their own classrooms or training events. Furthermore, the successful innovations soon spread and were adopted by the system. Selection 3 in Chapter Four has some especially useful suggestions in this regard, but the issue is also treated in Chapter Two, selection 2; Chapter Three, selections 4, 5, 6, and 8; Chapter Four, selection 2; Chapter Six, selection 2.

7. Innovations can be anxiety producing to a system and can induce resistance. Creative practitioners have found ways to reduce this risk by involving relevant elements of the system in planning, by keeping them well informed, and by establishing peer-support groups or networks (see Chapter Two, selections 2 and 6; Chapter Three, selections 4 and 6; Chapter Four, selections 1 and 3; Chapter Five, selections 1 and 4; Chapter Six, selections 1 and 3; Chapter Seven, selections 1 and 2; Chapter Eight, selection 2).

What Research Has Revealed About Andragogy. Of the several foundational elements on which the andragogical model is built, self-directed learning has attracted the largest volume of empirical research. Tough's seminal studies of this phenomenon (1967, 1971) and subsequent studies by Penland (1977) and Peters (1974) stimulated a rash of studies around the world. Tough (1979) cites twenty done in the previous decade. All these studies found that adults do indeed engage in self-directed learning outside of formal instructional programs but that they assume a dependent role when they enter into structured educational activities. Cheren (1978) investigated the process by which adults learn to take more control of their learning and discovered that there is a "transitional dynamic" that can be facilitated. There is now good reason to believe that self-directed learning is their natural mode when they undertake to learn things on their own. The andragogical model is, therefore, congruent with adults' natural way of learning.

The other elements of the andragogical model, and the assumptions on which it is based, have begun to receive the attention of researchers. Knights and McDonald (1977) found

that mature students in university courses possessed the characteristics described by the andragogical assumptions. Hadley's
(1975) Educational Orientation Questionnaire enables teachers
to be placed on a continuum between pedagogical and andragogical beliefs and has been used in subsequent research to distinguish between pedagogical and andragogical teachers (Jones,
1982; Logue, 1982). Zogas (1981) has developed an interview
guide for the same purpose. Kerwin (1979) adapted Hadley's
EOQ to measure students' perceptions of their teachers' practices and found that teachers tended to see themselves as more
andragogical than their students did.

Bowers (1977, pp. 221-224), in a study of 474 students at
Boston University, found that "adult students tend to respond
positively to andragogical methods regardless of age, marital
status, estimated grade point average, graduate/undergraduate
status, or class size" and that "application of andragogical principles in the university class tends to predict increased cognitive and affective learning as perceived by students." Bromley
(1972) followed students through andragogically designed
courses at Boston University and found that in a fifteen-week
semester they experienced three weeks of increasing confusion
and anxiety, two weeks of reorientation, and ten weeks of deep
involvement and excitement in learning. Beder and Darkenwald
(1982, p. 154) found that "teachers do in fact teach adults differently from children and adolescents." Specifically: "When
teaching adults, teachers appear to emphasize responsive,
learner-centered behaviors and deemphasize controlling and
structuring behaviors."

A number of other studies of the andragogical model are
in progress, and no doubt the volume of research on this subject
in the next decade will be double the volume of research in the
past decade.

*Adapting Andragogy to Future Education and Training
Needs.* Certain clearly discernible trends provide some security
in forecasting some future developments:

1. The volume of adults seeking continuing education
will continue to increase rapidly. We have already moved from
being a predominantly youth-centered society to being a pre-

dominantly adult-centered society, and we are rapidly becoming a predominantly older-adult-centered society. Perhaps even more important, with the accelerating pace of change owing to the knowledge explosion and the technological revolution, an increasing proportion of adults of every age cohort will be seeking to continue learning in order to avoid becoming obsolescent. Adult education will continue to be one of our greatest growth industries, not only in North America but around the world.

2. With the increasing importance of adult education as a movement, more creative professional practitioners will be attracted to it, and more researchers will discover its rich lodes to be mined. As a result, the pace of innovation in the designing and operating of adult learning resources will accelerate, and the breadth and depth of research will swell. Some of the major breakthroughs in new knowledge about adult learning will result from biological scientists' discoveries about the physiology and chemistry of learning. I fully expect the andragogical model to be modified, enriched, and perhaps superseded by new knowledge about learning in general and learning of adults in particular.

3. As more and more adults seek more and more opportunities to continue learning without interrupting home and work lives, it seems certain that we are entering an era of major transformation of our systems for delivering educational services. I believe we are nearing the end of the era of our edifice complex and its basic belief that respectable learning takes place only in buildings and on campuses. Adults are beginning to demand that their learning take place at a time, place, and pace convenient to them. In fact, I feel confident that most educational services by the end of this century (if not decade) will be delivered electronically—by interactive cablevision, satellite television, computer networks, and other means still to be invented. Our great challenge now is to find ways to maintain the human touch as we learn to use the media in new ways. Only the andragogical model provides guidelines for accomplishing this feat at this time.

What a world of infinite potential we are entering!

References

Adderley, K., and others. *Project Methods in Higher Education.* London: Society for Research into Higher Education, 1975.

Arends, R. I., and Arends, J. H. *Systems Change Strategies in Educational Settings.* New York: Human Sciences Press, 1977.

Baldridge, J. V., Kemerer, F. R., and Green, K. C. *The Enrollment Crisis: Factors, Actors, and Impacts.* AAHE-ERIC Higher Education Research Report No. 3. Washington, D.C.: American Association for Higher Education, 1982.

Baltes, P. D. (Ed.). *Life-Span Development and Behavior.* Vol. 1. New York: Academic Press, 1978.

Bandura, A. *Principles of Behavior Modification.* New York: Holt, Rinehart and Winston, 1969.

Barker, R. G., and Associates. *Habitats, Environments, and Human Behavior: Studies in Ecological Psychology and Eco-Behavioral Science.* San Francisco: Jossey-Bass, 1978.

Barney, G. O. *The Global 2000 Report to the President: Entering the Twenty-First Century.* Washington, D.C.: U.S. Government Printing Office, 1981.

Barrett, J. H. *Individual Goals and Organizational Behavior.* Ann Arbor: Institute for Social Research, University of Michigan, 1970.

Beder, H. W., and Darkenwald, G. G. "Differences Between

Teaching Adults and Pre-Adults: Some Propositions and Findings." *Adult Education,* 1982, *33* (3), 142-155.

Bellow, G., and Johnson, E. "Reflections on the University of Southern California Clinical Semester." *Southern California Law Review,* 1971, *44,* 664, 688-689.

Benne, K., Bradford, L. P., and Lippitt, R. *The Laboratory Method of Changing and Learning.* Palo Alto, Calif.: Science and Behavior Books, 1975.

Bennis, W., Benne, K., and Chin, R. *The Planning of Change.* New York: Holt, Rinehart and Winston, 1968.

Bernard, L. D. "Education for Social Work." In J. B. Turner (Ed.), *Encyclopedia of Social Work.* Washington, D.C.: National Association of Social Workers, 1977.

Birren, F. *Light, Color, and Environment.* New York: Van Nostrand Reinhold, 1969.

Boocock, S. S. *An Introduction to the Sociology of Learning.* Boston: Houghton Mifflin, 1972.

Borman, E. G. *Interpersonal Communication in the Modern Organization.* Englewood Cliffs, N.J.: Prentice-Hall, 1969.

Botkin, J. W., and others. *No Limits to Learning: Bridging the Human Gap.* A Report to the Club of Rome. Elmsford, N.Y.: Pergamon Press, 1979.

Boud, D. *Developing Student Autonomy in Learning.* New York: Nichols, 1981.

Bowers, R. D. "Testing the Validity of the Andragogical Theory of Education in Selected Situations." Unpublished doctoral dissertation, Boston University, 1977.

Boyatzis, R. E. *The Competent Manager.* New York: Wiley, 1982.

Boyd, R. D., Apps, J. W., and Associates. *Redefining the Discipline of Adult Education.* San Francisco: Jossey-Bass, 1980.

Boys, M. C. "Religious Education and Contemporary Biblical Scholarship." *Religious Education,* 1979, *74* (2), 182-197.

Bradford, L. P. *Making Meetings Work: A Guide for Leaders and Group Members.* La Jolla, Calif.: University Associates, 1976.

Bromley, J. "An Investigation of Some Changes That Take Place in Students as a Result of Their Participation in the

Graduate Program of Adult Education at Boston University."
Unpublished doctoral dissertation, Boston University, 1972.

Bronfenbrenner, U. *The Ecology of Human Development.* Cambridge, Mass.: Harvard University Press, 1979.

Brown, R. E. *Biblical Reflections on Crises Facing the Church.* New York: Paulist Press, 1975.

Cheren, M. I. "Facilitating the Transition from External Direction in Learning to Greater Self-Direction in Learning in Educational Institutions: A Case Study in Individualized Open System Postsecondary Education." Unpublished doctoral dissertation, School of Education, University of Massachusetts, 1978.

"The Coming Enrollment Crisis." *Change: The Magazine of Higher Education,* March 1983, pp. 14-51.

Connor, D. M., Searly, S. H., and Bradley, K. T. *Learning for Individual and Social Development.* Ottawa: Department of Regional Economic Expansion, 1970.

Cooke, B. J. *Ministry to Word and Sacraments: History and Theology.* Philadelphia: Fortress Press, 1976.

Cooke, B. J. "The Church, Catholic and Ecumenical." *Theology Today,* 1979, *36* (3), 353-367.

Corwin, R. G. *Education in Crisis: A Sociological Analysis of Schools and Universities in Transition.* New York: Wiley, 1974.

Cowan, J. "Freedom in the Selection of Course Content: A Case Study of a Course Without a Syllabus." *Studies in Higher Education,* 1978, *3* (2), 130-148.

Cronbach, L. J., and others. *Toward Reform of Program Evaluation: Aims, Methods, and Institutional Arrangements.* San Francisco: Jossey-Bass, 1980.

Cross, K. P. *Accent on Learning: Improving Instruction and Reshaping the Curriculum.* San Francisco: Jossey-Bass, 1976.

Cross, K. P. *The Missing Link: Connecting Adult Learners to Learning Resources.* Princeton, N.J.: College Board Publications, 1979.

Cross, K. P. *Adults as Learners: Increasing Participation and Facilitating Learning.* San Francisco: Jossey-Bass, 1981.

Darkenwald, G. G. "Factorial Structure of Differences in Teach-

ing Behavior Related to Adult/Pre-Adult Student Age Status."
Adult Education, 1982, *33* (4), 197–204.

Dave, R. H. (Ed.). *Reflections on Lifelong Education in the
School.* Hamburg, Germany: UNESCO Institute for Education, 1975.

David, T. G., and Wright, B. D. (Eds.). *Learning Environments.*
Chicago: University of Chicago Press, 1975.

Davis, G. A., and Scott, J. A. *Training Creative Thinking.* New
York: Holt, Rinehart and Winston, 1971.

Davis, L. N., and McCallon, E. *Planning, Conducting, Evaluating Workshops.* La Jolla, Calif.: University Associates, 1974.

Delbeque, A., and Van de Ven, A. "A Group Process Model for
Problem Identification and Program Planning." *Journal of
Applied Behavioral Science,* 1971, 7 (4), 466–492.

Deutsch, M., and others (Eds.). *Social Class, Race, and Psychological Development.* New York: Holt, Rinehart and Winston,
1968.

Draves, W. *The Free University.* Chicago: Follett, 1980.

Dubin, R., and Taveggia, T. C. *The Teaching-Learning Paradox.*
Eugene: University of Oregon Press, 1969.

Dubin, S. S. *Professional Obsolescence.* Lexington, Mass.:
Heath, 1972.

Eiben, R., and Milliren, A. (Eds.). *Educational Change: A Hu-
manstic Approach.* La Jolla, Calif.: University Associates,
1976.

Erikson, E. *Identity and the Life Cycle.* Psychological Issues
Monograph 1. New York: International Universities Press,
1959.

Etzioni, A. *Complex Organizations.* New York: Free Press,
1961.

Etzioni, A. *A Sociological Reader on Complex Organizations.*
New York: Holt, Rinehart and Winston, 1969.

Faure, E., and others. *Learning to Be: The World of Education
Today and Tomorrow.* Paris: UNESCO, 1972.

Ferrier, B. M., McAuley, R. G., and Roberts, R. S. "Selection of
Medical Students at McMaster University." *Journal of the
Royal College of Physicians,* 1978, *12* (4), 365.

Foeckler, M. M., and Boynton, G. "Creative Adult Learning-

Teaching: Who's the Engineer of This Train?" *Journal of Education for Social Work*, 1976, *12* (3), 37–43.

Fraenkel, G. J. "McMaster Revisited." *British Medical Journal*, 1978, *2*, 1072–1078.

Freire, P. *Pedagogy of the Oppressed*. New York: Seabury Press, 1970.

Gelfand, B., and others. "An Andragogical Application to the Training of Social Workers." *Journal of Education for Social Work*, 1975, *11* (3), 55–61.

Goulet, L. R., and Baltes, P. B. *Life-Span Developmental Psychology*. New York: Academic Press, 1970.

Greiner, L. E. (Ed.). *Organizational Change and Development*. Homewood, Ill.: Irwin, 1971.

Gross, R. F. "Faculty Growth Contracts." *Educational Horizons*, 1976, *55* (2), 74–79.

Group for Human Development in Higher Education. "Faculty Development in a Time of Retrenchment." Cited in *Professional Development Through Growth Contracts Handbook*, Gordon College, 1979, p. 9.

Guba, E. G., and Lincoln, Y. S. *Effective Evaluation: Improving the Usefulness of Evaluation Results Through Responsive and Naturalistic Approaches*. San Francisco: Jossey-Bass, 1981.

Hadley, H. N. "Development of an Instrument to Determine Adult Educators' Orientation: Andragogical or Pedagogical." Unpublished doctoral dissertation, Boston University, 1975.

Havighurst, R. *Human Development and Education*. New York: Longman, 1953.

Havighurst, R. *Developmental Tasks and Education*. (2nd ed.) New York: McKay, 1970.

Heron, J. *Experience and Method*. Guildford, England: Human Potential Research Project, University of Surrey, 1971.

Heron, J. *The Concept of a Peer Learning Community*. Guildford, England: Human Potential Research Project, University of Surrey, 1974.

Herzberg, F. *Work and the Nature of Men*. Cleveland: World Publishing, 1966.

Hewitt, D., and Mather, K. F. *Adult Education: A Dynamic for Democracy*. New York: Appleton-Century-Crofts, 1937.

Holmes, M. R. "Interpersonal Behaviors and Their Relationship to the Andragogical and Pedagogical Orientation of Adult Educators." *Adult Education,* 1980, *31* (1), 18–29.

Hornstein, J. A., and others. *Social Intervention.* New York: Free Press, 1971.

Houle, C. O. *The Inquiring Mind.* Madison: University of Wisconsin Press, 1961.

Houle, C. O. *Continuing Learning in the Professions.* San Francisco: Jossey-Bass, 1980.

Houle, C. O. "Three Kinds of Lifelong Learners." In R. Gross (Ed.), *Invitation to Lifelong Learning.* Chicago: Follett, 1982.

Howe, L. W., and Howe, M. M. *Personalizing Education: Values Clarification and Beyond.* New York: Hart, 1975.

Howe, M. J. A. (Ed.). *Adult Learning: Psychological Research and Applications.* New York: Wiley, 1977.

Hungerford, H. R., and Peyton, R. B. *Teaching Environmental Education.* Portland, Maine: J. Weston Walsh, 1976.

Hunt, D. E. "A Conceptual Level Matching Model for Coordinating Learner Characteristics with Educational Approaches." *Interchange: A Journal of Educational Studies,* 1970, *1* (2), 4.

Ickes, W., and Knowles, E. S. *Personality, Roles, and Social Behavior.* New York: Springer-Verlag, 1982.

Jones, E. "The Andragogical-Pedagogical Orientation of Faculty at a Land-Grant Institution." Unpublished doctoral dissertation, Oklahoma State University, 1982.

Kemp, C. G. *Perspectives on the Group Process.* Boston: Houghton Mifflin, 1964.

Kerwin, M. A. "The Relationship of Selected Factors to the Educational Orientation of Andragogically and Pedagogically Oriented Educators Teaching in Four of North Carolina's Two-Year Colleges." Unpublished doctoral dissertation, North Carolina State University, 1979.

Kidd, J. R. *How Adults Learn.* (2nd ed.) New York: Cambridge, 1972.

Kirkpatrick, D. L. *Evaluating Training Programs.* Washington, D.C.: American Society for Training and Development, 1975.

Knights, S., and McDonald, R. "Adult Learners in University Courses." Perth, Australia: Educational Services Resources Unit, Murdoch University, 1977.

Knowles, M. S. "Andragogy, Not Pedagogy." *Adult Leadership,* April 1968, *16* (10), 350-386.

Knowles, M. S. "Innovations in Teaching Styles and Approaches Based upon Adult Learning." *Journal of Education for Social Work,* 1972, *8* (2), 32-39.

Knowles, M. S. *Self-Directed Learning: A Guide for Learners and Teachers.* Chicago: Follett, 1975.

Knowles, M. S. *The Modern Practice of Adult Education: From Pedagogy to Andragogy.* (2nd ed.) Chicago: Follett, 1980. (Originally published 1970.)

Knowles, M. S. *The Adult Learner: A Neglected Species.* (3rd ed.) Houston: Gulf, 1984. (Originally published 1973; 2nd ed. 1978.)

Knox, A. B. *Adult Development and Learning: A Handbook on Individual Growth and Competence in the Adult Years.* San Francisco: Jossey-Bass, 1977.

Kolb, D. A. *Learning Style Inventory.* Boston: McBer, 1976.

Levinson, D. J. *The Seasons of a Man's Life.* New York: Knopf, 1978.

Levy, C. S. *Social Work Education.* Washington, D.C.: National Association of Social Workers, 1981.

Lewin, K. *Field Theory in Social Science.* New York: Harper & Row, 1951.

Lidz, T. *The Person: His Development Throughout the Life Cycle.* New York: Basic Books, 1968.

Lindeman, E. C. *The Meaning of Adult Education.* New York: New Republic Press, 1926.

Lippitt, G. *Organizational Renewal.* New York: Appleton-Century-Crofts, 1969.

Lippitt, G. *Visualizing Change.* Fairfax, Va.: NTL Learning Resources, 1973.

Logue, I. H. "An Examination of Pedagogical-Andragogical Principles in Teacher Inservice Courses." Unpublished doctoral dissertation, University of Pittsburgh, 1982.

Long, H. B., Hiemstra, R., and Associates. *Changing Approaches to Studying Adult Education.* San Francisco: Jossey-Bass, 1980.

McGregor, D. M. *The Human Side of Enterprise.* New York: McGraw-Hill, 1960.

Martorana, S. V., and Kuhns, E. *Managing Academic Change: Interactive Forces and Leadership in Higher Education.* San Francisco: Jossey-Bass, 1975.

Maslow, A. *Toward a Psychology of Being.* New York: Van Nostrand, 1962.

Maslow, A. *Motivation and Personality.* New York: Harper & Row, 1970.

Maslow, A. *The Farther Reaches of Human Nature.* New York: Viking Press, 1971.

Meltsner, M., and Schrag, P. "Report from a CLEPR Colony." *Columbia Law Review,* 1976, *76,* 584–587.

Meltsner, M., and Schrag, P. "Scenes from a Clinic." *University of Pennsylvania Law Review,* 1978, *127,* 32–33.

Mentkowski, M., and Doherty, A. *Careering After College: Establishing the Validity of Abilities Learned in College for Later Careering and Personal Performance.* Milwaukee: Alverno Productions, 1982.

Milley, J. E. "A Case Study Approach to the Evaluation of a Faculty Development Program Which Uses Individual Development Plans." Unpublished doctoral dissertation, Syracuse University, 1977.

Moos, R. H. *The Human Context: Environmental Determinants of Behavior.* New York: Wiley-Interscience, 1976.

Moos, R. H. *Evaluating Educational Environments: Procedures, Measures, Findings, and Policy Implications.* San Francisco: Jossey-Bass, 1979.

Moos, R. H., and Insel, P. M. *Issues in Social Ecology.* Palo Alto, Calif.: National Press Books, 1974.

National Association of Social Workers. *Standards for the Classification of Social Work Practice.* Washington, D.C.: National Association of Social Workers, 1981.

Neufeld, V. R. "The Three-Year Medical Curriculum at McMaster University." In *Proceedings of the Josiah Macy, Jr., Foun-*

dation Conference on Teaching the Basic Medical Sciences. New York: Josiah Macy, Jr., Foundation, 1973.

Neugarten, B. L. *Personality in Middle and Later Life.* New York: Lieber-Atherton, 1964.

Neugarten, B. L. (Ed.). *Middle Age and Aging.* Chicago: University of Chicago Press, 1968.

Patton, M. Q. *Utilization-Focused Evaluation.* Beverly Hills, Calif.: Sage, 1978.

Patton, M. Q. *Qualitative Evaluation.* Beverly Hills, Calif.: Sage, 1980.

Patton, M. Q. *Creative Evaluation.* Beverly Hills, Calif.: Sage, 1981.

Patton, M. Q. *Practical Evaluation.* Beverly Hills, Calif.: Sage, 1982.

Penland, P. *Individual Self-Planned Learning in America.* Washington, D.C.: Office of Education, U.S. Department of Health, Education, and Welfare, 1977.

Peters, J. M., and Gordon, S. G. *Adult Learning Projects: A Study of Adult Learning in Urban and Rural Tennessee.* Knoxville: University of Tennessee, 1974.

Pressey, S. L., and Kuhlen, R. G. *Psychological Development Through the Life Span.* New York: Harper & Row, 1957.

Rahner, K. *The Shape of the Church to Come.* London: SPCK, 1974.

Ray, W. S. *Simple Experiments in Psychology.* New York: Behavioral Publications, 1973.

Reich, C. "Toward the Humanistic Study of Law." *Yale Law Journal,* 1965, *74,* 1402-1403.

Reissman, F. "The 'Helper' Therapy Principle." *Social Work,* 1965, *10,* 27-49.

Rice, A. K. *Learning for Leadership.* London: Tavistock, 1965.

Rogers, C. A. *Client-Centered Therapy.* Boston: Houghton Mifflin, 1951.

Rogers, C. A. *On Becoming a Person.* Boston: Houghton Mifflin, 1961.

Rogers, C. A. *Freedom to Learn.* Columbus, Ohio: Merrill, 1969.

Rogers, C. A. *A Way of Being.* Boston: Houghton Mifflin, 1980.

Romey, B. *Confluent Education in Science.* Canton, N.Y.: Ash Lad Press, 1976.

Sheehy, G. *Passages: Predictable Crises of Adult Life.* New York: Dutton, 1974.

Simmons, H. C. "Human Development: Some Conditions for Adult Faith at Age Thirty." *Religious Education,* 1976, *71* (6), 563-572.

Simmons, H. C. "Building Maps for the Journey of the Middle Years." *The Living Light,* 1978, *15* (3), 337-347.

Smart, J. D. *The Strange Silence of the Bible in the Church: A Study in Hermeneutics.* Philadelphia: Westminster Press, 1970.

Smith, A. B. *Faculty Development and Evaluation in Higher Education.* Higher Education Research Report No. 8. Washington, D.C.: American Association of Higher Education, 1976.

Smith, R. M. *Learning How to Learn.* New York: Cambridge, 1982.

Stevens-Long, J. *Adult Life: Developmental Processes.* Palo Alto, Calif.: Mayfield, 1979.

Stolz, P. "Clinical Experience in American Legal Education: Why Has It Failed?" In E. Kitch (Ed.), *Law of the Future.* University of Chicago Law School Conference Series, No. 20. Chicago: University of Chicago Press, 1970.

Stone, A. "Legal Education on the Couch." *Harvard Law Review,* 1971, *85.*

Thompson, K. *Competency Profile for Field Instruction.* Athens: School of Social Work, University of Georgia, 1978.

Thorley, N. R., and Prosser, M. T. "Towards Student Self-Directedness in a First-Year Undergraduate Physics Course." Paper presented at the Fourth Annual Conference of the Western Australia Science Education Association, Perth, 1978.

Tough, A. M. *Learning Without a Teacher.* Toronto: Ontario Institute for Studies in Education, 1967.

Tough, A. M. *The Adult's Learning Projects.* (2nd ed.) Toronto: Ontario Institute for Studies in Education, 1979. (Originally published 1971.)

Tough, A. M. *Intentional Changes: A Fresh Approach to Helping People Change.* Chicago: Follett, 1982.

U.S. Forest Service. *Environmental Education for Teachers and Resource People.* Investigating Our Environment Series. Denver: U.S. Forest Service, 1975.

Vermilye, D. W. (Ed.). *Lifelong Learners: A New Clientele for Higher Education.* San Francisco: Jossey-Bass, 1974.

Warpinski, R. J. *Instruction-Curriculum-Environment.* Green Bay, Wis.: Project ICE, 1975.

Washburn, B. P. *Implementing Personalized Instruction.* Dubuque, Iowa: Kendall/Hunt, 1975.

Werdell, P. R. "Teaching and Learning: The Basic Process." In P. Runkel, R. Harrison, and M. Runkel, (Eds.), *The Changing College Classroom.* San Francisco: Jossey-Bass, 1969.

Woodward, C. A., and McAuley, R. G. *Performance of McMaster University Student Graduates During the First Post-Graduate Year.* Toronto: Ontario Ministry of Health, 1981.

Woodward, K. L., Mark, R., and Buckley, J. "Who Was Jesus?" *Newsweek,* December 24, 1979, p. 49.

Zogas, G. "An Analysis of Teaching Practices at Reading Area Community College as They Pertain to Adult Learning Theories." Unpublished doctoral dissertation, Center for Higher Education, Nova University, 1981.

Zurcher, L. A. *The Mutable Self: A Concept for Social Change.* Beverly Hills, Calif.: Sage, 1977.

Index

435